Women
and
Violence

Compiled by

Miranda Davies

Zed Books Ltd
London and New Jersey

Women and Violence was first published by Zed
Books Ltd, 7 Cynthia Street, London N1 9JF, UK, and
165 First Avenue, Atlantic Highlands, New Jersey 07716,
USA, in 1994.

Cover designed by Andrew Corbett.
Typeset by Derek Doyle and Associates, Mold, Clwyd.
Printed and bound in the United Kingdom
by Biddles Ltd, Guildford and King's Lynn.

A catalogue record for this book is
available from the British Library.

US CIP data is available from
the Library of Congress.

ISBN 1 85649 145 5 Cased
ISBN 1 85649 146 3 Limp

Contents

Acknowledgements

This compilation reflects the support, enthusiasm and co-operation of women all over the world. In addition to those whose words fill these pages, my special thanks go to Charlotte Bunch, who provided many early contacts as well as sending an encouraging letter at a time when I was wondering if I would ever get this project off the ground; to Jane Connors, whose generous input goes far beyond her written contributions to the book; and to Urvashi Butalia, who kindly researched and brought a stack of material from Delhi to London.

For further help in finding sources, thanks also to Eliz Martinez of Isis International in the Philippines, Susan Smith of Oxfam's Gender Development Unit, Shamima Ali of Fiji Women's Crisis Centre, Jane Cottingham, Nick Allen, Iheoma Obibi, Beena Sarwar, Sally Baden and Debbie Taylor.

Finally, a big thank you to Michael Reed, whose time and efforts greatly alleviated some of the inevitable problems of international communication; and to Anna Gourlay and Robert Molteno of Zed Books for their encouragement over the years and for suggesting I do the book in the first place.

Preface

In the past 20 years, in particular since gender-based violence was first established as a development issue at the United Nation's Decade for Women's meeting of 1985, women's groups and individual activists across the world have campaigned vigorously against abuses such as rape, wife-beating, sexual slavery and sexual harassment. Countries as far apart as the USA, Zimbabwe, France, Brazil and the Philippines have seen the problem raised onto the political agenda, both at a local and national level. Shelters for battered women have been set up, there has been an overall increase in counselling and popular education to encourage women and girls to speak out against victimization, and new laws have been implemented to extend and protect women's rights. In addition, persistent lobbying by feminists has recently succeeded in establishing official international recognition of gender-based violence as a fundamental violation of human rights. Yet, throughout the world, violence against women is still very much a hidden problem, the scale of which is vastly underestimated everywhere.

This anthology focuses on the universal nature of the problem through the experiences and analyses of individual women and women's groups from some 30 countries in Europe, Asia, Africa, the Pacific and North and Latin America. Starting from the premise that violence against women is rooted in the structural relationships of power, domination and privilege which exist between women and men in different societies, the book looks at some of these root causes and at ways in which women are attempting to develop effective strategies for change. In gathering material from very different sources, certain common threads have emerged which, I hope, contribute toward a better understanding of why the threat of male violence is a fundamental experience that unites women across barriers of race, culture and class throughout the world.

The division of chapters by theme, rather than country or region, is intended to highlight the extent to which violence touches on all aspects of women's lives. Whether the focus is domestic violence in Northern Ireland, French strategies against sexual harassment in the workplace or the maltreatment of Asian maids in Kuwait, the links between violence and economic exploitation are made clear. Similarly, the connections between violence and sexuality are revealed in accounts on such different topics as women and torture in Latin America, the relationship between militarism and the sex industry, women's reproductive health, and the complexities of female genital mutilation. The coercive birth control policies currently being imposed on Tibetan people by the Chinese as part of a policy of ethnic cleansing in Tibet, and the rape of women in Bosnia provide evidence of further links, this time between violence and ethnicity, similar to the type of motives based on class or caste discrimination used to justify sexual abuse in many societies. Lastly, there are connections between violence, religion and culture, here illustrated by the examination of traditional customs, such as widow-burning in India and, on a more positive note, attitudes to male violence among aboriginal communities in Canada. (I had hoped to expand this theme in a specific chapter, but was forced to abandon it for lack of material.)

Themes overlap. 'Wife-beating' – probably the most common manifestation of male violence, exacerbated by its hidden nature within the sacred confines of the family – crops up in virtually every chapter, as does the relationship between violence and women's health and sexuality. Nevertheless, I hope that the thematic structure is useful, not only in highlighting the scale of the problem, but in helping to identify some of the major issues that need to be understood in order to develop clear strategies for change. As illustrated by the final chapter's focus on popular education, this means not only changes in the laws and government policies of individual countries, but a change in public attitudes. In the words of Toronto's Popular Education Research Group, it necessitates the widespread challenge to 'patriarchal claims and images that suggest male violence against women is a "natural" state of affairs'.

Miranda Davies
London, 1994

Part 1
The Hidden Problem: Domestic Violence

Understanding the Problem
(From the United Nations resource manual *Strategies for Confronting Domestic Violence*)

The United Nations (UN) is one of a growing number of intergovernmental bodies concerned with the issue of domestic violence. Part of its strategy to deal with the problem (expressed in resolution 45/114 adopted by the General Assembly in 1990) has been to convene a working group of experts to produce a manual for practitioners on the subject. The resulting publication, entitled *Strategies for Confronting Domestic Violence: A Resource Manual* (United Nations, June 1993), draws on a wide range of information on action by police, prosecutors, health service workers, social service workers, women's groups and government agencies across the world. The following extract describes the hidden nature and effects of a problem that may be found in any home anywhere.

Nature and extent of domestic violence

The term 'domestic violence' is used to describe a variety of actions and omissions that occur in different relationships. The term is used narrowly to cover incidents of physical attack, when it may take the form of physical and sexual violations, such as punching, choking, stabbing, throwing boiling water or acid and setting on fire, the result of which can range from bruising to killing; what may often start out as apparently minor attacks can escalate both in intensity and frequency.

Some people use the term 'domestic violence' to include psychological or mental violence, which can consist of repeated verbal abuse; harassment; confinement; and deprivation of physical, financial and personal resources. Contact with family members and friends may be controlled. The forms of violation may vary from one society and culture to another. Other people use the term to describe violence against women in the family only, and for others it is a general label to cover any violation where the victim and perpetrator have some form of personal relationship or where they have had such a relationship in the past. Used in this wider sense, domestic violence encompasses child abuse, be it physical, psychological or sexual, violence between siblings, abuse or neglect of the elderly and abuse by children of parents. Here, however, the term 'domestic violence' means physical or mental assault of women by their male partners. In many countries the term 'wife assault' is used for this type of behaviour.

Domestic violence is a hidden problem. Research on domestic violence is fairly new, and has been undertaken perhaps only in the last 25 years. In the main, it has originated in Western Europe, North America, Australia and New Zealand. Most studies have concerned the dominant culture, although a growing number focus on native populations, and immigrant and refugee groups. An increasing number of studies are now being undertaken in the developing world. For example, comprehensive and systematic studies of domestic violence (defined in this case to include violence against women and men in the home) have been undertaken in Papua New Guinea.[1] In addition, a recent collection of essays published by the United Nations Development Fund for Women (UNIFEM) summarizes the research into domestic violence that has been undertaken in various regions of the developing world.[2]

While it can be stated that women are the usual victims of violence in the home and men are the usual perpetrators, it remains unclear which particular women and men are likely to be involved. Studies indicate that marital violence occurs in some communities in as many as one in three marriages.[3] There appears to be no part of the world where it is unknown.

It is difficult to estimate the actual incidence of violence in the household. Communities deny the problem, fearing that an admission of its existence is an assault on the integrity of the family, and few official statistics are kept. Current methods of estimating the number of women who are assaulted by their husbands are questionable. The statistics are based on reported incidents of abuse obtained, for example, from police, welfare and hospital records on the numbers of women using emergency housing or on self-reports from phone-ins or field surveys.

Statistics gathered from police records and other official sources

show that wife abuse does exist, but they are notorious for underrepresenting the problem. Victims are often reluctant to report that they have been violated: they may fail to report abuse because they feel ashamed of being assaulted by their husbands; they may be afraid; they may have a sense of family loyalty.

When women do report abuse, the statistics may be lost because the official fails to record the incident or records it in a way that is meaningless for research purposes. Criminal statistics, for example, although they could be a major source of comprehensive data on violence against women in the home, frequently fail to indicate the sex of the victim and of the assailant and rarely record the relationship between the two.[4] In these circumstances, it is impossible to distinguish wife assault from any other assault and thus, for statistical purposes, wife assault becomes invisible.

Self-reporting surveys also present problems. Women who have been abused may prefer to keep the fact to themselves. When they do respond, they may overestimate or, more commonly, underestimate the amount of violence they have suffered. For example, women may consider pushes and slaps to be insignificant and fail to mention them.

Phone-in surveys are restricted to women who have access to a telephone and who are willing to reveal intimate information to someone they do not know. Such surveys may also exclude women from ethnic minorities.

Surveys of couples currently cohabiting exclude evidence of violence in relationships that have ended. Studies of women who have used emergency housing are restricted to women who have already defined themselves as battered and so do not represent the population as a whole.

Notwithstanding these problems, anecdotal and other evidence, from most parts of the world, makes it clear that violence against women in the home is a serious problem.[5]

In Canada, on the basis of statistics obtained from doctors, lawyers and social workers and from police records, it has been estimated that one woman in ten is abused by her partner.[6] In Bangladesh assassination of wives by husbands accounts for fifty per cent of all murders.[7] In 1992, UNIFEM produced a factsheet on gender violence summarizing statistical evidence on the incidence of wife abuse worldwide. This revealed that wife-battering is common in Bangladesh, Barbados, Chile, Colombia, Costa Rica, Guatemala, India, Kenya, Norway and Sri Lanka.

The actual extent of violence in the home may never be accurately known, but it is clear that such violence is part of the dynamics of many family situations in both the developed and the developing world. In short, the research that does exist reveals that women are murdered, physically and sexually assaulted, threatened and humiliated within their own homes by men with whom they should enjoy the greatest trust. Sadly, this is not an uncommon or unusual occurrence.

Domestic violence can happen in families from any class. Given the limitations of existing research, it is difficult to generalize about the social position of victims of domestic violence. Some research shows an overrepresentation of victims who are economically disadvantaged or who might be described as lower-class or from younger age groups.[8] There may be more domestic violence in families that are economically disadvantaged or where the husband has had less education than the wife.

Much of the information that is available, however, is based on studies of people who come to the attention of officials. These people may be less able to protect their private lives from official scrutiny. For instance, women from the middle and upper classes are less likely to use women's emergency housing. In some countries, public hospitals are used primarily by the economically disadvantaged. The wealthy are able to take advantage of private doctors and clinics whose records are not usually open to researchers. Records from social work or welfare files, in general, contain information on less privileged groups who must respond to government enquiries in order to get government assistance. Wealthy people are more able to insulate themselves from government and police attention.

Anecdotal material and small research samples show that wife assault crosses all class, culture and colour barriers.[9] This research indicates that violence against wives is prevalent throughout the economic and social structure and appears to have no cultural barriers.

Effects of domestic violence

While it may not be possible to have a precise picture of the actual extent of violence against women in their homes, the results of this violence are fairly clear.

In addition to the physical injuries already noted, ranging from bruising to death, abused women suffer from health and psychological problems. They have a significantly higher level of anxiety, depression and somatic complaints than women who have not suffered such abuse.[10] They may often be paralysed by terror and under stress from the ever-present threat of an attack. They are more likely to be depressed, which may lead to higher rates of suicide than those found among women who have not been battered.[11,12]

The adverse consequences of violence in the family are not confined to the victim of the abuse. The abuser himself may suffer the consequences of his behaviour. Research indicates that women who kill their husbands do so more often than not in response to an immediate attack or threat of attack.[13,14]

Domestic violence is also hazardous for family members or others who seek to intervene, who may be hurt or killed by the abusive man. Children in families where the wife is abused run the risk of being injured or killed by the abuser if they become involved in an incident of violence, either by chance or in an attempt to protect their mother.

The effect on children who witness violence is the subject of much discussion. Some studies have established that children from homes where there is violence against the mother suffer significantly more behavioural problems and have less social competence than children from homes where there is no such violence. For example, a Canadian study suggests that observing parental conflict and violence during childhood is 'significantly predictive of serious adult personal crimes (e.g. assault, attempted rape, attempted murder, kidnapping and murder)'.[15] A high proportion of street children report marital violence in their family home. More systematic research into the real effect of family violence on children is required before categorical statements of sequelae can be made.

Beyond the enormous personal costs associated with domestic violence are the social and economic costs of the conduct. Social costs include the stigmatization of the individual family, social isolation and the temporary or chronic economic and psychological dependence of family members on support groups or the welfare system.

The cost to the community in financial terms is significant. Huge sums of money are being spent on police and court services, health and welfare services, women's emergency housing and social security benefits. One Canadian estimate suggests that, in 1980, Canadian taxpayers, through their local governments, paid at least 32 million Canadian dollars for police intervention in wife-battering cases and for related support and administrative services.[16] An Australian study found that the cost of services for 20 victims of domestic violence was well over 1 million Australian dollars.[17]

The causes of domestic violence

Although the causes of domestic violence may not be known, the need to take action is clear. There are many theories to explain the existence and extent of the problem. Some theories focus on the individuals and look for personal explanations such as the use of alcohol or drugs,[18] the victim's actions, mental illness, stress, frustration, underdevelopment[19] and violent families of origin.[20]

The pervasiveness and implicit acceptability of violence in the family directed at women has led some scholars to question the validity of explanations that are tied to personal and individual characteristics. They suggest a social and structural explanation. Violence in the home has its origins in an entire social context. Wife battery is a reflection of the broad structures of sexual and economic inequality in society. Studies show that rather than representing an aberration, violence in the home is widely accepted and tolerated. It is an extension of the role society expects men to play in their domestic sphere. In this analysis, the abuse of women can be seen as a display of male power, the outcome of social relations in which women are kept in a position of inferiority to men, responsible to them and in need of protection by them. These theories suggest that the social, political and economic dependence of women on men provides a structure wherein men can perpetrate violence against women.[21]

The origins of violence are located in the social structure and the complex set of values, traditions, customs, habits and beliefs which relate to gender inequality. The victim of the violence is most frequently the woman and the perpetrator the man and the structures of society act to confirm this inequality.[22] Violence against women is an outcome of the belief, fostered in most cultures, that men are superior and that the women with whom they live are their possessions to be treated as the men consider appropriate.

Finally, there is no single, simple explanation for violence in the home, and a focus on a search for causes can excuse inaction. Whatever the causes, individuals must accept responsibility for their own violent actions and societies must confront domestic violence.

Domestic violence and family privacy

The right to a private family life does not include the right to abuse family members. International and regional human rights instruments universally guarantee the right to a private life and to a home. The family is a private place, a source of comfort and nurture for the mutual growth of its members. Again, this value is enshrined in international and regional human rights instruments and acknowledged by the United Nations in, for example, the proclamation of 1994 as the International Year of the Family. While the importance of the family as a societal structure should not be underrated, excessive faith in its nurturing capacities may lead to efforts to sustain the family unit even where members are being victimized by other family members. Thus, the maintenance of the family as an intact unit may, in some cases of domestic violence, allow it to take precedence over the interests of the individual within it. The right to be free from domestic violence or the threat of domestic violence is a fundamental and universal human right.

Finally, any practitioner working in the area of family violence must recognize that a certain level of domestic violence is condoned by most societies. Physical disciplining of children is allowed and, indeed, encouraged in many legal systems and a large number of countries allow moderate physical chastisement of a wife or, if they do not do so now, have done so within the last 100 years. Again, most legal systems fail to criminalize circumstances where a wife is forced to have sexual relations with her husband against her will. Allied with this condemnation is denial that domestic violence is a serious issue which may have long-lasting effects on the victim, the perpetrator and other family members. Indeed, in the case of violence against wives, there is a widespread belief that women provoke, can tolerate or even enjoy a certain level of violence from their spouses.

These values, which legitimate a certain amount of family violence, shape the attitudes of the public practitioners in the context of the problem. They recur as themes when innovative strategies to confront domestic violence are considered and, moreover, combine to a large degree to undermine strategies that have been introduced.

In the main, domestic violence has been seen as a problem requiring legal solutions, but the policies that people involved in law-making and the approaches people within the legal system have pursued when grappling with the issue have not been uniform.[23] In all countries where domestic violence has emerged as a serious issue, people involved with the law have been forced to confront a central question, which is what role, if any, the criminal justice system should play in the management of domestic violence.

Notes

1. As discussed by Christine Bradley on pages 10–27. See also the following reports, published by the Papua New Guinea Law Reform Commission, Boroko: S. Toft (ed.), *Domestic Violence in Papua New Guinea*, Monograph No. 3, 1985; S. Toft and S. Bonnell (eds.), *Marriage and Domestic Violence in Rural Papua New Guinea*, Occasional Paper No. 18, 1985; S. Toft (ed.), *Domestic Violence in Urban Papua New Guinea*, Occasional Paper No. 19, 1986; *Interim Report on Domestic Violence; A Discussion Paper on Domestic Violence*; C. Bradley, *Final Report on Domestic Violence*, Report No. 14, in press.

2. M. Schuler (ed.), *Freedom from Violence: Women's Strategies from around the World* (New York, United Nations Development Fund for Women, 1992).

3. M. Borkowski, M. Murch and V. Walker, *Marital Violence: the Community Response* (London, Tavistock, 1983), p. 11.

4. Lorna Smith, *Domestic Violence*, Home Office Research Study 107 (London, Her Majesty's Stationery Office, 1989) reports that, with the exception of homicide, United Kingdom criminal statistics do not provide information on the sex of the victim, nor is the relationship between the victim and the offender routinely recorded.

5. United Nations, *Violence against Women in the Family* (Vienna, Centre for Social Development and Humanitarian Affairs, 1989; Sales, No. E.89.IV.5), pp. 18–20; see also 'Domestic violence: report of the Secretary-General' (A/CONF.144/17).

6. L. MacLeod, *Wife Battering in Canada: the Vicious Circle* (Quebec, Government Publishing Centre, 1980), p. 21.

7. Denise Stewart, 'The Global Injustice', *Viz-à-Viz* (Ottawa, Canadian Council on Social Development, 1989) quoted in *Women, Violence and Human Rights* (Women's Leadership Institute Report, USA Centre for Women's Global Leadership, 1991).

8. The studies by the Papua New Guinea Law Reform Commission reveal that domestic violence is more common in the lower and rural classes. See also D. Marsden, 'Sociological perspectives on family violence', in J. Martin (ed.), *Violence in the Family* (Chichester, Wiley, 1978).

9. G.R. Tocaven and M.L. Rodriguez, *Battered Woman Syndrome* (Mexico City, Attorney General of Justice, 1989).

10. P. Jaffe et al., 'Emotional and physical health problems of battered women', *Canadian Journal of Psychiatry*, No. 31, 1986, p. 625.

11. E. Hilberman and F. Munson, 'Sixty battered women', *Victimology*, No. 2, 1978, pp. 460 and 464–5; D. Counts, 'Female suicide and wife abuse in cross-cultural perspective', *Suicide and Life-Threatening Behaviour*, No. 17, 1987, pp. 194–204.

12. E. Stark, A. Flitcraft and W. Frazier, 'Medicine and patriarchal violence: the social construction of a private event', *International Journal of Health Services*, No. 9, 1979, p. 461.

13. The killing of abusive husbands by their wives is not confined to developed countries. Research by Ranjana S. Jain, reported in *Family Violence in India* (New Delhi, Advent Books, 1991), reveals that a number of female prisoners in Indian gaols are there because they have murdered husbands who have abused them. This pattern is common in Turkey also.

14. L. Bacon and R. Landsdowne, 'Women who kill husbands – the problem of defence', paper delivered at the 52nd Australia and New Zealand Association for the Advancement of Science Conference, Sydney, 1982; K. O'Donovan, 'Defences for battered women who kill', *Journal of Law and Society*, Vol. 18, No. 12 (1991), p. 219; P. Kivung et al., 'Women and crime, women and violence', in P. King et al. (eds.), *From Rhetoric to Reality? Papers from the Fifteenth Waigani Seminar* (Waigani, University of Papua New Guinea Press), p. 75.

15. D.G. Fischer, *Family Relationship Variables and Programs Influencing Juvenile Delinquency* (Ottawa, 1985), p. 41.

16. L. MacLeod, *Battered, But Not Beaten: Preventing Wife Battering in Canada* (Ottawa, Canadian Advisory Committee on the Status of Women, 1987), p. 35.

17. G. Roberts, 'Domestic violence: costing of service provision for female victims – twenty case histories', in *Beyond These Walls* (Queensland Domestic Violence Task Force, 1988).

18. *Violence against Women in the Family*; and L. Smith, *Domestic Violence*, Home Office Research Study 107 (London, Her Majesty's Stationery Office, 1989), pp. 29–30.

19. *Violence against Women in the Family*, pp. 28–30.

20. Ibid., pp. 27–8; and Smith, p. 30.

21. R.E. Dobash and R.P. Dobash, *Violence against Wives: a Case Study against the Patriarchy* (London, Open Books, 1980); Smith, pp. 23–30; *Violence against Women in the Family*, pp. 25–33; J. Ptacek, 'Why do men batter their wives?', in K. Yllö and M. Bograd (eds.), *Feminist Perspectives on Wife Abuse*, Focus Edition Series, Vol. 93, (Newbury Park, California, Sage Publications, 1988), pp. 133–47; and D. Adams, 'Treatment models for men who batter: a profeminist analysis', in Yllö and Bograd (eds.), pp. 176–99.

22. R.E. Dobash and R.P. Dobash, *Women, Violence and Social Change* (London, Routledge, 1992); H. McGregor and A. Hopkins, *Working for Change: the Movement Against Domestic Violence* (Concord, Massachusetts, Paul and Company Publishers' Consortium, 1992); and S. Schechter, *Women and Male Violence* (Boston, South End Press, 1982).

23. Editor's note: this point is illustrated in Part 5.

Why Male Violence against Women is a Development Issue: Reflections from Papua New Guinea

Christine Bradley

From 1986 to 1990 Christine Bradley was Principal Project Officer for the Papua New Guinea Law Commission, running a national programme on violence against women. She has a PhD in social anthropology, lived for eleven years in Papua New Guinea (PNG) and has also worked with battered wives in England. She is currently working as an international consultant on domestic violence in British Columbia, Canada.

The following contribution is updated by the author from a discussion paper prepared in 1990 at the request of the United Nations Development Fund for Women (UNIFEM).

In the industrialized countries of the West, male violence against women has been recognized as a serious social problem for some time. During the early seventies, research findings on violence against women in the family began to be published in the United States and, in 1974, Erin Pizzey's book *Scream Quietly or the Neighbours Will Hear* catapulted the topic into the limelight in the United Kingdom.[1] During the eighties, most developed countries introduced legislation and social measures aimed at giving women better protection against violence in intimate relationships. Less developed regions have been slow to recognize the extent of the problem in their own countries, and international development agencies working on behalf of women in those countries have, by and large, also hesitated to take a stand on this issue. In consequence of this neglect, the conditions of many women's lives have worsened, sometimes as a direct result of programmes intended to benefit them.

This chapter draws on experience in Papua New Guinea and presents some reasons why male violence against women should be recognized and addressed by governments and non-governmental bodies in developing countries, and also by the international organizations working in them. The main focus will be on wife-beating, since this is the most common form of violence against women and it has been thoroughly researched by the Papua New Guinea Law Reform Commission. As a United Nations publication pointed out in 1989, this work remains 'the only comprehensive and systematic study of violence against women in the home that has been undertaken by a developing country'.[2] Other forms of violence against women, such as rape, sexual assault and sexual harassment, will be considered more briefly, since fewer Papua New Guinean data exist on these topics.

Wife-beating in Papua New Guinea

Wife-beating is not a modern phenomenon in Papua New Guinea, but it has been exacerbated by modern conditions. By 1982, Papua New Guinea's National Council of Women was concerned enough to write to the Minister for Justice, asking the government to take action to protect women against violence by their husbands and boyfriends. In response to that request, the Law Reform Commission embarked on an extensive programme of research into domestic violence and other problems affecting marriage in rural and urban Papua New Guinea. Domestic violence was defined as physical violence between marriage partners, whether the couple had a legally recognized marriage or were simply living together as if they were married. Identical questions were put to men and women in most parts of the country, and four volumes of findings have been published.[3]

The research revealed that the majority of Papua New Guinean wives have been hit by their husbands. In a rural survey of 19 villages in 16 of Papua New Guinea's 19 provinces, 67 per cent of rural wives surveyed said they had been hit by their husbands, and 66 per cent of rural husbands said they had hit their wives. These figures are national averages which conceal a considerable variation between provinces, ranging from rates of between 90 per cent and 100 per cent as reported by wives (and confirmed by husbands) in some highland areas, down to a minimum of 49 per cent in one lowland village. The survey of urban low-income earners and spouses of low-income earners found that 56 per cent of wives claimed to have been hit by their husbands and 55 per cent of husbands admitted to hitting their wives. Amongst urban elites, males' and females' reports of wife-beating were identical, at 62 per cent. The very close match in responses between male and female informants (who were not necessarily married to each other and who were interviewed separately in privacy) suggests that they were being truthful in their answers.

Most wives in the surveys were hit more than once a year but not as often as once a month, except for a small minority of urban low-income wives who were hit more frequently. As to the severity of beatings, it was not possible to obtain meaningful data from rural areas. For urban wives, the surveys found that one in six had received medical treatment for injuries inflicted by their husbands, and that between 11 per cent and 18 per cent of the beaten urban wives had asked for police help, even though at the time of the surveys police had a policy of non-intervention in domestic assaults.[4] These figures indicate that beatings in an urban setting may often be quite severe.

Wife-beating – or 'wife-bashing', as it is popularly known – is a more serious problem in towns than in the villages, despite the fact that the proportion of wives affected is slightly lower in towns. Alcohol plays a large part in town life and was cited in both urban surveys as the main cause of wife-beating. Beatings may be more severe when husbands are drunk and less aware of (but not less responsible for) the damage they are doing. Another factor is that town wives are more dependent on their husbands, with fewer avenues of escape or sources of support than they would have at home in the village, and they are therefore obliged to tolerate a higher level of violence.

The research also showed that some Papua New Guinean women hit their husbands, with figures ranging from 30 per cent in rural areas to 50 per cent amongst urban elites. Yet this does not mean that Papua New Guinean men are being victimized by their wives. Wives mainly hit in self-defence and are generally far smaller, weaker and less practised in the use of violence than their husbands, who have often been trained to fight. A hospital survey in the city of Lae found that of all patients presenting for treatment for domestic violence injuries, 97 per cent were wives and only 3 per cent were husbands.[5] Similar findings were made during a police study, which showed that 94 per cent of domestic assault complaints were made by wives and only 6 per cent by husbands. Clearly, then, it is not husbands who are the main victims. The extensiveness of the Law Reform Commission's research and the consistency between male and female replies support the conclusion that wife-beating is indeed a widespread and serious problem in Papua New Guinea, one that directly affects two-thirds of all families in the country.

Why is wife-beating an issue at all?

Wife-beating in Papua New Guinea is so common that it is seen as a normal part of married life. Since it affects the majority, it is the statistical as well as the moral norm. In fact, the surveys found that 57 per cent of rural women and 67 per cent of rural men accept in principle the practice of wife-beating.[7] For town-dwellers the figures are lower, with fewer than half the surveyed population believing that wife-beating is acceptable. Amongst elites, the figures are 36 per cent and 41 per cent for females and males respectively, and 25 per cent and 42 per cent among low-income earners. Since over 80 per cent of Papua New Guinea's population live in rural areas, where a majority of people accept wife-beating and do not see it as problematic (except in extreme cases), it is appropriate at this point to ask why wife-beating is an issue at all. If the majority of the people accept it, why should anything be done about it?

This was the question asked by Members of Parliament when the Law Reform Commission presented its interim findings on domestic violence. Some argued that wife-beating is and should remain 'strictly a private affair', and that the law should not have the right to intervene in family life. Others asserted that there is nothing wrong with wife-beating provided the husband has 'a good reason', and a minister claimed that paying bride price makes the man the head of the family, so that husbands feel they 'own the woman and can belt her any time they like'. Another Honorable Member was annoyed that the nation's leaders were being asked to discuss something as trivial as wife-beating: 'We are wasting our time instead of discussing the development of the country. We should have something better to discuss than this!'[8]

The negative response from politicians prompted the Law Reform Commission to provide some answers to the question of what is wrong with wife-beating. What follows is the result of discussion sessions with hundreds of Papua New Guineans, though most or possibly all points would be universally valid.

Effects on the wife

Physical:

- injuries ranging from cuts, bruises, black eyes, burns, broken bones, internal injuries and brain damage (any blow to the head can cause minor brain damage such as loss of memory, difficulties in concentrating, mood changes etc., or can cause loss of sight or hearing);
- in the worst cases, death may result (just one blow can kill a person with an enlarged spleen), or the victim may commit suicide.

Psychological:

- love for the husband changes into fear of him, and of what might happen;
- confusion (because she often does not really know what brings on the violence);
- loss of confidence in herself (because her husband is always telling her it is her fault he hits her);

- feelings of helplessness (because her husband controls her through his violence);
- inability to make decisions on her own (in case he does not approve and punishes her); etc.

Because of these effects, a beaten wife finds it hard to help herself: for example, she may lay charges and then drop them, or leave her husband and then go back to him. This makes people who try to help her feel frustrated and less willing to help again.

Social:

- her work performance suffers, she may be absent a lot and may lose her job;
- she becomes isolated, as he controls whom she sees and where she goes.

Effects on the children

Physical:

- they may get hurt, even killed, during fights between their parents;
- they may be neglected because the mother is upset and may not take such good care of them;
- unborn babies may die if the mother miscarries because of being hit;
- some babies are born already injured because the mother was beaten when close to giving birth.

Psychological:

- they feel upset, worried about what might happen;
- their love for the father changes to fear or even hatred;
- they do not work well at school, are unable to concentrate;
- they may develop behaviour problems, becoming either aggressive and troublesome, or quiet and withdrawn.

Social:

- they may leave home early and get into trouble ('rascalism' or early pregnancy);
- when older, they repeat the pattern in their own marriages (unless they seek help to change their behaviour).

Effects on the husband

Physical:

- he may be injured, or even killed, if the wife retaliates;

Psychological:

- he feels alienated and insecure as he loses the love and respect of his wife and children, without necessarily understanding why;

Social:

- he tends to stay out more because of tension at home, and may become involved in drinking, or affairs with other women;
- he may lose his family altogether if the wife decides to leave, or if she finds someone else who treats her better. (The law allows a wife who has been treated badly by her husband to leave him, and to claim maintenance from him for any of the children the court says can stay with her.)

Effects on the family

- fear of the husband/father affects family life;
- possibility of family break-up: wife-beating is one of the main causes of divorce in Papua New Guinea.

Effects on the community

- disruptive of other families;
- intimidating for women;
- may escalate to involve relatives, or whole clan, in tribal war.

Effects on society

- helps to create a high level of violence in society, as children learn by observation how to use violence to get what they want;
- leads to family break-up, which creates instability in the society, causes social problems and contributes to the law-and-order problem;
- can result in high economic costs, in the many work hours (both garden work and paid employment) lost when victims are not well enough to work;
- also results in costs in the services to victims, such as medical treatment, assistance from the police, the courts, welfare services and so on;
- deprives the country of women's full potential for taking part in development;
- keeps women in their place as second-class citizens under men's control.

Why is wife-beating a development issue?

The first reason why wife-beating is a development issue is the most obvious: men's violence prevents or limits women's participation in development. Through the use of force and/or the threat of force, a man is able, if he wishes, physically to prevent his wife from participating in any development activities. Simply attending a women's meeting may be dangerous for a woman whose husband does not want her to go. In Papua New Guinea some husbands prevent their wives from attending meetings by locking them in the house, or by pulling them off the vehicle they have boarded to take them to the meeting, or even by pursuing them to the meeting and dragging them home, where further beatings are inflicted. If a woman cannot even attend a meeting to find some comfort, if not solidarity, from other women, she is doomed to an isolation that will almost certainly overwhelm any hopes she had of improving her situation.

Sometimes male force is used not to prevent wives from participating in development programmes, but instead to divert the benefits to themselves. It is not at all unusual, in Papua New Guinea as in other developing countries, for women to be allowed by their husbands to participate in income-generating schemes for women, only to find that the income is then taken from them by their husbands and spent on beer and cigarettes.

Sometimes male force is used in other ways to negate the effects of development programmes. For example, information about natural family planning methods, such as is frequently requested by the large number of Catholic women's groups in Papua New Guinea, is useless if the husband forces his wife to have sex against her will at the wrong time. In fact, a husband forcing his wife to have sex when she does not want to is one of the main causes of wife-beating in Papua New Guinea. Marital rape is very common in Papua New Guinea and is allowed by law. This situation has serious implications for the country's population growth (the population is expected to double in the next 25 years), as well as for the spread of AIDS in the country.

Another illustration of how wife-beating can negate women's advancement is provided by a recent study of female teachers in Papua New Guinea, who represent 39 per cent of the primary-school teaching force but less than 5 per cent of head teachers. One of the reasons given by married female teachers for their failure to apply for or take up promotions is their fear that it would provoke their husbands into more violence against them, to ensure that they (the husbands) retained control.[9]

Threats of violence control women's minds as much as do acts of violence, making women act as their own jailers. This means that a woman makes her choices based not on what she wants to do or

believes is best, but on what she thinks her husband will allow her to do. Of course, husbands have many other ways of controlling their wives as well as the recourse to violence, since in Papua New Guinea's predominantly patrilineal cultures a wife is socially, culturally and economically dependent on her husband (as is also the case for most women in the rest of the world). These aspects of male domination and female dependency are built into the social and cultural systems, but even if a woman is brave enough to challenge these and try to step out beyond the traditional female role, her husband can still exercise his ultimate control through force and re-establish the status quo, at least for the moment.

When a woman's economic and social dependency is backed up by physical force, even development programmes aimed at reducing the other dependencies cannot liberate a woman who is terrified to make any move for fear of her husband and what he might do to her. Although data on wives' education and employment were not asked for in the Law Reform Commission's questionnaire surveys, the commission has found through its legal advice programme that educated wives with jobs and therefore the potential for independence are just as likely – or even more likely, for reasons to be discussed below – to be beaten by their husbands as are less 'advanced' women.

Stress, development and wife-beating

The cause of wife-beating is complex. Cultural, social and psychological factors are involved, but the key to understanding why wife-beating happens lies in recognizing that wife-beating is an extreme expression of male dominance and that it is aggravated by stress. In societies where men are expected to be dominant – which includes most, if not all, contemporary societies – men may respond to any perceived threat to their superior position by using force and violence. During development or rapid social change, old norms are constantly being challenged by new circumstances, creating situations of stress and insecurity. Men frequently react to these stresses with increased violence towards their wives in an attempt to stay in control. Women, too, often respond with increased use of violence in stressful situations, but the whole question of how women deal with their own stress and anger lies outside the scope of this chapter. In any case, violence by women is minor when compared with violence by men.

While it is already accepted that conditions of underdevelopment and poverty produce stress that results in high levels of violence,[10] it has not yet been widely recognized that the development process itself can exacerbate violence against women. Development creates change, and change creates stress. Until systems and patterns of authority are stabilized, even participants in successful development programmes experience some degree of insecurity, which males may express through violence against their wives.

Unfortunately, wife-beating is a relatively recent field of study even in the more developed world. Insufficient attention has been paid so far to the question of how the nature and extent of wife-beating and other forms of violence against women change in relation to changing socio-economic circumstances. One interesting exception is a study by Benard which showed that the incidence of wife-beating among groups of Afghanis increased greatly after they were forced by the civil war to flee Afghanistan and live as refugees in Pakistan and later in the West.[11]

For Papua New Guinea no systematic comparisons of this kind have yet been carried out, but there are many indications that an increase in stress – whether induced by personal circumstances or by wider socio-economic conditions – can indeed cause an increase in wife-beating. For example, many wives have observed that their husband's violence against them increases when the husbands are out of work and when the wives are observing the taboos on sexual intercourse associated with pregnancy and breast-feeding. The period around the start of the new school year, when children's school fees must be paid, is a time of increased wife-beating, as couples argue about how the money is to be found. Although no hard data exist, it appears that working wives suffer more wife-beating than unemployed wives, because husbands feel threatened by the wives' potential independence and attempt to retain their control through physical dominance. In the East Sepik, women in a rubber development scheme report that a fall in the price of rubber causes their husbands to beat them more as a means of venting their frustrations.[12] Yet conditions of economic improvement such as in the gold strikes of Enga and the Southern Highlands can also lead to an increase in wife-beating, as husbands spend more on alcohol and beat their wives when drunk.[13]

Women's development and violence against women

If change and development in general can lead to an increase in wife-beating, programmes for women's development have the potential for creating even more stress and violence, because women's development threatens male authority. The purpose of women's development programmes is to improve the position of women. The position of women does not exist in a vacuum – it exists only in relation to the position of men. Therefore improving the position of women means improving the position of women relative to men. It means bringing about a change in the balance of power between men and women, although this is usually not stated explicitly and is even less frequently recognized consciously by the participants themselves.

Giving women more power over themselves means taking that power away from men. Eliminating all forms of discrimination against women means eliminating all forms of discrimination in favour of men. For example, if women participate more equally in politics, they will be taking up places in local and national government that are currently held by men. If more women enter the job market, they will be taking jobs away from men, unless there is economic expansion. If women are to participate more fully in development without overloading themselves intolerably, some of women's existing workload will have to be shouldered by men. Although some men are able to recognize that there are ways in which they too will gain from women's greater equality, the majority see only the ways in which they will lose. Their reaction is to try to retain or reassert authority over their own women by force, controlling their movements, preventing them from attending women's meetings, stepping up punitive or pre-emptive beatings and so on. Perhaps women's development programmes should carry a health warning: Beware! women's development can be dangerous to women's health!

Wife-beating – an invisible problem

The practice of wife-beating is particularly hard to tackle because many traditional and transitional cultures have a blind spot about wife-beating. Wife-beating remains hidden and invisible, not necessarily in the sense that it is covered up by victims and ignored by society (which is the case in the West), but in the sense that people see it as normal and therefore not a problem. Many people in developing countries believed that a man does have the right to control his wife, to be the head of the family, the 'boss'. This is part of the cultural nexus in which men are seen as having a natural right to control and discipline their wives, a right which in Papua New Guinea is legitimated in many peoples' eyes by the payment of bride price. It should not be forgotten either that even in the 'liberated' USA, a significant proportion of the population believe that it is acceptable for a man to use force on his wife occasionally.[14]

This kind of attitudinal obstacle does not apply in the same way for rape. Usually there is no difficulty arousing public concern about rape (although in individual cases there may be a tendency to blame the victim). In Papua New Guinea there are frequent calls from leaders and the general public for tougher penalties for rapists, even the death penalty. But the Law Reform Commission's proposals to introduce tougher legal action against wife-beaters have met with considerable opposition, mainly from men but also from women.

Even development organizations seem to have a blind spot when it comes to violence against women, particularly wife-beating. For example, the recent report by the Convention for the Elimination of Discrimination Against Women (CEDAW) on women as the 'invisible victims' of the worldwide economic crisis fails to mention that one of the major ways in which women suffer from the economic crisis is through increased violence from their husbands. In fact, CEDAW's whole current publicity package contains not one mention of violence against women. Not that the convention document itself is any better. There are three points under which wife-beating and/or other forms of violence against women could be considered – under Article 5 on sex roles and cultural practices that discriminate against women; under Article 12 on women's health; and under Article 16 on marriage and family law – but violence against women is not named explicitly as a problem under any of the articles. Another example of a blind spot is demonstrated by Britain's prestigious Open University, which has not one reference on violence against women in its 1989 reading list on women and development.

The UN Decade for Women eventually did recognize the problem of wife-beating and other forms of violence against women, at the mid-decade Nairobi conference. Some action has followed, notably the initiation of some research, some awareness programmes and the publication of an excellent survey of the problem and discussion of the main issues.[15] The Commonwealth Secretariat has put out the very useful manual, *Confronting Violence*, a training package for police and a curriculum package for legal professionals.[16] But considering the universality of male violence against women, remarkably few publications and programmes have been introduced by development agencies specifically to target this problem.

Sexual violence and development

Rape, sexual assault and sexual harassment have always existed in Papua New Guinea, but they have increased enormously over recent years. Traditionally, women and girls were only raped during tribal warfare, or in revenge for some wrong committed by their husband or member of their own clan. Also, amongst some cultures a husband could punish his wife for real or suspected adultery by giving her to a group of his clan-mates to rape. Outside these circumstances rape seldom occurred, mainly because females were strictly controlled and protected, and there were harsh punishments for those who insulted a clan by raping one of its women. When rape did occur, it was treated as an offence against the man or men who had rights over that woman (her husband if she was married, her father/brothers if she was not). Compensation would be paid to the males who had rights over her, but not, generally speaking, to the woman herself. In fact, the woman might even be made to marry her rapist, since being 'spoilt goods' no one else would pay full bride price for her.

Nowadays the situation is quite different. Rape, gang rape and sexual assault have become commonplace. Women or girls are raped when going about their ordinary business in daylight hours, such as going to or coming home from the trade-store, school, church, the food gardens, work, or when washing clothes at the river, visiting friends and so on. Even at home they are not safe: police statistics show that 45 per cent of rape victims were raped in or abducted from their own homes, or were attacked while in the company of others.[17] Pack rapes committed by gangs of 3 to 40 men are a phenomenon that appeared in the early eighties and has increased dramatically since then. The rates of armed highway robberies, muggings and burglaries have reached such levels that states of emergency have been declared or called for in several parts of the country. In these kinds of crime, female victims suffer far worse than men because as well as being robbed, they are frequently raped or pack-raped.

The sexual abuse of girls as young as 18 months – something which in the past is said only to have been committed very rarely and only by the mentally deranged – has become much more common. Figures on sexual assault collected by Port Moresby's General Hospital during the first three months of 1985 showed that nearly half the victims – 47 per cent – were under 16 years old; 22 per cent were aged between 12 and 15; 12 per cent were aged between 8 and 11 years; while a truly alarming 13 per cent were under 8 years old.[18]

The reasons for the increase in crimes of sexual violence against women and girls are complex. No firm answers can be given at this stage, since no systematic study of these phenomena has been undertaken in the country, but certain key factors can be identified. Modernization and development have enormously increased women's mobility and therefore their vulnerability to rape, sexual assault, sexual harassment and exploitation. At the same time, clan solidarity and the traditional systems of compensation and/or retaliation which once protected women have been severely weakened, whilst the state mechanisms for maintaining law and order are also inadequate and do not have the confidence of the people.

The spread of modern means of communication and Western-influenced media into previously isolated areas bombards men with powerful visual images of the often violent sexual abuse and degradation of women. Even in remote villages far from roads and electricity supplies it is not unusual to find someone with a television set and video machine powered by generator, batteries or solar power, from which the owner makes an income by showing videos obtained in town. These may well include pornographic and rampant macho videos of the Rambo type, which are available throughout Papua New Guinea despite the efforts of the Censorship Board. Even situation comedies, game shows and films approved as suitable for family viewing for Western audiences can contain displays of kissing, fondling and visual and verbal allusions to sexual practices that are at first profoundly disturbing to peoples accustomed to a great deal more reserve in relations between the sexes. For example, it is considered lewd in some rural societies for a husband and wife to sit side by side on the same bench or mat in public, and the common greeting between them if one has been away for a while is a handshake. Imagine then the impact on these unsophisticated audiences of the more explicit material shown on Australian and Guam television, which for the last few years has been receivable through satellite technology in many parts of Papua New Guinea, let alone the impact of the sex-and-violence videos, which may be shown over and over again on village video machines.

These foreign materials are particularly damaging in the Papua New Guinea context because local audiences generally lack sufficient experience of the outside world to enable them to distinguish between reality and fantasy. They therefore tend to believe that what they see is normal behaviour in the world beyond the village, and in the case of impressionable youth, to take this for a role model. In one recent case, a white woman living in Papua New Guinea was raped by six young Papua New Guineans, who told her while they were raping her that there was no reason for her to be upset, because they had often seen white women on films and videos having sex with many men and enjoying it.

Young men, who no longer have the outlets for their sexuality and aggression that were available to them in traditional times, such as warfare, long initiation rituals and formal preparation for manhood, hazardous trading voyages, arduous hunting trips, regular courting rituals and so on, are especially likely to be influenced by sexually stimulating and/or violent materials and to seek an outlet through rape or sexual assault. But older, married men may also be affected, and their wives complain of being forced into strange and humiliating sexual practices that their husbands have seen on video.

This is not to suggest that rape and other forms of sexual abuse of women are predominantly sexual phenomena. They are predominantly acts of domination and control, providing for the perpetrator a sense of personal power that compensates for his relative powerlessness in other areas of life. Modernization and development contribute to the sense of powerlessness experienced by many males in Papua New Guinea.[19] In cultures where men's identity and pride were based largely on their role as warriors and protectors, the suppression of tribal fighting and the decline of male cults have left many men feeling insecure and looking for other ways to reassert themselves. There is also a high level of frustration and boredom amongst young men who have struggled through the education system only to find that there are hardly any jobs available, at least of the kind that they aspire to. Against this background, typical of many developing countries, programmes for women's development can and do arouse a great deal of suppressed or overt hostility from men. One of the expressions of this hostility – perhaps its main expression – is through increased violence against women. Increases in sexual violence against women and, as has already been remarked, in wife-beating are the hidden costs that many women have to pay for modernization and development.

Conclusion

This brings us to the crux of the whole problem of violence against women, whether in the form of wife-beating or rape and sexual abuse. The essence of male violence against women is the sense of inadequacy, of vulnerability, of helplessness, of weakness, and of sheer naked fear that men inspire in women when they threaten or use violence against them. The use of brute force by men makes women *feel* inferior.

It leads women to accept male control (by fathers, brothers, husbands) as the price of their protection from aggression by other males. For this to be achieved, a woman does not necessarily have to experience the violence herself. Knowledge of other women's experiences through stories or even rumours has the same effect of producing a sense of fear and inadequacy in women which controls their minds and their behaviour. This is not a response peculiar to Papua New Guinean women. At a recent workshop on women's non-formal education held in China for 12 countries in the Asia-Pacific region, participants were asked to say what for them was the worst aspect of being female. Fear of male violence was the almost unanimous answer, even from those participants who had little or no direct experience of male violence themselves.[20]

Violence against women denies women basic human dignity by reducing interaction to the level of animals. It is a return to the law of the jungle, where might is right and the weak do the bidding of the strong. It is the antithesis of all that women's development programmes are trying to achieve. Violence against women is the most fundamental form of discrimination against women that exists, because it has the potential to destroy, and often does destroy, women's sense of self. The fact that widespread violence against women exists, and may be socially approved in some of its forms, is a denial of even the hope of autonomy and equality for most women. As long as they are kept under men's control by fear of what their husbands or other men will do to them, women will never achieve their full potential either as persons or as agents for development.

Recommendations

Much more information is needed about the forms and conditions of violence against women in developing countries. More information about wife-beating and other forms of violence against women is urgently needed, especially diachronic studies tracing changes through time. The necessary information can only be collected through original research, since in developing countries there may be no existing systems of data collection on forms of violence against women. Where systems do exist, for example the rape statistics kept by the police, they may give a misleading picture of the real situation. The research will need to be funded by outside donor agencies, partly because social research is seldom given high priority by governments with severe financial constraints, and partly because governments may be unwilling to admit that there is a problem that needs to be addressed. In Fiji, for example, government funding for the Women's Crisis Centre was withheld in an attempt to get the centre's name changed to something less challenging, such as Women's Welfare Centre.

International development agencies must explicitly recognize violence against women as a serious problem impeding development as well as a human rights issue for the female half of the world's population. These agencies must make clear and unambiguous statements condemning violence against women, and must design and support programmes for eliminating it as an urgent priority.

Programmes to eliminate violence against women must be aimed at men as much as or even more than at women, and must involve men in their implementation. Unless men change, women will continue to suffer. In fact, for the reasons described earlier in connection with wife-beating, it is not only women who suffer from the violence against them but the whole society. Therefore violence against women must be seen as a problem of society, and not just of women. The women's movement of the West has been responsible for drawing attention to violence against women as an issue, but to continue with a separatist approach would be counter-productive, particularly in those countries such as Papua New Guinea and others in the Pacific region where there is as yet no strong women's movement.

Case studies of developing countries' initiatives to combat the various forms of violence against women need to be identified, published and widely circulated, with some evaluation of the reasons for their success or failure, so that developing countries can learn from each other's experiences. At the moment, almost all available information derives from wealthy, developed countries and is largely inappropriate for the very different cultural and socio-economic conditions prevailing in less developed countries. Developing countries trying to develop their own programmes of action often feel as if they are floundering in the dark, as I can certainly attest from our experience in Papua New Guinea. An international information exchange and support network linking developing countries and specifically targeting male violence against women is urgently needed.

Notes

1. In the US, these studies included notably R. Gelles, *The Violent Home: a Study of Physical Aggression Between Husbands and Wives* (Beverley Hills, Sage, 1972) and S. Steinmetz and M. Straus, *Violence in the Family* (New York, Harper and Rowe, 1974). Pizzey's work, based on her experiences working with battered wives in London, is published in the UK by Penguin.

2. United Nations, *Violence against Women in the Family* (Vienna, Centre for Social Development and Humanitarian Affairs, 1989).

3. S. Toft and S. Bonnell (eds.), *Marriage and Domestic Violence in Rural Papua New Guinea*, Law Reform Commission Occasional Paper No. 18, 1985; S. Toft (ed.), *Domestic Violence in Urban Papua New Guinea*, Law Reform Commission Occasional Paper No. 19, 1986; S. Toft (ed.), *Domestic Violence in Papua New Guinea*, Law Reform Commission Monograph No. 3, 1985; and S. Toft (ed.), *Marriage in Papua New Guinea*, Law Reform Commission Monograph No. 4, 1986.

4. C. Bradley, 'Wife-beating in Papua New Guinea – Is It a Problem?', *Papua New Guinea Medical Journal*, Vol. 31, No. 4, 1988, p. 258.

5. A. Ekeroma, 'Spouse-beating: a hospital study,' in S. Toft (ed.), *Domestic Violence in Urban Papua New Guinea*.

6. E. Kaetovuhu and R. Tyrer, 'Domestic violence in Papua New Guinea: the reporting of incidents to the police' (unpublished paper, Research and Planning Section, Department of Police, Konedobu, 1987).

7. S. Ranck and S. Toft, 'Domestic Violence in Urban Context with Rural Comparisons', in S. Toft (ed.), *Domestic Violence in Urban Papua New Guinea*.

8. Papua New Guinea *Hansard*, 2 March 1987.

9. M. Gibson, 'Equity for female teachers: a national survey of employment, training and promotional opportunities for community school teachers in Papua New Guinea'. (Unpublished draft Report No. 65 of the National Research Institute, Educational Research Division, 1990.)

10. United Nations, 1989, p. 29.

11. C. Benard, 'Patterns of violence against women in the family', Working Paper on the Nature and Effects of Physical Violence and Coercion Against Women in the Family, Expert Group Meeting of Violence in the Family with Special Emphasis on its Effects on Women, Vienna, 8–12 December 1986.

12. Elizabeth Cox, resident development consultant, personal communication.

13. Susanne Bonnell, resident social worker, personal communication.

14. According to Straus et al., one in three husbands and one in four wives interviewed in a survey of 2,143 couples in the United States believed that under certain circumstances, couples slapping each other was 'necessary, normal or good'. See M. Straus, R. Gelles and S. Steinmetz, *Behind Closed Doors – Violence in the American Family*, (New York, Anchor Press/Doubleday, 1980), p. 47.

15. United Nations, 1989.

16. Commonwealth Secretariat, *Confronting Violence – A Manual for Commonwealth Action*, 1987; Commonwealth Secretariat, *Guidelines for Police Training on Violence Against Women and Child Sexual Abuse*, 1988; and Commonwealth

Secretariat, *Violence Against Women – Curriculum Materials for Legal Studies*, n.d.

17. Published in the Papua New Guinea *Post Courier*, 13 November 1986.

18. I. Riley, D. Wohlfahrt and E. Carrad, 'The management of rape and other sexual offences in Port Moresby', report of a workshop held on 4 June 1985, Department of Community Medicine, University of Papua New Guinea, Port Moresby General Hospital, p. 3.

19. Papua New Guinean women also experience powerlessness to a greater extent than do men, although they still retain a basic sense of female identity through motherhood. Further discussion of this issue is not possible in this context.

20. Workshop organized by the Asia-South Pacific Foundation for Adult Education, on 'Strategies and Innovations in Nonformal Education for Women', Guangzhou, China, November 1988.

Domestic Violence: the Northern Ireland Response
Women's Aid

Our experience is that Women's Aid can dramatically change women's lives and has changed the lives of thousands of women and children as they discover an alternative to living with a violent partner. It changes lives in a way not understood by those who seek to dominate women, whether personally or through the workplace, through laws or services administered by government. That is the great hope of the Women's Aid Movement.
Jane Hutt in Ginny Nicarthy, *Getting Free: a Handbook for Women in Abusive Situations* (London, Journeyman Press, 1991)

Britain's leading organization dealing with domestic violence, Women's Aid, provides a wide range of services for women and children who have been abused within the home, and for agencies who come into contact with them. The following text, reprinted with kind permission from the Women's Aid Federation of Northern Ireland, forms part of a domestic violence training and information pack produced by Women's Aid in Belfast in 1991.

In 1857 a man could beat his wife 'providing the stick was no thicker than his thumb'. Although today in Northern Ireland wife assault is no longer legally permitted, its recognition as a criminal offence appears to have had little impact on the widespread practice and

27

extent of the problem, which affects hundreds of women and children throughout Northern Ireland. The existence of large numbers of women and children suffering persistent physical, emotional or sexual abuse within the family has been largely ignored. Indeed, domestic violence is only beginning to be a matter for public and government concern and part of the 'public agenda'. Since 1975 Women's Aid in Northern Ireland has been the primary agency working in this field providing a specialized service of support and protection to women and children at risk from violence within the home.

The 1970s: the beginning of the movement

The Women's Aid movement in Northern Ireland is part of a widespread movement which began in the United Kingdom in the early 1970s. The first refuge was set up in Chiswick in autumn 1971, as a centre where women would meet, talk and seek help with their problems. It soon became evident that the primary need of the women contacting the centre was for refuge for themselves and their children and this became the focus of their work. The intense media attention given to this refuge during the early 1970s was very effective in raising the awareness of the great need for more refuges. Throughout the mid-1970s independent refuges for women and children were being set up as part of an international movement which included Britain, Ireland, the USA, Canada, Australia and many European countries. In Britain many of these groups came together to share their experiences and used the name Women's Aid.

In Northern Ireland the growth of the movement has been dramatic. The first refuge opened in 1975 in Belfast but unfortunately closed after 19 months as the small terraced house was unsuitable for the purpose. The experience of running a refuge and the demand for its services had proved the necessity of making provision for women and children who suffered from domestic violence. During 1977, Women's Aid groups were set up in Derry and Coleraine and with Belfast Women's Aid they formed the Northern Ireland Women's Aid Federation. The role of the federation was to act as a co-ordinating and development body and also to maintain contact with sister federations which now existed in England, Scotland and Wales.

The campaigning years

The year 1978 was a significant one for Women's Aid in Northern Ireland, with Belfast opening a larger refuge and new refuges opening in Coleraine, whilst the Derry refuge had opened six months earlier. Despite the availability of refuge provision, the political climate in Northern Ireland at this time was largely unsympathetic to the needs of abused women and children. The late 1970s was therefore a period of intense campaigning to extend legal protection and welfare rights for women being abused by their partners. Progress did not always come quickly and the significant advances gained during this period were gained primarily through the efforts of Women's Aid and abused women themselves. Sometimes the results of the campaigning were dramatic – a campaign resulted in the exercise of the royal prerogative and secured the release of a young woman who had been given a seven-year jail sentence for stabbing her father, who had persistently sexually abused her and her sisters.

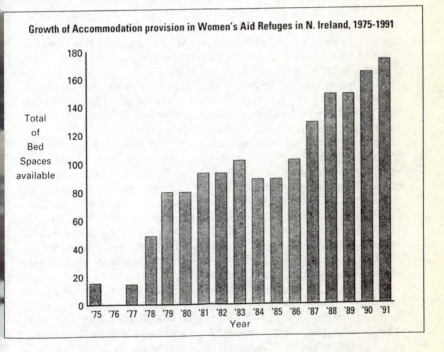

Growth of Accommodation provision in Women's Aid Refuges in N. Ireland, 1975-1991

Legal protection with an automatic power of arrest was introduced in 1981, although cohabitees were not included until 1983. Housing policies were amended to include abused women and children as a priority category. The financial position of women and children in refuges was improved to assist with the additional expenditure essential for living in temporary accommodation and for families moving out to set up home on their own. But these gains have now been set in reverse and the position of women and children in refuges is currently one of great financial hardship.

The 1980s: a decade of regional development

By 1980 the demands on the three refuges in Northern Ireland were immense and it was obvious that facilities were hopelessly inadequate in responding to need. The 1975 government report by the Select Committee on Violence in Marriage had recommended there should be one family space per 10,000 population. Applying this to Northern Ireland meant a minimum target of 150 family spaces or 450 bed spaces. As Northern Ireland had only 25 family places, the overriding priority for the 1980s was to extend the provision throughout the province. Help from established refuges was crucial during this period of regional development: they provided expertise, support and advice for the new groups which were set up in Omagh and North Down (1982), Newry (1983), Ballymena and Enniskillen (1984), Antrim (1986), and Craigavon (1988). Whilst not all of these groups survived, the diagram on page 29 illustrates the success of the policy giving priority to the establishment of refuges.

By adopting the principles of self-help within a supportive structure and women-only environment, Women's Aid has provided one of the most innovative and effective models of working to be seen in either the voluntary or statutory sectors in recent years.

The pioneering work that characterized the 1970s was not forgotten during the 1980s; a conference on sexual abuse was held in Belfast in 1985 and led to a refuge specifically for victims of incest and sexual abuse being opened by Belfast Women's Aid in 1986, one of the few in the UK. Concern over the response of other agencies, particularly the police, to domestic violence prompted a research initiative on police response in 1987. The role of Women's Aid in providing training and awareness to outside agencies was also developed during this period and included training with police officers, social workers, health visitors and others.

The funding of refuges, which was a source of constant difficulty, continued to place Women's Aid groups in great economic insecurity. However, with the growing recognition of the expertise that Women's Aid had to offer statutory agencies, securing funding, albeit at a minimum level, became somewhat easier. In 1989, with the introduction of the Homeless Persons Act, Women's Aid in Northern Ireland was fortunate to retain funding for the care elements of the work whilst the Northern Ireland Housing Executive took responsibility for the accommodation costs. This dual funding mechanism reflects the diverse elements in the service Women's Aid provides. It is primarily the result of the open and honest working relationship that has been established and maintained over the years between Women's Aid and a wide range of voluntary and statutory agencies.

By the end of the 1980s, Women's Aid was and is still today the largest provider of temporary accommodation in the voluntary sector with over 70 family spaces including a provision for women and children who have been victims of incest and sexual abuse.

The 1990s: looking to the future

With the start of the 1990s Women's Aid's priority was still firmly with the needs of women and children coming to refuges. A particular feature of Women's Aid in Northern Ireland has been a deep commitment to a high standard of refuge accommodation which can provide a safe and positive environment for women and children. This has been made possible first through the housing associations who purchase and renovate suitable properties. Second, permanent funding enables Women's Aid to employ committed and experienced staff who can offer a professional and caring service to women and children.

The political situation in Northern Ireland has implications for those concerned in responding to domestic violence. It can limit the availability and response of police officers in certain areas and this can restrict a woman's choice about involving them. However, the service provided is used by women from all communities as well as from both urban and rural communities. Indeed, a positive aspect of our work is that the common experience of domestic violence brings women together and friendships and networks are formed despite the divisions and conflicts within Northern Ireland communities.

In the 1990s the issue for Women's Aid will be to develop mechanisms which lie outside refuge support systems. The Women's Aid movement is still developing, but we need to assist and encourage other agencies in developing positive responses to domestic violence. The recent guidelines issued by police forces throughout the UK are an encouraging sign.

Whilst the availability of Women's Aid refuges in Northern Ireland in the last 16 years has provided a powerful catalyst in challenging male violence within the home, refuges on their own provide only part of the solution. Responding to domestic violence is about addressing the needs of women and children who are at a crisis point in their lives; it is also about addressing the actions of those who use violence against their partners. Meeting these challenges will require clear policies, a multi-agency approach and a commitment to bring about change. There is greater awareness than ever before of the need for a concerned response to be made.

In Search of Solutions: Women's Police Stations in Brazil

Dorothy Q. Thomas

In April 1991, the Women's Rights Project, together with the Americas regional division of Human Rights Watch, travelled to Brazil to assess the response of the Brazilian government to the problem of domestic violence. This article, focusing on the role of the women's movement and the impact of women's police stations, is compiled from a 70-page report of that mission.

The report's author, Dorothy Thomas, is director of the Women's Rights Project, established in 1990 to monitor both violence against women and gender discrimination committed or tolerated by governments throughout the world. The project grew out of Human Rights Watch's recognition of the epidemic proportions of such abuse and of the past failure of human rights organizations, and the international community, to hold governments accountable.

On 5 August 1988, in the Brazilian city of Apucarana, João Lopes (nicknamed 'Joe Slick'), after spending two days in search of his wife, Terezinha Ribeiro Lopes, arrived at a hotel where he believed her to be with her lover, José Gaspar Felix. A bellman took him to the room of two people answering to their description. At the bellman's request, the door was opened by José Felix who, with no forewarning, was stabbed repeatedly in the chest by João Lopes. Lopes then ran after his wife, who fled naked from the room and out of the hotel. Lopes chased his wife into the streets and caught up with her at the door of a hospital, where he killed her with two knife wounds.

The all-male jury accepted the argument advanced by the defence that Lopes had acted in legitimate defence of his offended honour in killing the two victims, and unanimously absolved him of the double homicide.[1] The state appellate court in Paraná upheld this decision.

The Federal Public Ministry responsible for prosecuting the case sought recourse to the Superior Tribunal of Justice, Brazil's highest court of appeal. The tribunal accepted the prosecution's appeal, and on 11 March 1991 overturned the lower court's decision and ordered a new trial.[2] In so doing, the tribunal declared that murder cannot be conceived of as a legitimate response to adultery and that what is being defended in this type of crime is not honour but 'self-esteem, vanity and the pride of the lord who sees his wife as property'.

Love yes, beating no. *Movimiento Manuela Ramos, Peru.*

The Superior Tribunal's decision represented an historic moment, both for the Brazilian judiciary and for the feminist activists who waged a 20-year-campaign against the honour defence and against the proprietary attitudes towards women on which it is based. However, despite such welcome progress, the reality is that in Brazil – as elsewhere – wife murder is still considered an appropriate response to alleged unfaithfulness. On 29 August 1991, the Lopes case was retried in the state court of Paraná, and Lopes was again acquitted of the double homicide on the grounds of legitimate defence of honour. The decision perpetuates a culture of impunity in wife murder crimes sanctioned by the Brazilian courts and represents a victory of social prejudice over the rule of law in Brazil.

The role of the women's movement

The Superior Tribunal's rejection of the honour defence in the Lopes case follows a decades-long struggle by Brazilian feminists to de-legitimate the 'legitimate defence of honour' and to force the state to prosecute wife murder and other domestic violence crimes to the full extent of the law. This effort began in connection with two famous cases in Rio de Janeiro and São Paulo.

The first involved Raul Doca Street who in 1979 murdered his lover after she decided to break off their relationship. During Street's first trial the defence argued he had acted in legitimate defence of his offended honour. While the court ultimately did not accept the honour defence, it did accept the notion that Street acted in a moment of 'violent emotion' (discussed below), which it took as a mitigating factor justifying a sentence of only two years for the crime. The decision was appealed and at Street's second trial in 1980, thousands of women gathered outside the courthouse protesting against the earlier decision. Street ultimately was sentenced to 15 years in prison – the standard sentence for intentional homicide.

The second case, which took place in 1981, involved Lindomar Castilho, a famous Brazilian singer who shot his wife, Eliane, and her cousin, who Lindomar believed was Eliane's lover. Eliane died but her cousin survived. In the pre-trial phase, the defence argued that the crime had been motivated by 'violent emotion due to the unjust provocation of the victim', whereas the prosecution charged that the crime was premeditated and that Eliane's active nightlife and love relationship were 'not valid reasons for a crime of this magnitude'. The judge ultimately accepted violent emotion as a factor in the crime. Women's rights activists immediately protested against the judge's ruling. In 1984, when the case was finally brought to trial, the jury rejected the 'violent emotion' defence and Lindomar was sentenced to 12 years in prison.

These two cases, together with two similar cases heard at the time in Minas Gerais, galvanized a national women's movement to protest against domestic violence and the inadequate, often discriminatory response of the Brazilian police and judiciary.

This movement against domestic violence emerged, in part, against the background of Brazil's military dictatorship and in the context of the gradual liberalization which began in the late 1970s and culminated in the 1985 indirect election of a civilian president and the creation of the new Brazilian Republic. Reports on sexual abuse, torture and murder of political prisoners during the dictatorship led to a national debate about violence and, in the mid-1970s, to the creation of a number of non-governmental human rights organizations in which women were very active.

With the development of the broadly based pro-democracy movement, 'the debate on violence enlarged to include many forms of its exercise, besides those which occurred directly at the hands of the authoritarian state'.[3] Women's organizations proliferated during this period, particularly SOS-Mulher, a nationwide organization devoted to combating violence against women.[4] As a result of these developments, gender-specific issues which had previously been considered 'private' or 'personal', such as domestic violence, emerged as major public policy concerns.

Active women in both urban and rural areas and across racial and economic divides seized on domestic violence and used it successfully to propel gender concerns into the broader public policy debate. A series of local demonstrations led to several nationwide protests against domestic violence from which emerged the anonymous slogan that became the *crie de coeur* of the Brazilian women's movement: 'Those who love don't kill.'

The 1982 elections, which represented the first direct balloting for state governor since 1965,[5] demonstrated the emergence of the women's movement as a major political force. Women were very

If anyone hits you, denounce him. *Irene Rojas, Movimiento Manuela Ramos, Peru.*

active during the campaign, and gender-specific demands were for the first time integrated into the platforms of the various political parties. As a result of the 1982 elections several opposition candidates won state governorships, most notably in São Paulo and Rio de Janeiro. Women's demands were soon institutionalized in these states through the creation of state councils of women.

The first state council (Conselho Estadual da Condição Feminina) was created in São Paulo in 1983. Its primary goals were to increase women's access to the policy-making process and to promote women's interests within the state administration. It was followed by the creation of similar councils in many other states and, in 1985, under the auspices of the first civilian President, Tancredo Neves, by the creation of a National Council for Women's rights (CNDM), one of the very few things Neves did before his tenure as President was cut short by his death in March of that year. The CNDM was a federal body 'in charge of designing and developing public policy to improve the condition of women'.[6]

A major goal of both the state and national councils was combating violence against women. CNDM president Jacqueline Pitanguy put gender-specific violence at the top of the council's political agenda, launching a 'say no to violence against women' campaign and compiling several documents detailing violence against women and criticizing the inadequate penal and judicial response.

During this period, women also began to be better represented in professional and political life. According to research conducted in 1984, 'the female economically active population (EAP) went from 18.5 per cent in 1970 to 26.9 per cent in 1980, a proportion which accounts for 41 per cent of the increase in the total EAP over the decade'.[7]

The type of women's employment also changed. 'The share of female EAP increased in administrative occupations (from 8.2 per cent in 1960 to 15.4 per cent in 1980) and in professions of higher prestige (engineers, architects, doctors, dentists, economists, university professors and lawyers which went from 19,000 in 1970 to 95,800 in 1980).'[8] In 1980, the number of women enrolled in Brazilian universities almost equalled the number of men.[9] According to statistics compiled by the Inter-American Commission on Women, women now represent 52 per cent of Brazil's voting population.[10]

Women's increased economic and political power, coupled with the development of autonomous and state-affiliated women's institutions, enabled the women's movement to press for fundamental changes in the state's response to gender-specific violence. In 1985, women's groups, together with the state council on women, persuaded São Paulo's opposition party mayor to establish a woman's police station, staffed entirely by women and dedicated solely to crimes of violence against women, excluding homicide, which was not viewed as a gender-specific crime.[11] By late 1985, eight women's police stations (Delegacias de Defesa Da Mulher, hereafter *delegacias*) had opened in the state of São Paulo, and by 1990 there were 74 throughout the country.[12]

The impact of women's police stations

The women's *delegacias* represent an integrated approach to the problem of domestic violence. They were designed to investigate gender-specific crimes, and to provide psychological and legal counselling. The female police officers (*delegadas*) were to receive training in all aspects of domestic violence, from its psychological impact to the legal remedies available to the victim. The medical practitioners at the Medical Legal Institute (IML), charged with certifying the nature of physical injuries to the police, were also to receive such training. Finally, the *delegacias* were to integrate perspectives gained in their work into the activities of the other stations and, in some states, a permanent commission was formed to ensure these objectives were met.

Prior to the creation of women's *delegacias*, police stations rarely investigated crimes of violence against women that occurred in the home. In many cases, police officers were actively hostile towards female victims seeking to report such abuse.

The national anti-violence network SOS-Mulher, which was created in 1981 and aided over 2,000 victims of domestic violence in its first year, found that 'violence against women continued in the regular *delegacias* when they tried to report aggressions'. The SOS network reported:

> Battery, rape and death threats are routine facts in the lives of many women ... Every time women go to the regular *delegacias* looking for support and protection, they suffer another type of violence. This is the violence of refusing to register their complaints, the suspicion cast upon them making them responsible for the crimes they suffered ... Such behaviour of the authorities reinforces and legitimizes impunity for violence against women and makes them hesitate to fight for their rights.[13]

A 1983 follow-up study in Minas Gerais by the Centre for the Defence of Women's Rights found that the police often turned female victims away, on the grounds that domestic violence was 'a private problem'. When police did register domestic abuse crimes, they frequently failed to follow standard procedures, leaving out pertinent information about the circumstances of the abuse. In addition, they often subjected the victim to abusive treatment aimed at implicating her in the crime.[14]

An Assistant Secretary of Public Security, who served as Secretary of Public Security in Pernambuco prior to and during the creation of the women's *delegacias*, told Americas Watch that 'the *delegacia* was created because of the failure of regular police to investigate crimes ... The woman was seen as something her husband can beat on. She could be a victim of violence and then have it be perceived by the police as normal. There's a song that says you don't beat a woman even with a flower, but the reality is different.'[15]

In the context of such overtly discriminatory attitudes on the part of police, the creation of women's police stations to deal exclusively with violence against women constituted a major victory for women's rights advocates. As noted by Sonia Alvarez, 'the ground-breaking recognition of this gender-specific aspect of crime by the State [was] unprecedented in Brazil and indeed the women's precinct structure is unparalleled anywhere in the world'.[16]

Brazil's most recent census (1988), coupled with reports gathered from the women's *delegacias*, reveals a high level of domestic abuse among reported crimes of physical violence against women. A 1987 study of over 2,000 battery cases registered at the São Paulo *delegacia* from August to December 1985 found that over 70 per cent of all reported crimes of violence against women occurred in the home. Almost 40 per cent of these registered incidents involved serious bodily injury, usually committed by the accused's own feet or fists.[17] The 1988 census generally corroborates these figures. These statistics give the first in-depth picture of domestic violence in Brazil.

In the six years since their creation the *delegacias* have succeeded not only in expanding the definition of criminal activity in Brazil to include violence against women, but also in altering the traditional perception of wife-beating as socially acceptable. According to former National Council of Women President Jacqueline Pitanguy:

> The existence of the *delegacias* means that certain acts [which were not and still are not in many cases] perceived as criminal behavior by the regular police, by the accused and frequently by the victim are now qualifying as criminal behaviors. And they are being punished as such. In this sense the *delegacias* combat not only crime but also its definition, changing the border of accepted/non-accepted social behavior.[18]

Despite the *delegacias'* considerable accomplishments in responding to women victims and raising the visibility of domestic violence, Americas Watch found that the actual criminalization of such abuse has not markedly increased. Several researchers told Americas Watch that in general the *delegacias'* impact 'has been more psycho-social than criminal. They created a space within the police system which is dedicated to recognizing crimes of violence against women, but have not necessarily worked as an effective deterrent to such violence.'

Sociologists, researchers, attorneys and women's rights advocates interviewed by Americas Watch estimated that only 20 to 50 per cent of the domestic abuse cases reported to the *delegacias* are ever investigated. Figures from the main São Paulo *delegacia* show that of 2,573 corporal-lesion cases registered in 1989, only 1,135, or less than 50 per cent, were ever investigated by the police.[19]

The reasons for these low investigative rates are complex and vary from police station to police station and from state to state. However, general trends are discernible. Most people familiar with the *delegacias* attribute this problem less to the failings of the *delegacias* themselves (although they are a contributing factor) than to the limitations imposed on the *delegacias* by the institutional and social context within which they operate. Many people we interviewed, including *delegadas*, attribute low investigation rates primarily to shifting and often diminishing economic and political support from the state and federal governments, low police morale, and lack of training about domestic violence at the police academy.

The effectiveness of the *delegacias* depends on the importance local authorities ascribe to them. There are only 74 *delegacias* in all of Brazil's 24 states and two territories and they are not equally distributed throughout the country (over 50 are located in the state of São Paulo). Nor do they receive equal support *vis-à-vis* each other or the regular police stations. Pitanguy notes that 'the prestige of the women's police stations inside police structures varies, but in general they are not given the importance of traditional specialized police stations like those for homicide or drugs'.[20]

In the state of Rio de Janeiro, for example, the first women's police station opened in 1986 and was soon followed by two more. After a change in government, however, only one *delegacia* was added during the next four years. In the same period, the state of São Paulo added 19 stations. This may be due partly to economic factors, as Rio suffered a severe economic crisis in the late 1980s. However, the number of *delegacias* is also a function of political will. The new Rio state government – elected in 1990 – has already added two additional women's *delegacias* and plans to add five more by the end of 1991. Rio Secretary of Public Security Nilo Batista told Americas Watch that 'the demand is very great'.[21]

Several *delegadas* we interviewed spoke of the discriminatory treatment they experience from many of their police colleagues as a result of choosing to work in the women's police stations. One *delegada* told us that the *delegacias* are treated like 'the kitchen of the police'. A women's rights activist who works closely with the *delegacias* told Americas Watch, 'The *delegacias* are not a career police thing. There is a stigma attached to working in a *delegacia*. The *delegadas* do not like the work because of discrimination in the police force.'[22]

While diminishing resources and poor morale are key factors in low investigative rates by the police, the most regularly cited problem is that many women police serve in the *delegacias* without receiving adequate specialized training. Sonia Alvarez points out that although 'in some cases feminist scholars and activists were brought in to train female police at these specialized precincts, feminists were marginalized from most, as the selection and training of staff was entrusted to the local force'.[23] In São Paulo and Rio for example, early attempts to have material on domestic violence incorporated into the police training manuals, while successful at first, suffered from both lack of institutional support and financial cutbacks, and were ultimately dropped.

In some *delegacias*, particularly in the early years, lack of police training was offset by the presence of social workers who were trained to respond in domestic violence cases. However, financial cutbacks and lack of internal support have scaled down the capacity of the *delegacias* to provide psychological aid as originally intended. Some cities and states, like São Paulo and the small city of Santo André outside São Paulo, continue to retain social workers in the *delegacias* to assist victims. In the states of Belo Horizonte and Rio de Janeiro, however, *delegacias* no longer provide this service. Overall, the psychological aid provided at the *delegacias* is minimal.

These institutional constraints limit the capacity of the *delegacias* to move beyond raising the visibility of domestic violence to increasing the actual criminalization of such abuse. Attorneys with whom we spoke believe that, in particular, the *delegadas'* lack of training perpetuates a reluctance by police authorities, regardless of their gender, to see domestic violence as a crime. According to Pitanguy 'police women still need to perceive certain violent behaviour as crimes'.[24] As one attorney who frequently represents domestic violence victims in civil cases told Americas Watch, 'the *delegacias* normally don't register the crime ... There doesn't exist any mentality in the *delegacia* that a crime has occurred ... Even the *delegacias* don't consider domestic violence a crime. Even registered cases don't go forward; they get shelved. It's a question of mentality. It's family, it's not a crime.'[25]

Even when domestic abuse is perceived as a crime, these attitudes can carry over into the police's choice of the crime to be charged. There appears to be a tendency to file reduced charges in cases of domestic abuse. In the 1987 São Paulo study cited above, for example, researchers noted that in 30 per cent of the cases classified as 'serious threats' and 36 per cent of those classified as 'misunderstandings', the police record included complaints of physical abuse that apparently had not been reflected in the crime charged.[26]

These reduced charges are to some extent attributable to lack of training. Detectives, who are often the first to interview the victim, are not always versed in the law pertaining to the classification of domestic abuse offences. Although women police chiefs are required to have legal degrees and should correct improper classifications before they are forwarded for prosecution, this is not always the case.

Available data indicates that reduced charges are also the result of the police's reluctance to investigate reports of domestic abuse. Researchers at the University of São Paulo Centre for the Study of Violence found that 'the women police showed a lot of disrespect for the victims. They were not sympathetic, sort of fed-up. They ended up blaming the victims for their own fate.'[27] One researcher noted that certain 'informal mechanisms' exist to file lesser charges in cases of domestic abuse so that they can be registered as private action crimes which depend on the initiative of the victim, not the state, for prosecution.

This reluctance to investigate is often due to the *delegadas'* assessment that domestic abuse will not be prosecuted. As one scholar noted, 'the *delegadas* are in a double bind. They want to help the victim but they do not want to mislead her about the likelihood that her assailant will be punished.'[28] One victim of domestic violence interviewed by Americas Watch had just come from a *delegacia* where the *delegada* told her 'it would not do any good to register the crime because 70 per cent of such cases are dropped'.[29]

Brazil's first chief of a women's police station, Rosemary Correa, now a deputy in the São Paulo State Legislature, estimates that 40 per cent of domestic abuse cases are prosecuted. However, the main *delegada* in Rio told Americas Watch that of the over 2,000 battery cases she investigated in 1990, none resulted in punishment of the accused. Similarly, the US State Department's human rights report for 1990 noted that in the main *delegacia* in São Luis, Maranhão, of over 4,000 complaints registered by women from 1988 to 1990, only 300 were forwarded for processing by the court and only two men were convicted and sent to prison.[30]

Women police officers in several cities told Americas Watch that even when they investigate cases in a timely manner and forward them for prosecution they do not hear from the prosecutor for months and then he or she is usually seeking additional information.[31] One *delegada* said the prosecutors often sent the files back to the police 'due to a backlog in the courts. It's sent back [to the *delegacia*] to buy time.' One police chief told Americas Watch that in cases where 'it takes a long time, the case can kind of go away'.[31] According to one criminal court judge, 'someone commits a crime and it takes an eternity for it to get a response. This is a great discredit to judicial power.' The day before Americas Watch's visit he was presiding in the trial of a case which occurred 17 years ago. While he was quick to point out that this kind of delay 'is the exception', he noted that 'a lot of these trials go on for years. It's really a structural problem.'[33]

The failure to prosecute can also be attributed in part to the nature of domestic violence. In the first place, both prosecutors and judges drop cases when they believe the couple will reconcile. Moreover, in the courts as with the police, there is a persistent failure to see domestic battery as a crime. Judges receive no training on domestic violence. A defence lawyer representing domestic violence victims in Rio de Janeiro told Americas Watch that the 'judiciary takes a benign view towards violence against women'.[34] Professor Silvia Pimentel told Americas Watch, 'Domestic violence is not sufficiently followed by the state. We are seeking improvements in the law and its implementation, but it requires more than a change in legal framework. It requires a whole change of attitude: a man should not be able to beat and/or kill his wife with impunity.'

Notes

1. Not all jurors in Brazil are male. The defence attorney in the Lopes case felt the sex of the jurors had 'nothing to do' with the decision. He chose two women jurors for the trial, but they were rejected by the prosecution.
2. Under Brazilian law, prosecutors have a right to appeal an acquittal when the decision is made against all available facts in the case.
3. Jacqueline Pitanguy (former president of the National Council of Women's Rights), 'Violence against women: addressing a global problem', report to the Ford Foundation, 1991, p. 2 (mimeo).
4. Sonia Alvarez, writing in 'Politicising gender and engendering democracy', in Alfred Stepan (ed.), *Democratising Brazil*, (Oxford, OUP, 1989), p. 211, notes the 'presence of over 400 feminist groups in the major Brazilian urban centres' in the mid-1970s.
5. Thomas E. Skidmore, in Stepan (ed.), p. 23.
6. Pitanguy, p. 2.
7. Renato Paul Boschi, 'The art of associating: social movements, the middle class and grassroots politics in urban Brazil' (Final Report for the Tinker Foundation, December 1984), quoted in Alvarez, p. 211.
8. Ibid.
9. Ibid.
10. Comissão Interamericana de Mulheres, Brazil report, July 1990.
11. In general, the responsibilities of the *delegacias* include crimes involving bodily wounds, threats and sexual crimes, including rape.
12. Pitanguy.
13. Letter sent to the Secretary of Public Security by the SOS Mulher Chapter in Belo Horizonte, October 1982, cited in *Crimes Contra A Mulher: A Violência Denunciada*, (provisional title), unpublished report by Maria da Conceição Marques Rubinger, et al., with support from the Ford Foundation, 1991.
14. *Crimes Contra A Mulher*, Introduction.
15. Assistant Secretary of Public Security Marini de Figueired, Recife, interview with Americas Watch, April 1991.
16. Sonia E. Alvarez, *Engendering Democracy in Brazil* (New Jersey: Princeton University Press, 1990), p. 218.
17. Fundação SEADE, Conselho Estadual Da Condiçao Feminina, *Um Retrato Da Violência Contra A Mulher* (CIP International, 1987).

18. Pitanguy, p. 5.
19. Assessoria Especial Das Delegacias De Defesa Da Mulher Do Estado De São Paulo, General Statistics, 1989.
20. Pitanguy, p. 6.
21. Secretary of Public Security Nilo Batista, interview with Americas Watch, April 1991.
22. Cida Medrado, interview with Americas Watch, April 1991.
23. Alvarez, p. 246.
24. Jacqueline Pitanguy, interview with Americas Watch, April 1991.
25. Cecília Texeira Soares, Pró-Mulher, interview with Americas Watch, April 1991.
26. *Um Retrato Da Violência Contra A Mulher*, p. 44.
27. Nancy Cardia, sociologist, University of São Paulo's Centre for the Study of Violence, interview with Americas Watch, April 1991.
28. Professor Silvia Pimentel, interview with Americas Watch, April 1991.
29. 'Marta', interviewed by Americas Watch at Pró-Mulher, a legal and social assistance office in Rio de Janeiro, April 1991.
30. United States Department of State, Country Reports on Human Rights Practices for 1990, February 1991, p. 531.
31. Under the law, police have 30 days to complete an initial investigation when the suspect is not detained, and the prosecution has another 30 days to conduct its own investigation and recommend charges. However, these limits are regularly exceeded, often without the required judicial authorization.
32. Detective Inspector Mary May da Silva Porto, interview with Americas Watch, April 1991.
33. Judge Roberto Ferreira Lins, interview with Americas Watch, April 1991.
34. Attorney Leila Linhares, interview with Americas Watch, April 1991. Linhares is a criminal defence attorney who works for CEPIA, an organization which monitors, among other things, penal and judicial response to crimes of violence against women.

India: From Sati to Sex-Determination Tests
Sakuntala Narasimhan

Religion and culture have been used, more than any other reasons, to defend practices oppressive to women around the world. Sakuntala Narasimhan, an Indian journalist and author of four books, including *Sati – A Study of Widow-Burning in India*, discusses three such practices below.

One thinks of violence mostly in terms of physical battering, or rape, but there are other kinds of violence that spring from a particular mind-set based on the cultural perceptions of a woman's place in

Women and Violence

society. One such manifestation in India is sati, the rite of widow immolation. The other is bride-burning (also known as dowry death).

When a man dies, if his wife burns herself to death on the same pyre she is said to become a sati, a paragon of connubial devotion and an exalted, deified woman. The rite was banned by law in 1829 during British rule, but incidents of sati continued to be recorded right up to September 1987 when an 18-year-old girl named Roop Kanwar burned to death on the funeral pyre of her husband in Rajasthan state in western India. In the wake of this incident the government passed a Sati (Prevention of Glorification) Act, but several thousand supporters of the custom congregated in protest demonstrations, claiming that sati was part of Hindu religious observances and that the law amounted to interference in religious beliefs. The frenzied emotions that the nationwide debate on the issue whipped up all through 1988 showed that the worthlessness of a woman's life, except in the service of her husband, is still a pervasive belief governing social perceptions.

The case of Roop Kanwar

Roop Kanwar and her 24-year-old husband Maal Singh had been married for less than eight months when he died on 4 September 1987, reportedly of gastro-enteritis. Dressed in bridal finery and followed by a crowd said to have been 4,000 strong, Roop Kanwar walked to the funeral platform that had been erected in the middle of the village, and was burnt to death along with the body of her deceased husband. Money began to pour in almost immediately for the erection of a marble temple to commemorate her deification. As news of the incident spread, women's groups in the state capital, Jaipur, an hour and a half away by road, demanded the arrest of those who had been a party to this roasting alive of a young girl, but apart from a few token arrests (of the brother-in-law who had lit the pyre and the father-in-law, both of whom were later released on bail) the state machinery turned out to be powerless as thousands of visitors began to gather from nearby villages to begin preparations for the thirteenth-day 'glorification' ceremony in honour of Roop Kanwar. Although all public buses were stopped on the road to the village, some 250,000 people turned up for the ceremony, and over 30,000 copies of a colour photo-collage showing her in the middle of the flames with her husband's head on her lap were sold. Roop Kanwar had become a *sati-mata*, a deified woman endowed with miraculous powers to grant boons, because she had died on her husband's pyre.

44

Dowry deaths

This same exaltation of the married state as the only desirable or socially acceptable state for women has also spawned the problem of dowry deaths. If marriage is imperative for a girl, parents suffer social censure if they have not found a suitable husband for their daughters. Parents of girls therefore offer a dowry, in cash and kind (household goods, gadgets, luxury items, gold) as enticements to prospective bridegrooms. The groom's family in turn makes demands or dictates 'terms' on which they will agree to the marriage, and this often forces a girl's family to go heavily into debt in order to perform the marriage to the satisfaction of the in-laws. (Marriages are still mostly arranged by the parents, especially in the villages and smaller towns.) When the demands are not met satisfactorily, the bride is harassed by her in-laws and pressured to get more from her natal home. Since every bride has it impressed upon her that walking out of a marriage, whatever the provocation or distress, would disgrace her parental family (a 'good' woman is one who is stoical; to shirk suffering is to be 'unfeminine') she kills herself when the harassment becomes unbearable, or is doused with kerosene and set alight by her in-laws who then claim that it was a 'kitchen accident' (most middle-class homes use kerosene stoves for cooking). The man soon marries again, and receives another dowry.

There were 922 officially recorded dowry deaths in 1988, and 792 in 1987[1] (but these do not take into account the hundreds of cases where a woman's death by burns is recorded as 'suicide', even if she was driven to death by the physical and mental torture inflicted on her by her husband and/or in-laws because she could not bring him a refrigerator or scooter or colour television).[1] In the state of Karnataka during 1992 there were 14 dowry deaths in January alone, and in 1991 there were 221 dowry deaths and 892 cases of 'harassment'. A Dowry Prohibition law was passed in 1961, but the law has made no difference – in fact, dowry deaths have proliferated in the years since then because of the spread of a materialistic outlook and rising expectations among the middle classes. The cultural pressure to conform to the ideal of the submissive, uncomplaining, self-effacing wife is so strong that even highly educated women (medical doctors, lawyers, high achievers in various fields) have become bride-burning casualties over the years.

The cult of the virtuous wife

Underlying both sati and dowry deaths is the concept of *pativrta*, the virtuous woman who is unreservedly devoted to her husband, the

"DOWRY DEATHS" IN VISAKHAPATNAM DISTRICT (1985–1988) A REPORT

Andhra Pradesh Civil Liberties Committee, October 1989.

apotheosis of traditional Hindu womanhood. For the *pativrta*, there is – there ought to be – no existence apart from that of her husband. A *pativrta* need not visit temples or go on pilgrimages because worshipping and serving her husband brings her greater merit. The ancient law-giver Manu, whose codes still form the basis for many of the statutes governing Hindus, said, 'A wife's marital duty does not come to an end even if the husband were to sell or abandon her.' Another text, the *Shuddhitattva*, declares, 'If her husband is happy, she should be happy, if he is sad she should be sad, and if he is dead she should also die. Such a wife is called *pativrta*.'

Right from childhood, little girls are taught to pray for the long life of their husbands-to-be (whom they do not even know yet), because widowhood is seen as the worst possible punishment a woman could suffer. Young schoolgirls observe fasts so that in later life they may be spared the indignities of widowhood. There are no corresponding fasts observed by boys for their wives' longevity. 'Deergha sumangali bhava' (May your husband live long) is the traditional blessing uttered by elders every time a girl prostrates herself before them on ceremonial occasions. '*Sumangali*' is a typically Indian concept, denoting the 'auspicious woman'. Only married women whose husbands are living can be *sumangalis*. A widow is '*amangali*', inauspicious, unfit to participate in festivities and weddings (even of her own children). A woman who dies while her husband is still alive (with her *suhag*, or auspicious mark, still intact) is considered 'blessed'.

Mythology reinforces these perceptions. Sita and Savitri are two characters held up as ideals of Indian womanhood. Sita was Rama's wife in the epic *Ramayana*; though she was a princess she insisted on following her husband into the forest when he was banished for 14 years. There she was abducted by Ravana who coveted her, but she refused his advances and was ultimately restored to Rama after a battle in which Ravana was vanquished. However, since she had been in Ravana's custody for a while, she had to prove her fidelity and chastity by undergoing a trial by fire. Savitri, the other ideal, insisted on marrying Satyavan although she knew he had no more than a year left to live; as a *pativrta* she could not think of anyone else as her husband once she had come to look upon Satyavan as her husband-to-be. By the power of her devotion to her husband she vanquished even Yama, the harbinger of death, when he came to take Satyavan's life. 'Grant me a boon,' she said, and he agreed, 'as long as she did not ask for Satyavan's life.' 'Grant me the good fortune of mothering a hundred sons,' she said, whereupon Yama had to grant Satyavan long life, for how could a virtuous woman have a hundred sons unless her husband were alive?

The word *sati* means literally, in Sanskrit, a 'virtuous woman'. It came to be identified with 'a woman who immolates herself' because of the confusion with Sati in a mythological story, who reduced herself to ashes by invoking a divine fire because her father Daksha insulted her husband Shiva by refusing to invite him to a grand sacrificial ceremony he was performing, and she was infuriated by this insult to her consort. She did not immolate herself on her husband's pyre, nor was she a widow, but the term 'becoming a sati' has come to mean not merely a virtuous woman but one who burns herself to death.

From scriptures to economics

The pro-sati faction insists that the scriptures enjoin immolation, and quotes Sanskrit texts. But several scholars have pointed out that the Vedas, which are the most important of Hindu scriptural texts, do not exalt sati and in fact urge a widow to 'get up and make a life of her own' and even mention remarriage.[2] Even the famous couplet that is quoted as enjoining a widow to 'walk into the fire' is believed to be a misreading, either deliberate or inadvertent, of the word *agrey* (meaning 'to come forward') as *agney* ('into the fire'); one small change in the alphabet, and enough mischief done to send thousands of women down the ages to a fiery death. Some of the other verses quoted in favour of sati are either interpolations of a later period (when the position of women is believed to have deteriorated following invasions by alien hordes) or of dubious authority.

In the Bengal region of eastern India, and in Rajasthan in the west, sati incidents were particularly frequent during the late eighteenth and early nineteenth centuries. The belief that a widow who burned would enjoy 'heavenly bliss' in her next seven births was only part of the reason. In Bengal, where the *dayabhaga* system of inheritance was applied (under which a widow could inherit her husband's property, overriding the claims of his other relatives), there was an economic reason for urging a widow to burn: the vested interests of the relatives in the joint family. In Rajasthan, valour for the men lay in death on the battlefield (Rajasthan's history is full of martial confrontations and feuds which were always to the death), whilst for women a corresponding exaltation lay in choosing immolation rather than widowhood. Folklore and popular legends all reiterated this theme.[3]

A voluntary act?

A really chaste and virtuous woman, the argument goes, cannot conceive of a life after her husband is dead; she therefore 'voluntarily' chooses to burn. Such a resolve requires divine inspiration and suprahuman courage; therefore her act deserves veneration and glorification, they say. But has sati always been a voluntary act? Eyewitness records of the early nineteenth century show that child widows, some aged eight and ten, were forced onto the pyre; any who tried to escape were physically bound hand and foot and thrown into the fire so that the family would not be disgraced by her desire to live on after her husband's death.

Some widows who walked apparently voluntarily to their deaths were drugged with opium, so that they were only half conscious of what was happening. And layers of mystique were added to the rite to divert attention from, and downplay, the horror of a woman roasting to death: she is decked in bridal finery because she is 'going to heaven to reside eternally with her husband', there is music, and offerings are brought to her by friends and family, and the whole event, with chanting by priests, and gongs and sandal paste, is treated as an awesome spectacle, a miracle taking place. This kind of frenzied seduction, at a time when she is under shock of bereavement and in addition can look forward to only a future of unmitigated misery as a widow, could even make a woman walk voluntarily to the pyre, no doubt.

Eyewitness accounts of the Roop Kanwar incident of 1987 say that she flailed her hands in the air as the flames caught her.[4] (She was buried under a mound of coconuts: coconuts are traditional offerings brought by devotees, and coconuts, being rich in oil, burn well!) One high-ranking official whom women activists confronted with this fact declared that she had flailed her arms not in distress but 'to bless the crowds gathered to witness her immolation'. Such hijacking even of suffering into mystique lends a horrible dimension of deceptive gloss to a gruesome event.

Even if a woman does walk willingly to the pyre, the question arises: Why does she? Isn't it because life as a widow would be far more of a misery than a quick death by fire?

Widows cannot wear coloured clothes or finery. They are allowed no adornments. Although widow remarriage has been legal since 1856, even today it is only the socially modern and the intrepid who dare to remarry. (For men, on the other hand, remarriage is not merely allowed but enjoined, because a wife's presence beside the husband is essential for the performance of religious rites.) A widow has her bangles ceremonially broken to signify her wretched status. In some communities she is forbidden to eat twice a day: only one meal is permitted. Bengali widows are forbidden fish (because fish is a symbol of fertility). Tonsure of widows (shaving of the head) used to be a common practice (one can still see some elderly widows with their heads shaved). All this was supposed to be 'for her own protection', so that she does not attract male attention and 'go astray'. The word for 'widow' in Tamil, Telugu and Kannada languages is an insult flung even at men; in Tamil a widow is also referred to as 'the woman who does not live' (although she is very much alive!). A Rajasthan widow is required to confine herself to a dark corner of the house, never to show her face outdoors. She is shunned as inauspicious and polluted, an ill omen (especially if she happens to cross the path of someone setting out on an important mission) and a harbinger of bad luck. No wonder, then, that some widows preferred death to life as a widow. As one widow commented wryly after the Roop Kanwar incident, 'It would have been very easy to throw myself onto the pyre when my husband died; it required greater courage to live on and face life – I decided to live on only for the sake of the children.'

This, then, is the crux, the reality of a widow's life, rather than religious or economic considerations. The crushing distress of worthlessness and guilt heaped on a widow (guilt that she is still alive when her lord and master is no more) is as much a kind of violence as physical assault, and perhaps more reprehensible because it is not perceived as violence. The ideal of sati is still very much part of the indoctrination of every Hindu girl.

It is estimated that Rajasthan has had at least one sati case every year in the four decades since independence.[5] However, it is not the actual numbers but the strength of the tide of pro-sati sentiment that comes as an eloquent comment on the social contumely to which widows are subjected, even today. The Shankaracharya of Puri, one of the religious leaders of the Hindus, has filed a case in the Supreme Court challenging the government's ban on sati glorification as unconstitutional; and for a democratically elected government dependent on votes to stay in power, considerations of expediency override any avowed declarations about 'improving the status of women'.[6] And fundamentalist forces have found it convenient to hijack the rite too, in their 'defence of the purity of Hinduism' against 'degenerate modern trends that devalue our glorious heritage'. Young, restless adolescents, looking for causes, in search of diversion from the monotony or tensions of daily life in the current ethos, become easily proselytized into this fundamentalist stream. Roop Kanwar, for instance, had young Rajput boys carrying drawn swords surrounding her as she walked towards the cremation ground and 'protecting her' from interference in the carrying out of her 'divine mission'. Had she wanted to back out, those sword-carrying youths would have made sure that she did not.

A temple could not be raised to commemorate Roop Kanwar's immolation as planned because of the government's ban, but the place still continues to draw crowds of visitors and worshippers – on average 100 people per day, five times as many on special days like the eleventh day of the lunar calendar. Puja, with incense and flowers and coconut offerings takes place every day, notwithstanding the presence of a posse of policemen (in fact, several policemen have themselves spoken appreciatively about the 'virtuous custom of sati'). Visitors seek the deified woman's blessings and intervention in having their wishes fulfilled; and the local residents I spoke to seemed proud of the fact that their village had 'become world-famous' after the sati incident.

Sex determination tests and abortion

Sex-selective abortion is yet another atrocity against the female. With the aid of modern technology which makes it possible, through an examination of the amniotic fluid, to know the sex of the foetus, thousands of women have terminated their pregnancies because the foetus was female. Abortion is legal in India, and in one study conducted in Maharashtra, in western India, out of 8,000 foetuses aborted, 7,999 were female (the one exception was that of a Jewish mother who wanted a daughter).[7] Clinics used to advertise their MTP (medical termination of pregnancy) facilities with the slogan 'Better to spend Rs500 today [on sex determination test and abortion] rather than Rs500,000 at the time of the girl's marriage' (to meet dowry demands). Daughters are perceived as economic and social burdens and, in addition, the cultural preference for sons is strong for religious as well as economic reasons: only sons can perform the rites for the souls of deceased parents and ancestors, and only sons can offer security in old age, since daughters are 'given away' in marriage and no longer belong to their natal families. (Conservative parents even today will not eat or drink in their married daughter's house, much less expect her to support them financially in their old age.) A daughter is seen as a liability, a burden.

Even a woman who does not mind giving birth to a girl is often pressured by her husband or in-laws into have sex determination tests and aborting the foetus if it turns out to be female. One cabinet minister has declared that he sees 'nothing wrong' in such sex determination tests followed by female foeticide because, according to him, 'it will solve the population problem' (people go on conceiving only because they keep trying for sons) and also make women 'more valuable' by reducing their supply in the long run (as if women were some commodity governed by supply-and-demand equations)! The devaluation of female lives that these tests intensify seems entirely lost, even on some of the doctors who perform these tests. 'It is better for an unwanted girl not to be born than to suffer later in life,' says one doctor. The sex ratio (number of females per 1,000 males), which was recorded as 933 per 1,000 in the 1981 census, has fallen to 929 according to the census of 1991, making India one of the few countries with such an adverse ratio. Activists and feminist groups had the sex determination test banned in Maharashtra in 1988, but those wanting the test need only go into an adjoining state. So long as women's lives are devalued, so long as unquestioning self-effacement, suffering and sacrifice are held up as the exalted ideals of womanhood, and girls continue to be indoctrinated with such ideas, such aberrant manifestations will continue to be part of the Indian ethos. Basic alterations in our social perceptions are needed.

Notes

1. These dowry death statistics are from the union minister in Parliament; and, for the state of Karnataka, the home minister in the state legislature.

2. For instance Swami Agnivesh, an ascetic and activist who leads a progressive movement against bonded labour and exploitation, has pointed out that the Vedas do not require widow immolation. Another scholar, Swami Ranganathananda of the Ramakrishna movement, has also condemned sati as barbaric.

3. See Sakuntala Narasimhan, *Sati: a Study of Widow-burning in India* (India, Viking/Penguin, 1990; USA, Doubleday/Anchor, 1992).

4. Such eyewitness accounts were reported in the *Times of India* and the *Indian Express*, September 1987. Also see *Trial by Fire*, a report by the Women and Media Committee of the Bombay Union of Journalists, 1987.

5. See *Trial by Fire*, quoted in Narasimhan.

6. See interview with the Shankaracharya of Puri in the *Illustrated Weekly of India*, 1 May 1988.

7. From a widely quoted report publicized by feminist groups in Bombay.

Part 2
Beyond the Family

Maltreatment of Maids in Kuwait
Michele Beasley

This is the introduction of a newsletter produced by Middle East Watch and the Women's Rights Project for which Michele Beasley, the author, is a staff attorney. The newsletter goes on to document various individual cases of severe human rights violations, from illegal employment practices – debt bondage, passport deprivation, illegal confinement – through to rape and physical assault, none of which ever appear to lead to the punishment of abusive employers.

Ambia Khatum told us she was subjected to repeated attempted rape by her male employer. She said that on one occasion, '*Baba* wanted to have sex with me and he took a knife and put it to my throat. That time he broke my thumb. My Madame came and took the knife so he wouldn't cut me.' ... She said, 'My Madame wanted to send me home, but the *baba* refused.' She said that sometimes her male employer also beat her with a plastic water pipe that left her legs bloody. We noted visible scars on her legs. Interview with Ambia Khatum, Kuwait City, May 1992 (She has since returned to the safety of Bangladesh)

Since the liberation of Kuwait in March 1991 to the present, nearly 2,000 women domestic servants,[1] mainly from Sri Lanka, Bangladesh, India and the Philippines, have fled the homes of abusive Kuwaiti employers and sought refuge in their embassies. This mass exodus of maids is the culmination of a longstanding problem of abuse of Asian women domestic servants[2] and occurs at a time of general hostility towards foreigners that has escalated since liberation.[3]

In April 1992, Middle East Watch and the Women's Rights Project, both divisions of Human Rights Watch, conducted a two-week fact-finding mission in Kuwait to investigate reports of abuse of Asian women domestic servants. Participating in the mission were Patt Derian, a member of the board of directors of Middle East Watch and of the Women's Rights Project's Advisory Committee, and Michele E. Beasley, staff attorney for the Women's Rights Project.

We found that while not all domestic servants in Kuwait suffer at the hands of their employers,[4] a significant and pervasive pattern of rape, physical assault and mistreatment of Asian maids takes place, largely with impunity.

To our knowledge, only a handful of the charges against abusive employers have ever been investigated or prosecuted. We have submitted formal requests for information on cases in which allegedly abusive employers have been prosecuted, but the Kuwaiti government has yet to respond to those requests.[5] Moreover, we found that, rather than investigate or prosecute alleged abusers, Kuwaiti authorities often detain maids seeking to report crimes to the police or simply return them to their employers. Worse, there have also been credible reports of abuse of women domestic servants in police custody that likewise goes unpunished.

In addition to failing to provide abused domestic servants with justice under applicable criminal and civil law, the government of Kuwait has explicitly excluded them from the protection of the country's labor law. The law covers most other workers (including expatriates), and regulates working conditions, providing for civil arbitration in the case of employment disputes. The domestic servants' exclusion from the labor law has created a widespread attitude that the maids are not entitled to the same rights as other workers. This has rendered them particularly vulnerable to abuse, and has simultaneously limited possible remedies, like arbitration. Only criminal or civil sanctions remain and they, as noted, are rarely applied and can often backlash on the abused women.

Ultimately, abused maids had little alternative but to flee to their embassies or to shelter with friends. Many sought to settle their disputes or to find new jobs. Others simply wanted to return home. Initially, the al-Sabah government foreclosed all these options. Arbitration was unavailable, job transfer exceedingly difficult to secure, and the government flatly denied exit visas to many maids seeking to leave. The result was that, unless the maids could find informal means of resolving their difficulties, as some did, they languished in ever increasing numbers at their embassies.

Eventually, in the week prior to our mission, Kuwait deported

VIOLENCE AGAINST WOMEN

Legal Rights of Women in Pakistan.

over 800 maids, mostly from their embassies.[6] The deportation relieved the immediate problem, but raised a number of important concerns. Prior to deportation, the Kuwaiti government made no systematic effort to document abused women's criminal complaints or civil claims. Upon investigation, we found these had been effectively dropped. In addition, for those women desiring to remain in Kuwait, alternatives to deportation such as job transfer were never made available, despite the fact that they had had a legitimate rationale for leaving their employers. Finally, deportation seems to have allowed the Kuwaiti government to wash its hands of the maids' problems without addressing the underlying causes of their abuse. The government has yet to punish known abusers or implement the legal and practical reforms necessary to ensure that the pattern of abuse and mistreatment of Asian maids with impunity does not recur. According to sources in Kuwait, new maids seeking refuge appear daily at the Asian embassies.[7]

Middle East Watch and the Women's Rights Project recognize that Kuwait has experienced enormous loss and upheaval in the years since liberation and that it is still in the process of rebuilding and restructuring its society. But if, as part of this process, the Kuwaiti government fails to take the necessary steps towards addressing and preventing abuse of Asian women domestic servants, in the words of one Asian official, 'This will go on forever.'[8] We urge the al-Sabah administration to ensure that abuse and mistreatment of Asian women domestic servants is punished, adequate protection against abuse is provided, and all Asian maids' international human rights to due process and equal protection of the law are guaranteed.

Background

The abuse and mistreatment suffered by Asian maids in Kuwait is occurring in the context of hostility towards expatriates that has increased since liberation in 1991.[9] Kuwait has long depended upon expatriates to provide the backbone of its labor force.[10] By 1990, prior to the Iraqi invasion of Kuwait, foreign workers and their dependants, also referred to as expatriates, accounted for nearly 62% of Kuwait's population.[11] Large numbers of these workers come from India, Sri Lanka, Bangladesh and the Philippines.

Until the mid-1970s, Asian women came to Kuwait as dependants of their husbands, fathers or other male relatives, but were not themselves a significant percentage of the foreign labor force.[12] Since that time, increasing numbers of Asian women have joined Kuwait's labor force in their own right, the total growing from 1,000 in 1965 to over 72,000 in 1985.[13] The numbers of Asian women workers continued to rise through the late 1980s.[14] By 1992, the number of Asian maids reached roughly 75,000 to 100,000, approximately one for every seven Kuwaiti citizens (men, women and children).[15]

In the wake of its liberation, Kuwait has embarked upon a concerted campaign to rectify what it sees as a dangerous imbalance in its population. A report prepared by the government's Higher Planning Council concluded that the high numbers of expatriates are 'a threat to national security' because they outnumber Kuwaiti citizens. The government, by taking steps to limit immigration of foreign workers and to curtail employment benefits for expatriates, is actively seeking to invert the pre-war population ratio so that by 1995 Kuwaitis will constitute 60% of the population.

New policies restricting immigration of foreign workers include women domestic servants. The government has reportedly stopped granting permission to bring over more maids to families that already have one or more.[16] However, this new restructuring apparently has yet to significantly affect the number of Asian maids in Kuwait. Asian women domestics are in increasing demand as more Kuwaiti women enter the workforce or choose to employ a maid,[17] and much of Kuwait's social structure remains dependent upon the presence of domestic servants who care for the homes and children of Kuwaiti families.

To some degree, however, these new policies do reflect what the maids we interviewed perceived as a sea-change in the way their employers treated them. Of the women who spoke to us, those who worked in Kuwait both prior to and following the Iraqi invasion cited a marked deterioration in their treatment after the war's end. This heightened abuse may have accounted, in part, for the flight of the maids to their embassies, a phenomenon that occurred in pre-invasion Kuwait, but increased dramatically in the post-war period.

According to information we obtained from embassies, Asian diplomatic officials, journalists, the US Department of State and Kuwaiti government officials, over 1,400 Filipinas – between 14 and 20% of the estimated number of Filipina maids – fled their employers between May 1991 and April 1992. During the first four months of 1992, we determined that at least 300 Sri Lankan maids ran away from their employers to the Sri Lankan embassy, most of them complaining of rape and mistreatment. The US State Department told us that large numbers of Bangladeshi and Indian women also fled to their embassies during this time period. The Bangladesh embassy sheltered 20 women a day,[18] while there were 10 to 20 women at the Indian embassy at any given time.[19]

It is difficult to say precisely what proportion of those maids who fled experienced abuses and mistreatment, because it was not possible in the two weeks we were in Kuwait to pursue every reported case. However, our investigation revealed a significant and pervasive pattern of rape, physical assault and mistreatment of Asian maids by their Kuwaiti employers, largely with impunity.

One-third of the 60 cases we investigated directly involved the rape or sexual assault of maids by their employers or a man with access to the employer's house. Well over two-thirds involved physical assault, including kicking, beating with sticks, slapping and punching. Almost without exception the women we interviewed spoke of non-payment of salary, passport deprivation and near-total confinement in their employers' homes. Asian embassy officials and other sources reported to us that these findings held true across the larger population of maids who fled their employers.

We found every indication that such abuses are underreported.[20] Impediments to the maids' reporting abuse or mistreatment, such as confinement in the homes of their employers or police refusal to investigate their complaints, as well as the social stigma attached to certain types of abuse, particularly sexual assault, present serious disincentives to the reporting of employer abuse to the authorities.

The abuse of Asian maids is not limited to sexual or physical assault. Underlying abuses, such as debt bondage, passport deprivation and confinement, are also common and create conditions for the maids to suffer assault in near total isolation from the outside world. The maids' exclusion from the labor law paved the way for this isolation and denied the maids even minimal protection against unfair practices. The government, by virtue of having excluded the maids from the labor law in the first place, has effectively disclaimed responsibility for the abusive practices that have arisen directly and indirectly from that exclusion.

Exclusion from the labor law

Kuwait's Private Sector Labour Law No. 38 of 1964 (hereinafter 'the labor law') governs working conditions for most workers – including expatriates – in the private sector. It explicitly excludes domestic servants from its provisions.[21] According to Meshari al-Osaimi, a prominent attorney and president of the Kuwait Lawyers' Association, many of the problems facing the maids in Kuwait stem from this exclusion:

> It affects the atmosphere of work and the sense of what treatment maids are entitled to. In 1964 there were only a few hundred maids, today there are 200,000;[22] now their exclusion from the law is a human rights issue.[23]

The labor law contains rules governing the maximum daily and/or weekly hours an employee can be required to work,[24] employees' entitlement to overtime,[25] and provisions for weekly and annual leave.[26] If employers violate these requirements, the law provides workers with access to the Ministry of Social Affairs and Labour to air their grievances about working conditions and have them investigated or arbitrated by the ministry.[27]

The exclusion of domestic servants from this protection has created a widespread attitude that the maids are not entitled to the same rights as other workers. This renders them not only especially vulnerable to the abuses against which the labor law protects, but also largely powerless to combat them. As a group, women domestic servants have no right to organize,[28] no power to bargain for fair employment terms or to enforce the terms their employers agreed to when they were hired. Nor do they have access to the government facilities for arbitration of employment disputes. This has clearly created an atmosphere in which the maids can be, and often are, overworked and ill-treated by their employers at whim with little expectation that the state will intervene.

Notes

1. This estimate is based on the official lists given to us of maids deported in the weeks surrounding and during our mission, the records of the Asian embassies, our inter-

views with the Asian ambassadors and Western diplomats, and newspaper accounts.

2. Reports of rape, assault and other forms of mistreatment of Asian maids have been aired since 1988. See, for example, Lee Stokes, 'India bans women from working in three Persian Gulf states', *United Press International*, 23 September 1988. In two 1989 cases, Asian maids died as a result of the abuse inflicted on them by their employers (*US Department of State Country Reports on Human Rights Practices for 1989*, p. 1,464).

3. Middle East Watch has recently released a report on the general situation of expatriate workers in Kuwait.

4. Our best estimate, based on our research into this and other expatriate issues in Kuwait, is that something less than half of domestic servants, including chauffeurs, are men. The focus of this report is the treatment of women domestic servants.

5. Letter to Abdul Aziz Dikheel al-Dikheel, Undersecretary, Ministry of Justice (26 May 1992); letter to International Organizations Liaison Office, Ministry of Interior (26 May 1992); letter to International Organizations Liaison Office, Ministry of Interior (7 June 1992).

6. Although we have records and information establishing that nearly 2,000 maids have fled their employers since liberation, we were unable to determine in each case what happened to the woman. It is our understanding that in hundreds of cases the Asian embassies repatriated maids at their own expense, helped them to resolve disputes or find new employers, while other maids returned to their employers or informally found other jobs.

7. Interview No. III–9, Washington, DC, June 1992.

8. Interview No. I–1, Kuwait City, April 1992.

9. See note 3.

10. The demand for foreign labor in Kuwait originated with the development of oil resources following World War II. Migration to Kuwait from Asia accelerated in 1974 and 1974 when escalating oil prices, surplus capital and labor shortages produced the need for large-scale importation of workers. See Ian J. Seccombe, 'Economic recession and international labour migration in the Arab Gulf', *Arab Gulf Journal*, April 1986, p. 46.

11. Population Estimates, Ministry of Planning (1990). The Ministry of Planning estimated in mid-1990 that out of a total population of 2,142,600, 1,316,014 were foreigners, 517,436 of whom were women.

12. Nasra Shah, Sulayman S. Al-Qudsi and Mahkdoom A. Shah, 'Asian women workers in Kuwait', *International Migration Review* (Fall 1991), p. 466.

13. Ibid., pp. 464, 466–7.

14. Seccombe, pp. 44–5. See also Frank Eelens and J.D. Speckmann, 'Recruitment of labor migrants for the Middle East: the Sri Lankan case', *International Migration Review* (Summer 1990), p. 299.

15. Hard facts about exactly how many Asian maids are currently working in Kuwait are nearly impossible to obtain. The Kuwaiti government's official current statistics indicates that there are 30,036 Indian, 5,433 Sri Lankan, 11,428 Bangladeshi and 25,699 Filipino male and female domestic servants now working as servants in Kuwait (letter from the International Organizations Liaison Office, Ministry of Interior, to Middle East Watch and the Women's Rights Project, dated 15 July 1992). However, these figures differ significantly from those given by Asian embassy sources, who place the population of women servants alone nearly as high as the government's figures for both male and female servants, with the exception of the Indians (interview with US Department of State, Washington, DC, May 1992). Media estimates of the total population of Asian maids have ranged as high as 250,000. See, for example, 'Cabinet acts on domestics', *Arab Times*, 4 May 1992. Our research indicates that the number ranges between 75,000 and 100,000.

16. 'Hold on family visit visas confirmed', *Arab Times*, 1 May 1992.

17. Ibid., pp. 468–9.

18. Interview with US Department of State, Washington, DC, June 1992.

19. Ibid. Asian officials were reluctant to let us talk to women staying in their

embassies or to give us concrete information about their numbers or complaints.

20. It should also be noted that domestic violence and rape are two of the most underreported crimes internationally. See United Nations, *Violence Against Women in the Family* (New York, United Nations, 1989), p. 17.

21. Law No. 38 of 1964 Concerning Labour in Private Sector (as amended through 1989), Chapter 1 (Scope of Implementation), article 2(e) (hereinafter 'Law No. 38'): 'The following categories shall not be subject to the applications of this law's provisions. Domestic servants and those having their status.'

The law also excludes government workers (who are predominantly Kuwaiti at this time), seasonal laborers, sea laborers and owners of non-mechanical minor business concerns (i.e. people who work in small shops). Government workers are covered by other labor laws and sea laborers by traditional law. Only shop workers and seasonal laborers also work without the protection of a labor code.

22. As noted earlier, the exact number of Asian maids in Kuwait is difficult to establish.

23. Interview with Attorney Meshari al-Osaimi, president of the Kuwait Lawyers' Association, Kuwait City, April 1992.

24. Law No. 38, Article 33.

25. Ibid., Article 34.

26. Ibid., Articles 35–39.

27. Ibid., Chapter XV (General Provisions), Articles 95 and 96.

28. Maids are denied the right to organize because labor organizations are only authorized under Law No. 38, from which the women are excluded. However, even if they were covered by Law No. 38's provisions, their ability to organize would still be effectively foreclosed because Kuwaiti unions can only be established by Kuwaiti employees and, to our knowledge, there are no Kuwaiti women working as maids. See Law No. 38, Chapter XIII (Organization of Laborers and Employers), Articles 69–74. The effective denial of the right to organize is a problem in other expatriate-dominated industries in Kuwait, such as the oil refineries and manufacturing, as are the substantial restrictions on expatriate workers' freedom of association. See Statement of Don Stillman, director of Governmental and International Affairs, International Union, UAW, to the Overseas Private Investment Corporation, *On Worker Rights in Kuwait* (12 November 1991).

Women's Organizations against Rape in India: Report of a National Meeting
Forum against the Oppression of Women

This report of a meeting held in April 1990 in Bombay was written by a group of participants from Delhi, on the basis of discussions and notes provided by the Forum against the Oppression of Women, and individual members of the group. The original report was produced by India's first women's publishing house, Kali for Women.

'... I used to fearlessly go and lie under a tree and sleep in its shade. Then an incident happened ... today I have fear, disturbance ... what bloody right does anyone have to do this to me? To take away my sense of security?'

'Rape is a weapon all men use against all women ... so long as one woman is raped, all women live in the fear of rape. It keeps all women in their place – below men ...'

'If I were raped, would I make it public? Is rape a fate worse than death? Isn't it more important to stay alive?'

'Rape is probably the only crime in which the victim is treated like the criminal.'

'What does a rape victim get? No compensation. And the rapist? Punishment, maybe?'

'When was the first law about rape codified and defined as a criminal offence?'

'It's up to a woman to decide what that assault means to her ... if she doesn't want to feel hassled, then she should not allow herself to feel that it's the ultimate violation.'

At a National Meeting on Rape held in Bombay, 23–25 April 1990, several women's organizations met to discuss the issue of rape and review the response of the women's movement to it, especially over the last 10 years. Mathura, Rameeza bi, Maya Tyagi, Suman Rani, Mukti Dutta and countless others that came to our notice, and the equally countless ones that did not, had galvanized the women's movement into campaigning nationally against this assault on women, and in effecting some changes in the Rape Law. But, despite the campaigns and legal amendments there has been a startling increase in rapes reported, in the exploitation of loopholes in existing legislation and legal procedure, and a realization that rape has the kind of social, economic and political ramifications that require us to review our strategies and methods of protest, and action in challenging it.

The Forum against the Oppression of Women (FAOW), Bombay, called a national meeting to discuss the issue and raised the following questions: Can we work towards a better definition of rape? Can the burden of proof be shifted to the rapist? How successful have we been in our consciousness-raising? In our dealing with the legal system? Have we been able to deal satisfactorily with individual rape cases? Are our strategies effective? Have we been able to provide adequate support to raped women?

About 80 women from various organizations, with a range of experience on the issue of rape, talked at length during the three days of the meeting; the discussion was marked by intensity and depth, with individual women recounting personal experiences of rape or sexual assault, often for the first time, and organizations describing the cases they had handled and the problems they had faced while trying to grapple with the fundamental questions: how do we redefine rape and what are the strategies for tackling it that emerge from such a redefinition?

The meeting began with a brief and quick recall of how the women's movement had orchestrated its campaign against rape, given it wide publicity through the Mathura case, agitated to have the Rape Law amended, and brought the issue of custodial rape into focus. (Mathura's was an example of police rape of a minor in custody.) Over the years, the large number of rapes of different categories that women's organizations have had to deal with indicate the enormity of the problem. These are:

- communal rape
- gang rape
- political rape
- rape of minors
- marital rape
- army rape (in situations of war or 'peacekeeping')
- institutional rape (in hospitals, remand homes, prisons, etc.)
- rape in economically dependent circumstances
- rape within political organizations.

Action by women's groups over the last decade seems to have made only a very minor dent in the system: some concessions were granted in the amended rape law, but the major changes asked for in the law of evidence, in the burden of proof, in the moral character and sexual conduct of the woman and in minimum punishment were bypassed. On the part of the autonomous women's movement, it was felt that one very real failing in our strategies has been the absence of concrete and adequate support to rape victims.

It was also felt that, really speaking, we have not been able to get much legal redress either, in most cases. Many women's groups expressed in some detail their disillusionment with the law and the legal process. Years of litigation resulted in financial hardship for the woman and did nothing to remedy the social stigma and loss of dignity that are imposed on her. The crisis within the legal system and the failure of the law to deliver justice, adequately and in good time, have led to a deep sense of frustration with strategies that look to the law for redress. They have also led to dissatisfaction with the definition of rape as it exists; most people felt that its emphasis on penetration reflected a male and patriarchal bias, that it did not make sufficient acknowledgement of other forms of sexual assault (which are equally degrading and violent even though they may not culminate in penetration) and that therefore a reassessment of the issue from a women's and feminist perspective becomes necessary, in order to work out future definitions and strategies.

The context for this reconceptualization was individual experience and reflection as well as detailed analyses of several cases put forward by the different groups present, each of which highlighted the particular problems that arose, and that linked the case to the larger social and political reality. The attempt was always to keep the issue of rape in its political and economic and social ramifications at centre stage. 'Rape is not only sexually motivated – it is a weapon of power … it is violation of a physical and mental nature.'

A nine-months-pregnant domestic servant is raped repeatedly by her employers – nothing comes of her case; the Speaker of the Goa Assembly tries to sexually assault a young woman in his employ; a terrible tale of familial rape is brought to another organization in Bangalore – the father rapes his daughters, the grandfather rapes his grandchild; Suman Rani's rapists have their sentence reduced by half because the judges find her 'conduct' questionable; an activist is raped by some Communist Party (Marxist) (CPM) cadre workers; any number of minor children are raped daily, in and out of wedlock; the IPKF routinely rapes in Sri Lanka (Perumal says, 'They may have raped – so what?'); an Air India air hostess is lured into a room, forced to drink and then molested – the management does nothing; a student of Elphinstone College is gang-raped – her father denies that anything ever happened; an 8-year-old and a 13-year-old in Delhi rape their 8-year-old playmate while playing; a young woman developed VD, contracted from her husband – the list is endless.

Of the many accounts that were shared, eight cases are briefly recounted here, because they highlight the complexities of dealing with rape, and allow us to question our own strategies.

Rural Women's Labour Movement (Tamil Nadu)

A construction worker is forcibly taken into a room and raped. She brought her rape to the notice of the Rural Women's Labour Movement (RWLM) who took the case before the village panchayat. ('Our strategy is never to go to the police.') The woman asked for, and obtained, compensation in the form of a share of the rapist's property. Asked if she would like him to marry her, she refused.

Generally, however, in the experience of the RWLM, the rapist is made to marry his victim, after they have the woman's consent: if she is willing, the group arranges the marriage. Sometimes, she may even be the rapist's second wife. Women feel they cannot live with dignity after a rape; no one will agree to marry them, they are like social outcasts – and so are open to such marriages. The question arose as to how a woman can agree to marrying her rapist? The women replied: She has been made socially unfit, she cannot live in the same village, 'so he better marry her and take away some of her shame. We make him sign an undertaking that he will not abuse or mistreat her.' In many instances women would otherwise see suicide as the only way out. 'Even in Tamil films, so deep is the hold of the concept of "honour" that, at the end of the film, the rapist marries the woman – these are the messages.'

Bailancho Saad, Goa

In Vasco, a nine-months-pregnant domestic worker was gang-raped by her employer and three of his friends. She said it was 'fate'. She asked the neighbour for a sari – he informed the police. 'We took up her case; there was a lot of public protest. One of the rapists was connected to a politician, tried to buy her silence, offered her thousands. We had to keep making sure she wasn't bribed and didn't leave Vasco. We tried to make it a legal case, but are stuck because the chemical analysis wasn't conclusive. She keeps saying, 'Why do you bother, my problem is getting my next meal. At least I didn't die.' What do we do? How do we help her?'

Narvekar, a Speaker of the Goa Assembly, was accused of sexually assaulting a female employee. The Bailancho Saad women's group raised a hue and cry, embarrassed him publicly, kept up social pressure against him through press reporting and widely publicizing the case. 'This time we refused to file a case because we knew it would fall through – he had too many connections – and we would have had to prove his wrongdoing. We said, let *him* file a case for defamation if he wants, we're going to insist that he did molest her. Of course he didn't file, and we campaigned against him in the elections. Our success was that he was defeated, on grounds of morality in public life.'

In the two cases above, Bailancho Saad consciously used two completely different strategies – one (arguably) successfully, the other not. 'But for us, the dilemma is: when do we take a case to the police? The woman who was gang-raped didn't ask us to go to them. And we couldn't do much for her. In fact nobody consults these migrant workers about whether they want their cases reported or not; and were they to be asked, they would say, "Baba, leave us alone, going to the police or the courts isn't a solution." And in Narvekar's case, again, all that the girl had asked for was a job transfer.'

Vimochana, Bangalore

Vimochana recounted a series of cases, each more harrowing than the last. A reputed doctor with NIMHANS infected his wife with VD he had contracted from a prostitute – said he had to go to her because his wife had gone home for her confinement and he needed sex every 24 hours.

A six-and-a-half-year-old child was raped by her 75-year-old grandfather. 'We went and met the old man. At the police station, he told the S.I., stroking his grey beard, 'I've read Vivekananda and Tagore. Could I do something like this?' They registered a case of VD for the child but the Inspector said, "Can such an old man have an erection?" We can't even get custody of the child for the mother. The father is "respectable", has a good job.'

A schoolgirl is repeatedly harassed and raped by a friend of the family. Her brother is a doctor, but the girl couldn't bring herself to talk about it. 'It was very torturing to sit and question her about exactly what had happened. She would say, "He used to come at night and leave after 15 minutes." God knows how long this had been going on. We confronted the brother. He was very rude, he said, "This is a family business. How dare she come and talk to you." Poor girl was locked up.

'Sometimes we don't know what to do as a women's organization. There are intimate relatives involved, there's violence, complicated by the woman's economic powerlessness. We get tortured by what's happening and we don't feel like insisting that the case be taken up unless that's what the woman wants.'

These stories raise more difficult questions of rape in the family context and the dilemmas presented to women's groups in responding to these women. Family pressures may silence the woman, and even if she isn't silenced, her words will not be believed because of social prejudices and notions of privacy. How do women's groups help a raped woman challenge her own family when it is the basis of her social and economic survival?

Elphinstone College rape, Bombay

At the college, a student was raped by six fellow students. The girl's father swiftly removed her from college and denied she had been raped – said it was just 'misbehaviour'. Other students took up the case, protested vociferously and boycotted the exams. It was picked up by the press and given wide coverage. The gang leader was expelled from college (although he still visits the place), as were three others, but they got admission elsewhere. Women's groups wanted very much to take up the case, but the girl's family ensured that she was silenced and not traceable.

Maithreyi, Hyderabad

A young woman is kidnapped by her fiancé who takes her to his house and rapes her. When his mother finds out, she refuses to let the marriage take place. When her father hears this, he throws the girl out of his house. Now she is determined to get the man to marry her, and only her, as her revenge: 'My ultimate victory will be when he puts a mangalasutra around my neck.' She came to a women's organization for help. Maithreyi says, 'We were completely taken aback by this kind of demand. We demonstrated in front of the boy's college during his medical exams. Subsequently, an attempt was made to pour acid on Manjula. The police arrested the boy but let him out on bail. Our demand was: punishment for the rapist. We hoped Manjula would change her mind in course of time ... the charges against him have been proved, he's in jail, but she still wants to marry him. He's demanding 30 lakhs in dowry to marry her! The case became notorious, political interest came in – we didn't know how to tackle the issue.'

The political factor, notoriety, differences in strategies and perceptions, were present in the Mukti Dutta case as well, which threw up equally intractable questions regarding the involvement of women's organizations in such cases.

Mukti Dutta, Delhi

A young, articulate social activist was molested by the Union Minister for Environment, Z.R. Ansari, in his private chamber in his office, where she had gone to see him on official business. She sought redress from senior bureaucrats and secretaries in the government, asking for a public apology and the denial of a ticket from the Congress I to the minister to contest the forthcoming elections. She also approached women's groups, some of whom advised her to go to the press and file a case with the police. She resisted doing the latter, saying, give them time, they will respond, but did go to the press. Once the issue was publicized, there was an attempt to communalize it (Ansari is a Muslim) and claims were made regarding Mukti Dutta's own motives. Some women's groups felt that in this case, there was a difference in the choice of strategy made by Mukti Dutta and what women's groups might have opted for. This difference of perception, the political factor and the strategies used finally made it difficult for women's groups to pursue the case.

The question for the groups was: should they put time and energy into banner cases like this one where the interest of the woman seems to be at variance with women's organizations, and the issue is confused by political ambiguities?

Suman Rani review petition, Delhi

In 1984 a minor girl, Suman Rani, was raped by two policemen who were then convicted to 10 years imprisonment by the trial court. This was the first conviction in custodial rape which used the amended Rape Law to pronounce the new minimum obligatory sentence in police rape. The amendment had been won after a long, concerted agitation by women's groups in response to the acquittal of the guilty constables in the historic Mathura/Tukaram case.

The High Court upheld the sentence but the Supreme Court bench reduced it to five years: the Supreme Court judges argued that since Suman Rani filed a case a full week after the rape, her 'conduct' was questionable, despite recorded evidence that it took her a week to return to her family who then helped her file the case. Predictably, a review petition by women's groups was struck down.

The key issue in this case was that even an amendment won by the women's movement worked against us because of a very basic male bias in the legal system.

Kashtakari Sanghatan activist's rape by CPM cadre members, Dahanu (Maharashtra)

The issue of rape by party workers was highlighted in the case of an activist of the Kashtakari Sanghatana being raped by CPM workers, and the party taking no action at all against them. Although the issue was raised repeatedly by women and men activists from a range of groups, to date the question has not been resolved satisfactorily. The CPM in Dahanu has denied responsibility, women's and other groups have issued a fact-finding report, but there has been no impact on either the CPM or the legal machinery.

Some of the broader questions that arose from a discussion of these and other cases were:

- Should one have recourse to the law or not?
- How should women's groups respond when conflicting demands are made on them?
- In cases of marital, familial, minor rape what should our response be?
- How does one deal with mass/gang/political /communal rape?
- How do we work with the law, as it is?
- What alternative strategies have proved more effective than legal remedies?
- If the woman doesn't want to file a case, how should women's groups proceed?
- How effective have our forms of protest been?

- Have we made any headway in providing counselling, crisis centres, support, to rape victims?

Among the first issues to be taken up was that of redefining rape. We broke up into three groups of roughly 20–25 women each, and then regrouped to share our thoughts.

The question of redefinition

Why do we feel the need to redefine rape in the first place? Are we doing so only at the conceptual level? Are we linking it up with the legal system? Are we throwing out the legal system, saying that's what's been defining it and giving inadequate redressal? Is rape really a fate worse than death or have we simply internalized patriarchal notions of rape and reacted accordingly? ('I would consider assault causing injury to my brain as worse than assault causing injury to my vagina, which will get OK in 15 days, maybe.') Do we have to be actually raped or is any assault or harassment with sexual intent not equally offensive?

It was clear that ten years of dealing with the issue of rape at all levels – state, society, legal and political systems, strategies evolved by the women's movement itself – have left us with a sense of dissatisfaction at the existing state of affairs, and compelled us to look for alternatives in tackling the problem. At the very outset, it was felt that we should try to redefine rape this time, beginning with women's experience of violation, not only of their bodies but of their very being, in order to reconceptualize the issue and review strategies.

The discussions therefore, took place at two levels: the contextual and the conceptual. Very broadly, these could be separated in the following way:

Contextual: Individual cases – Women's experiences – Campaigns by women's groups – Strategies and tactics.
Conceptual: Redefinition – Patriarchal controls – Rape as power – Social, economic and political ramifications – Women and violence.

A recounting of the cases mentioned earlier (together with many others not set out in detail here), and the strategies and campaigns around them, provided the context from which group discussions on redefinition took off.

Quite predictably, the three sub-groups emphasized different aspects of the problem in their discussions; the attempt here is to try and present the range of the discussions in order to give some idea of the ground covered, and then to summarize the outcome of these separate discussions.

Group discussions – a summary

'This business of dishonour – it's more than chastity. We have to fight rape within ourselves and outside. It's not like theft or burglary, we know it is no ordinary crime. How do we define rape in law and for ourselves, for society?'

1. The current and conventional linking of rape with penetration; the notion of it being a fate worse than death; the question of 'honour' and revenge; the evolution of rape from the concept of 'theft'; rape itself as a crime connected to the ownership of women and women's sexuality – all these, it was felt, are male-oriented and male-defined notions. In order to challenge them, we must extend our definition, set our terms for it, perhaps even move away from the words and language we have so far been using. The term 'assault' could be considered more encompassing from women's point of view.

2. Although women's sexuality *per se* was not discussed generally, one group did touch upon the principle of sexual pleasure and gratification, in itself and *vis-à-vis* rape. Women, it was felt, could experience pleasure through physical intimacy without desiring intercourse. Thus, rape – marital rape particularly, because it presumes consent and asserts 'rights and privileges' – is repeated violation: it is often a violent assertion of power and it denies women the right to intimate and pleasurable sexual activity, especially within marriage. It violates and brutalizes at the same time. The issue here is one of consent; because men equate women's sexual pleasure with their own, consent is simply assumed. Within marriage, marital rape would be better viewed if we discussed the unequal power relationship between men and women. Our choice of strategy could enable us to assert ourselves, voice our feelings, seek fulfilment in this union which has thus far been determined by the man.

Power: For men their sexuality and pleasure are defined in terms of the power of an erection, and aggression. For a woman, this becomes an assault, until and unless there is consent on her part. That is why consent is so central to the whole question of rape.

3. As far as the law is concerned, rape becomes a crime only when it is reported. What means do we have to gauge its criminality in cases of minor/child rape, marital rape, mass rape, communal and political rape, rapes by armies, gang rape? In the case of the last few mentioned, we have already moved beyond the individual woman's case to the social, political – even religious – sanction of rape as a political weapon. Which court of law will dare to try the raping soldiers of the IPKF in Sri Lanka or the soldiers of the Pakistan army who raped Bangladeshi women – dead and alive – to dishonour the 'enemy' publicly? In the Thangamani rape case in Kerala, 14 policemen mass-raped village women after their men had fled in fear. They then raped some nuns in their hostel. In spite of the findings of

the Sridevi Commission, all 14 policemen were promoted. It was said, 'These Marxists have cooked up the whole story.'

4. Any violation should be considered a rape. Getting in and out of buses in big cities is like being raped. 'It's a systematic way of destroying a woman's well-being – the motivation behind eve-teasing is the same as that behind rape.' Without intending to deny the trauma experienced by women who have been raped, we discussed the commonalities between all forms of sexual assault. There was considerable discussion on the question of how women perceive rape and other offensive activities with sexual overtones, all as being a violation, thus minimizing the importance of the legally critical fact of penetration in placing rape on a higher scale of violence. In this view, molestation, eve-teasing, obscene gestures and behaviour, sexually aggressive postures during festivals, etc., all assume a similar significance. The question raised was why men felt they had the power to degrade and humiliate women, and why women feel so powerless in stopping them. If sexual activity, or the power to control it, is a male prerogative both inside the home (legitimately) and outside it (illegitimately) should women not challenge all expressions of that power?

5. It was generally felt that it is society, with its patriarchal attitudes, that stigmatizes a raped woman and then withholds justice from her for a crime visited upon her. She is thus twice victimized. If this is so, should our strategy not be to refuse society's humiliation, to deny rape its false importance in social terms, to not be cowed down? 'It's up to a woman to decide what that assault means to her, whether it is the ultimate violation.' The objective is to redefine the social understanding of any violation as a violation of an individual woman's physical integrity and shift the stigma to the rapist.

During discussions in the larger group it was felt that one possibility would be to de-link any definition of rape from penetration; this would take rape beyond the present, very male perception and definition of rape. It was also felt that one approach would be to de-link the sexual aspects from the violent aspect of the crime. This approach raised several problems which came up for discussion – the critical one being that emphasizing rape as only an act of *violence* would eclipse the reality of how much of men's violence against women is *sexual* in nature. The fact that rape is sexual is itself significant.

At another level it was pointed out that although the above strategy might be a panacea for individual women, it would make little impact on the existing power structure of caste, class or community rape – nor would it take on the whole range of rapes classified as custodial, institutional, army, gang, etc.

Again, it was thought that such an extension of the definition of rape would further liberate society, the legal system and men in general from any accountability at all, allowing them to shrug off a responsibilty that they are even now extremely reluctant to shoulder. Furthermore, we would need to consider the impact of this definition on the question of redress: if a whole spectrum of offences from eve-teasing to rape resulting in death were collapsed under 'sexual assault', what form of punishment would fit the crime? How would we deal with pregnancy or grievous injury resulting from actual rape? How would we deal with child or marital rape? How would we deal with making all of these criminal offences? Can we say that we do equate the significance of eve-teasing with that of raping?

The question thus is: say, we are for the moment able to work out an extended definition for ourselves, how would we hold society and the legal system responsible? By the same token, how would we then fight structural violence – all those rapes committed as a direct assertion of power or right: custodial, institutional, political, communal, state? It is important to recognize that these rapes take place because their intention often is to humiliate and crush, through the ultimate violation of their women, men belonging to the other group. To take revenge. To terrorize. To silence. Nothing less symbolic or violent than actual rape will serve this purpose – why else would conquering or retreating (or, for that matter, 'peacekeeping') armies rape their enemies' women? And why would the mothers of children so conceived be forever stigmatized, while their rapists are publicly honoured?

One possible alternative would be to have degrees of seriousness on this index of 'sexual assault' for the purposes of redress, but we were not able to discuss this in any depth or detail at the meeting. What we concluded, therefore, was that though it was necessary for us to redefine rape, we should locate this redefinition in the larger socio-legal context rather than view it in isolation. In other words, we move from the individual woman's *violation* to the *rape* of women generally, so that the issue itself always remains in focus. This is as important conceptually as it is for deciding on strategies to resist.

Strategies

Although no consensus was reached on how we would redefine rape, a discussion on strategies for resistance did take place on the second day of the meeting. Once again, we broke into subgroups and regrouped for a final session.

Both legal and alternative strategies were discussed, keeping two things in mind: the problem of the individual woman's rape and how women's groups have dealt with cases that have come to them; and rape as an issue to be addressed in the social–legal–political–economic context. Both sets of strategies would need to look at how we have dealt with these aspects in the past, how our campaigns have evolved and how we should strategize in the future. Again, the discussions were not conclusive but various questions were raised and debated.

'There is a lot of hope and expectation from women's groups. Cases keep coming into women's centres but it is not possible to take up each one. We have not been successful in creating activists who could take up various issues by themselves. Perhaps we need to shift the responsibility to society and the men who commit the crime – women's groups can't take on the whole burden.'

'It is necessary to shame the man – many groups have used this tactic. But men don't always feel ashamed of what they have done and so punishment is also important.'

'How do we make the link between individual cases and the concept of rape? We need to find a *via media* between our different strategies. In the Kashtakari Sanghatana case, should we see it as an individual story or as rival party aggression?'

'We seem to be rather negative about our achievements in the last 10 years, but there has been a fantastic rise in consciousness. Battering away at the legal system has helped the movement.'

'How do we work with other groups with different political interests?'

The question of individual women

It was suggested that there could be three ways of looking at an individual woman's problem: through her own understanding of sexuality (this is particularly important with regard to marital rape); her class/cultural position; her need for shelter, counselling and rehabilitation.

One of the main criticisms about our response to rape is that sometimes it is removed from the individual context of the victim. For example, in the Narvekar case from Goa, though the local group was effective in being able to publicize the case, the victim subsequently stated that she would have preferred not to have come to the women's organization. The effect of the publicity was that she gained notoriety and had to break off with her fiancé since his family did not want such a 'famous' daughter-in-law; all she had wanted was a job transfer. In the case of the migrant labourer who was raped in Vasco, the incident was viewed by her as an act of fate. For her, questions of survival were more important.

The Maitreyi group from Hyderabad also raised the issue of how to reconcile the victim's response with the group's response. Although in their case the rapist is currently serving a sentence in jail, the victim's sole demand was to get the rapist to marry her so that he would be bound to her and unable to marry any other woman. Ironically the rapist is demanding a 30-lakh dowry in return! Such situations have an individual as well as a social context, not always easy for a feminist group to address.

Campaigns/community response

Criticism arose at the inability of women's groups to carry on a sustained campaign against an individual rape until the conclusion of a case. Even then, such campaigns generally addressed themselves to well-known or politically sensitive cases such as the Suman Rani, Kashtakari Sanghatana, or Air India cases. There was negligible response to lower-class, lower-caste, ordinary rapes by both the press and women's groups, rapes which take place every day. This highlighted the importance of keeping both the banner cases as well as the issue of rape in mind, and perhaps devising strategies that could work in tandem.

There was need for a long-term educative process which would mean involving individual communities in rape cases in their area, and a need to dispel the notion of rape as being irredeemable.

The importance of the media was stressed in rendering men more accountable by putting the rapist in the limelight, rather than the woman and her rape. While there was a need to publicize a case, there was also the fear of the media being a double-edged sword which could verge on sensationalism and insensitivity, as has clearly happened in the case of the Air India hostess. Journalists also cautioned that the media itself operates within a power structure beyond individual persuasions.

Provisions for shelter and counselling are pressing needs for most victims, though there was some fear as to the effect of uprooting a rape victim from her natural habitat, how 'short-term' shelter would be defined, and whether such a shelter would be cross-class and cross-caste. Counselling should ensure that the victim does not fall prey to the notion that she is thereafter worth nothing.

The question of legal redress

'All men from judges downwards have oppressed women, and they are the ones who give justice. What chance do women have?'

'The history of rape law is a history of disbelieving what women say.'

'The legal process can take up to fifteen years and then you get five years for the rapist. I say, what the hell?'

'Ninety per cent of men arrested on rape charges are released on bail.'

'The judge said to the woman, "Every day you come with a new story." She was so upset she opened her blouse and bared herself – she had cigarette burns all over. The judge charged her with misconduct in court.'

An extended discussion on the law and the possibility of obtaining adequate and timely justice for a raped woman from the existing legal system indicated the general disillusionment with legal redress that most of us felt. Every aspect of the law – its definition of rape, due process, the law of evidence, the burden of proof and, not least, the evident prejudices of the judiciary – militated against victims of rape. In seeking justice from a patriarchal state, we will need to devise strategies that can work in a court of law that is almost entirely male, from top to bottom. Any changes in legislation will have to keep in mind that women can make use of male jurisprudence only up to a point. Should we not therefore de-emphasize legal remedies, and concentrate our energies on mobilizing support for raped women, on counselling and rehabilitation, which are a more concrete and necessary form of assistance to them? Money raised to help a woman now when she needs it is more useful to her than her rapist getting five years, ten years imprisonment after he committed the rape, for example.

All its disabilities notwithstanding, it was felt that the importance of challenging the legal system is symbolic, as well as strategically necessary. Legal and religious texts are among the most important codes that we are governed by, that regulate society and social and moral conduct. Both have defined and institutionalized women's subordinate status, then ensured that they remain subordinate through elaborate, interrelated and very patriarchal mechanisms. They embody the power of men over women, and if we are challenging the assertion of this power in other domains, how can we not do so in law? Thus, even while we recognize the difficulties of overthrowing powerful, vested interests, the fight to change the status quo has to continue. Take, for instance, the question of burden of proof. Shifting the burden of proof to the accused is an important actual and psychological shift, because it presumes the man rather than the woman guilty, and acknowledges that, unless proved otherwise, a crime has been committed. The same is true with regard to consent, conduct and all the other burdens that the woman currently bears.

Apart from the definition of rape itself, other changes suggested were: amendments in the Evidence Act; making rape a non-bailable offence; inducting feminist judges; making payment of compensation to the woman compulsory; creating alternative courts for rape trials; and pressing for time-bound judgements. Although these are not new demands, women's groups have so far met with little success on them, even from 'progressive' lawyers.

Social pressure

As an alternative to purely legal solutions, a great deal of emphasis was placed on innovative forms of redress. We may briefly recapitulate these:

1. In the case reported from the RWLM (Tamil Nadu) the village panchayat decided that the rapist would have to transfer a share in his property to the victim, as compensation.

2. The Rural Women's Liberation Movement often arranged marriages between the accused and the raped woman, if this was what the woman insisted on. (There was some debate on the desirability of this option, as many felt that it was like colluding with practices that only further entrenched structures of oppression.)

3. A third alternative was the social boycott – *jati bahar* – of the rapist; many rural groups, in particular, were persuaded of the effectiveness of this as a punishment.

4. In the Narvekar case in Goa, the strategy was to defame the assailant and publicly embarrass him. This worked well in this case, because it was a politically sensitive issue, and the accused was a public figure. Although the group, Bailancho Saad, gained credibility and public support, the strategy backfired somewhat on the woman herself, who acquired unwelcome notoriety.

What became abundantly clear is that all of these solutions are still situated within a patriarchal context, and it is here, too, that women's groups should seek alternatives. What these could be and how they should be implemented are subjects for further, in-depth discussion. Meanwhile, we realized that what we had done was merely to scratch the surface; a number of issues remained to be dealt with, and we had been silent on many others, indicating how difficult it is to make a breakthrough. Child marriage, for instance, is still considered more a social misdemeanour than the more serious crime of child rape that it is. An overwhelming 50–70 per cent of reported rape cases are of minors, predominantly between the ages of 5 and 16 years. Yet the Rape Law makes no distinction between adult and minor rape, and the majority of the accused even in the cases brought to court are never convicted. Mass and political rape have still to be addressed by women's groups in a concerted manner. Such offences constitute human rights violations (especially rape by armies) and can avail of constitutional remedies, at the very least.

Should our consciousness-raising activities not begin within the family, where so much incestuous activity takes place?

How do we provide for access to information on laws and issues in rural areas? And so on. All these simply serve to illustrate how deep-rooted the problem is.

Evaluation

The general feeling was that the two days had made for some very fruitful exchange of experiences and points of view, and had, for the first time, provided a sympathetic, almost intimate environment in which to share doubts, fears, confidences. The issue is complex, complicated and so widespread in its ramifications that two days can only mark a beginning, a tentative attempt at defining our perspective.

The rural groups, particularly from the south, felt that the discussions tended to become monotonous – skits or songs or some cultural inputs would have enlivened them and created a greater sense of participation – and that the session on defining the concept of rape and its elaboration was not really relevant to rural women. For them, solutions needed to be concrete, immediate, and capable of offering genuine relief, economic or otherwise. They also felt that there was too much emphasis on the individual woman's body, rather than on its social construction. Some participants were of the opinion that if this had been anticipated, a *via media* could perhaps have been thought of.

Nevertheless, there is an awareness now of not just rape but the attempt to rape, and other forms of sexual assault. Again, marital rape is now being articulated by women themselves as a pervasive problem.

It was agreed that the discussions should be continued at different places, with different groups, using this meeting as a starter.

Finally, almost all of us felt the need for long-term optimism, even in the face of all the odds, and to introduce fresh militancy into the movement by involving younger activists.

How Common is Sexual Harassment in Tanzania?
Tanzania Media Women's Association

In October 1991, the first ever crisis centre dealing with sexual harassment, domestic violence and discrimination against women and children opened in Tanzania. In the words of the Tanzania Media

Women's Association (TAMWA) under whose umbrella the centre was started: 'This event heralded a new era for women in Tanzania, taking into consideration the fact that they can discuss issues like rape, domestic violence and other forms of discrimination openly and that they have somewhere to go and seek help.'

TAMWA has long been instrumental in bringing the issue of violence against women to the public, through its magazine *Sauti ya Siti*, radio programmes, brochures, popular education material, workshops and seminars. In November 1992, *Sauti ya Siti* devoted a special issue to violence against women. Included in its pages was Chemi Che Mponda's article reprinted below, commemorating the death of a young woman student driven to suicide by persistent harassment from a group of male engineering students at the University of Dar es Salaam. The harassment in this case formed part of a systematic campaign of violence against women known as Punch. Having singled out a particular woman – she might excel at her studies or show Westernized attitudes – members of Punch would research into her past: where she came from, what school she went to, the grades she achieved, her family situation, details about her love life. At an appointed time this information was broadcast throughout the university, always distorted and often totally invented; it would then be featured on huge placards on a high wall where it could be read but not taken down. Alongside this type of public ridicule, Punch sustained its reign of terror by demanding that women submit to their sexual demands for fear of being 'Punched' themselves or, as in some cases, raped.

Levina Mukasa remembered

For two decades almost every female student who studied at the university's main campus (popularly known as the Hill) suffered sexual harassment. They were subjected to ridicule, sexual threats or outright assault and rape. However, it wasn't until a young woman killed herself, on 7 February 1990, that the issue became the focus of public outrage.

A first-year education student, Levina Mukasa had been severely harassed over a long period by a group of male engineering students and the clandestine satire group Mzee Punch, which specializes in producing pornographic wall literature about selected female students. Their aim is mainly to make female students give in to the sexual demands of Punch members or to make successful women students perform badly. Their efforts, according to several ex-students at the campus, have been highly effective.

'My grades suffered terribly; I was really demoralized,' says one ex-student who faced the torture of Punch. She is now a successful

Cover of Women's Crisis Centre pamphlet.

businesswoman in the city, but when asked if she would be identified in the press she said, 'For heaven's sake, No! No! No! My name has been tarnished enough. Don't you know that once Punched you have been Punched for life?'

Though Punch existed at the UDSM campus for a good 20 years no one ever thought of seriously banning it because its victims were women. Originally a political instrument to ridicule a government policy, it evolved into a major instrument of sexual harassment and repression of women. Even when Levina Mukasa killed herself by taking an overdose of chloroquine tablets (used to cure malaria) there was still hesitation in banning the organization. Cries from women leaders and women's groups to put an end to Mzee Punch fell on deaf ears. It was only later that year, when President Ali Hassan Mwinyi and other top government leaders were targeted, that the group was officially banned. At the same time the university was closed down for one year on the grounds that it was being repaired and students needed to learn manners. All students, men and women, were expelled.

After Levina's suicide, a probe team was formed to investigate the causes of her death. The team recommended that a then second-year engineering student be expelled for harassing her two days before [her suicide]. It also recommended that two others be suspended. The main accused was expelled, but reinstated in 1991 following an appeal through the male-dominated court system. The others have completed their studies.

Levina killed herself because when she pleaded for help no one listened. Mzee Punch had threatened to Punch any female student seen walking with her. Terrified, the women heeded the call and Levina was left to walk alone, shunned. She was haunted by knocks on her room door at night. Obscene messages and threats were stuck on her room door. She was featured as the next person in the Punch programme prominently displayed throughout the campus.

An emergency meeting of women which was called after Levina's death accused the then student government (MUWATA) of silently watching sexual harassment and even sometimes collaborating with the perpetrators. They said that female victims who attempted to get help from MUWATA would only find themselves in deeper trouble – instead of receiving support they were lectured on the superiority and invincibility of Mzee Punch.

How common is sexual harassment in Tanzania?

Violence against women students has received increasing attention in the past few years, especially in the United States where research by institutions such as the Center for Women Policy Studies (see p. 200) has focused, among other things, on the frequency of so-called acquaintance rape on university campuses. As an organized system Punch represents an extreme and particularly terrifying manifestation of the problem. In 1992 TAMWA decided to conduct its own survey of the wider issue of sexual harassment in Tanzania.

Of 300 women, schoolgirls and students interviewed, over 90 per cent have experienced sexual harassment at one time or another. They experienced it in their homes, in the streets and in institutions of learning. The majority had experienced sexual harassment in language and through the media. Some had been through it in marriage and nearly all the women out of the 200 women working outside homes questioned for our survey said they had been sexually harassed in their places of work or as a result of their jobs. This happened even if the harassers were not their colleagues in the course of their work. And they all felt two things in common: anger and helplessness.

Nearly all the women working outside homes in the sample said sexual harassment was a serious problem for women who are employed, that it curtails women in career advancement (some resign) and that it makes the atmosphere at work 'so miserable and depressing' that their productivity is reduced, sometimes to zero point, as a result of being undermined by male colleagues or even being outright molested.

Quite a large number of the schoolgirls interviewed out of a sample of 50 said they were not aware of the concept of sexual harassment, that is, they had not internalized the fact that sexual harassment is an aberration and when it did take place, they accepted it as the norm, thinking that is how men ought to behave towards women and that women are supposed to absorb it passively or even to respond 'favourably'.

Nearly 90 per cent of the 200 working women interviewed said sexual harassment threatens their jobs and their economic survival. Most of them related experiences of emotional upheaval which made their work suffer. Some of them were bypassed in promotions because they were not 'forthcoming' or 'responsive' to the propositions put across to them. The rest, about 8 per cent, said if they had no alternative 'what with being a single parent and the state of inflation being what it is, it is better to flirt with the boss/colleague or even sleep with him rather than lose my job!'

In the sample of 50 housewives taken for this survey, all admitted to being sexually harassed in the streets. Over 60 per cent said they had been harassed in abusive language and 6 per cent said they had also experienced it in the home from cousins, uncles, brothers-in-law or even (in the case of one), from a father-in-law. This establishes that even those women who do not work outside their homes in male-dominated establishments are not safe from sexual harassment. So the belief that only women who leave the 'safety' of their homes to seek employment outside are in peril of being sexually harassed is not correct. From the survey, we learned that women of all age groups, both employed and unemployed, schoolgirls and even the aged and nuns, run the risk of being sexually harassed.

Definition of sexual harassment

In its simplest definition, sexual harassment means 'unwanted sexual attention'. It can take the form of direct verbal propositioning or physical contact, that is, groping, touching of hair, slapping of bottoms, etc. Or it can take an indirect form: rude language about women's anatomy, backbiting with intent to defame, direct verbal abuse of victims, showing of women's anatomy in pornographic pictures, or hanging pictures of nude women in lewd positions, at workplaces.

In the streets, it takes the form of passing ribald comments when a woman passes, sometimes direct touching of women's bodies in public transport or direct assault.

OTTU (the trade union movement) has issued a *Trade Union Guide on Sexual Harassment at Work*, which defines sexual harassment thus:

> Any repeated and unwanted verbal, physical or gestural sexual advances; sexually explicit derogatory statements, or sexually discriminatory remarks made by someone in the workplace which are offensive to the worker (victim) involved; which cause the worker to feel threatened, humiliated, patronized or harassed. Or which interfere with the worker's job perform-ance, undermine job security or create a threatening or intimidating work environment.

A survey conducted by TAMWA (1988) for a seminar 'The Portrayal of Women in the Mass Media and Language' showed that the media plays a major role in undermining women's image of themselves as well as society's image of women. That goes for language too. Most of the abusive terms are female-oriented, in which parts of women's anatomies are mentioned explicitly and in a derogatory way. Dr Ruth Besha in her paper for this seminar said that whenever society wants to abuse a person (man or woman), his/her mother's anatomy is brought into focus, not his/her father's anatomy.

> This serves to perpetuate the notion that women are just sexual objects and also that they are objects of ridicule who don't merit societal respect! Even their [women's] reproductive function is undermined when a victim is abused/insulted by mentioning his/her mother's genitals and the fact that she gave birth to him/her!

'For years it has been kept under wraps, most women didn't dare talk about it ...' sums up the whole notion of sexual harassment, that although it is not a new problem and in fact has been existing for years, most women have been either too embarrassed to bring it out in the open or have accepted it as the norm.

It is only in recent years that the term 'sexual harassment' has been used formally in Tanzania, largely as a result of the upsurge of women's pressure groups formed to fight against all types of discrimination, of which sexual harassment is the most common.

Power play

Sexual harassment is one of the oldest forms of power play, with women reduced to the role of victims while the men (the perpetrators) are in the role of intimidators. In its most basic form,

Myths About Sexual Harassment

MYTH: Sexual harassment only happens to women who are provocatively dressed.

FACT: Sexual harassment can happen to anyone, no matter how she dresses.

MYTH: If the woman had only said "NO" to the harasser, he would have stopped immediately.

FACT: Many harassers are told "NO" repeatedly and it does no good. NO is too often heard as YES.

MYTH: If a woman ignores sexual harassment, it will go away.

FACT: No, it won't. Generally, the harasser is a repeat offender who will not stop on his own. Ignoring it may be seen as assent or encouragement.

MYTH: All men are harassers.

FACT: No, only a few men harass. Usually there is a pattern of harassment: one man harasses a number of women either sequentially or simultaneously, or both.

MYTH: Sexual harassment is harmless. Women who object have no sense of humor.

FACT: Harassment is humiliating and degrading. It undermines school careers and often threatens economic livelihood. No one should have to endure humiliation with a smile.

MYTH: Sexual harassment affects only a few people.

FACT: Surveys on campus shows that up to 30 percent of all female college students experience some form of sexual harassment. Some surveys of women in the working world have shown that as many as 70 percent have been sexually harassed in some way.

In Case of Sexual Harassment: a Guide for Women Students, Center for Women Policy Studies, USA.

when it is direct assault, sexual harassment brings into focus the helplessness of women: because they are physically weaker, because they do not hold positions of authority at places of work or at home, and because they are suppressed in society – 'When a man talks, a women is not supposed to answer back.' All that the victims (women) can feel is anger and impotent rage. Very few have taken the step of fighting back against the vile practice.

'Men tend to call us by derogatory names like '*shangingi*' or belittle us by calling us *mtoto*. They whistle as we walk by, or pass vulgar comments or stare at our breasts and buttocks while talking to us. All this is to emphasize that we are just sexual objects, to remind us that we are not to be taken seriously.' Songs play their role in perpetuating this notion too, when singers (male) sing about women who 'eat' men's money and don't 'deliver the goods'.

Asha (26), secretary – lives in Kariakoo

'My boss, an Italian expatriate, always makes passes at me. Once he asked me to stay behind in the afternoon and after everyone had left, tried to assault me. He kept chasing me around his desk and I couldn't get out of the room as he had locked the door. I told him I would scream, and he didn't believe me. I did scream and the watchman came to the door to inquire. I told him in Swahili what was happening and he told the boss to open the door. The boss opened the door and I rushed out and went home. When I told my husband about it, he said that I must have been behaving like a prostitute. It was a very bad experience for me and I had hoped to get sympathy from my husband, but he only blamed me. Now I am so depressed, if only I could afford to stop working. But we need the extra income. My husband has now become very suspicious and watches my movements all the time. The boss is still there, I wish he would get recalled to Italy. He still propositions me and has even offered me money. I told him I am a respectable married woman, but he wouldn't listen.'

Mwamvua (16), schoolgirl – lives in Temeke

'My stepfather always paws me when my mother is on duty. She is a nurse and sometimes works the night shift. He buys me presents and gives me money to spend which I always give back to him. He says I shouldn't be afraid of getting pregnant, that he knows how to prevent pregnancy. I hate him. I am too scared to tell my mother, I don't think she would believe me. My father died when I was small and three years ago my mother remarried.

'He gets angry when I speak to boys and once slapped me as I walked home from school with a male classmate. He tells my mother that I am cheap and she shouts at me.'

Maumba, defiler of schoolgirls

Athumani Ally Maumba, a Dar es Salaam tailor, was convicted of defiling primary schoolgirls below the age of 14. He is serving a seven-year sentence after luring young girls to his shop and offering them money (in the range of 100 shillings to 1,200 shillings) for having sex with him.

It is said that some of the girls suffered from venereal disease and one got pregnant. One of the girls was 12 years old and had been failing her exams. Her teacher decided to investigate the girl's laxity and discovered that she was one of Maumba's victims.

After Maumba was brought before the law, a large section of the community treated him as a hero with some people shouting, 'Maumba oyee', 'Viva Maumba', 'Maumba Superstud', etc.

The sentencing judge, Lugakingira, said Maumba was 'a perverted criminal ... who has to be removed from society ... so that children get a chance to grow up in dignity and with a hope for the future'.

According to reports, the schoolgirls who were Maumba's are doing well in their lessons now that Maumba has been put away. In all, he is alleged to have defiled over 30 young girls, all below the age of 14.

Maria (27), 'job for sex' – lives in Kipawa

'I went for an interview in a parastatal to get a job as an accountant. I'm fairly well qualified, having studied at the College of Business Education in Dar es Salaam. The manager looked me up and down and I felt he was undressing me. After the interview, he called me aside and offered to buy me drinks after office hours. When I sounded reluctant, he told me pointedly that I might not get the job. I questioned him further and he said other people had been interviewed before me and they were men and more qualified, but he liked my looks and thought that we could become more intimate. I refused and he told me not to go near his office again. Needless to say, I didn't get the job.'

Sexual Harassment at work in France: What Stakes for Feminists?

Marie-Victoire Louis

Marie-Victoire Louis is a French sociologist, editor of the feminist journal *Projets féministes* and president of the European Association Against Violence Against Women at Work (AVFT) which she set up with two other women, Joelle Causin and Yvette Fuillet, in 1985. In her own words: 'We wanted to expose, analyse and denounce as unacceptable the hitherto unrecognized existence of violence against women in the workplace, and to give it a name, something which the term 'sexual harassment' (borrowed from Anglo-Saxon vocabulary) enabled us to do. The central question was not how the problem was discovered, but what kind of complicity of interests had managed to conceal it for so long.'

The following translation focuses on the principles and working method of AVFT, which both campaigns for the reform of labour laws and the penal code to take into account the problem of sexual harassment at work, and takes up individual cases. The article is based on the text of a paper first presented by Marie-Victoire Louis at an international meeting on sexual harassment in Rome in December 1990 and later published in the journal *Chronique féministe* (No. 44, July 1992).

Aims and principles of AVFT

In establishing AVFT, we began with the need to define various aspects of the problem and to understand the obstacles faced by women on the receiving end of sexual harassment. We were also interested in analysing the reactions of institutions, such as trade unions and employers, and the response of the judiciary.

In 1989 in Paris we organized the first international meeting on Violence, Harassment and the Abuse of Power at Work, which gave rise to a book on the same theme.[1] The Employment Ministry and the Secretary of State for Women's Rights funded a study based on the analysis of 140 cases of sexual harassment in the workplace, with the aim of better recognizing the various forms of abuse that constitute sexual harassment, the kind of reactions to be expected from sources mentioned above and the effects of harassment on women's careers and health.[2]

We also published a journal, *Cette violence dont nous ne voulons plus*, dedicted to the analysis and denunciation of violence against women. The themes, covered over twelve issues, included sexual harassment and protection, sexism and trade unions, violence in marriage and prostitution.[3]

In relation to the judiciary, we suggested legal reforms of both penal and labour codes, based on the needs for the following:

- a definition of sexual harassment;
- the penalization of sexual harassment;
- recognition of the existence of aggravating circumstances – when the person accused of harassment is in a position of power over the woman (as employer, deputy, doctor, teacher, priest, functionary, proprietor, etc.), and when she loses her job or becomes ill or depressed as a result;
- the protection of witnesses, without whom it is impossible to develop a strategy against sexual harassment;
- acknowledgement of a boss's responsibility for the well-being of his workforce, beyond the limitations of company policy.

This last point is crucial, for to judge a case according to company policy runs the risk of diverting a tribunal's focus away from the concrete facts and onto the issue of whether the employer in question actually had any publicized policy on sexual harassment. (Does a statement on some noticeboard amount to a definite policy?) Above all, such a shift in emphasis is likely to divert attention from the true debate, which concerns working methods and the legitimacy of a given company's hierarchical structure.

Finally, we also insisted – and this should apply to all types of violence against women – that a woman's sex life, or indeed any questions about her private life leading up to the incident, should not be taken into account.

These legal proposals, later used by the government who actually based their proposals on our own, were disseminated through the press, deputies and government ministers. We also suggested specific changes to the Labour Code. Sexual harassment is a problem connected to work conditions, hygiene and security, the abuse of power, and management of personnel, all of which are ultimately the employer's responsibility. As well as fighting against the consequences of sexual harassment it is essential to establish a clear

Open Training and Education Network, Australia, 1992.

prevention policy.[4]

The arguments that 'women feel ashamed, guilty, afraid, keep silent ...' are unacceptable. As soon as women realize that complaining can have positive results, that the risks of speaking out are not insurmountable, that it is within their power to survive the human costs of appearing before a tribunal and that there is a chance that the system might actually guarantee the rights they have previously been denied – namely the right to a life protected from male violence – many more will be prepared to state their cases. Arguments about female culpability and responsibility have served to justify the abuse of power against women for centuries.

Working methods

Initially subsidized by the European Community (EC), AVFT is nowadays funded jointly by the Secretary of State for Women's Rights and the Ministry of Employment. Two paid workers work part-time with the support of around ten volunteers. Though the project is essentially run by women, it is a deliberately mixed organization. Refusing to trap men as they have trapped women in a negative image of themselves, and in opposition to the type of biological determinism that denies freedom of the individual, not to mention the pessimism that excludes any chances of improving gender relations, we wish men to have a role in AVFT. I do not mean a role based on gender, but on their commitment as lawyers, trade unionists, work inspectors, journalists, husbands or partners ... who support and agree with some, if not all, of our work. Where gender relations are concerned, we deliberately try to guard ourselves against any kind of 'siege mentality'. We also endeavour not to fall into the role of providing 'charity' – something feminists have not yet fully broken from – nor of some avant-garde or band of social workers.

Open Training and Education Network, Australia, 1992.

The work of AVFT is carried out on a contract basis. Our aim is to help modify the power structure of gender relations, a project for which we believe we have a certain competence. The contract is explicit: this is who we are, this is what we do, this is how we can advise you, offering suggestions that you can take or leave. Now we need to know who you are, what has happened, what you want to do and what we can do together. Our function is to supply advice to those who want it, maintaining a visible profile and remaining anonymous only in exceptional cases. We work in partnership with the people who come to us, as two entities, each with their own interests and constraints. We also reserve the right to refuse certain cases, for example those involving women with definite psychological problems or dealing with vengeance, where a woman's motives for complaint rest entirely on revenge. Our aim is the systematic defence of individual human rights.

Sexual harassment cases are often complex and last a long time. They usually constitute an attack on workers' rights and include a number of protagonists, often with conflicting interests (witnesses, hierarchy, colleagues, parents, unions etc.). Having agreed to take up a case, we tend to start by focusing on a careful reconstruction of events in order to put the entire situation into perspective. Without careful study of the background to each individual case it is difficult to refute the 'incompetence' argument, often raised suddenly following years of approval for a woman's 'loyal and excellent service'. Shifting the harassment problem away from the protagonist towards the inadequacies of the harassed woman is often the only response from a company hierarchy determined to cover up incidents of harassment that it either doesn't know how to or else refuses to tackle – partly out of reluctance to puncture a likely front of male solidarity. Consequently, we are careful to question any claim that a woman's dismissal is based on nervous depression or absenteeism (both consequences of sexual harassment) and look beyond for the cause. Whatever the situation, it is essential to seek out witnesses, create support networks and officially take on the employment hierarchy.

Our main reference point is always the word of the woman who claims she has been harassed. A man often tries to gain a woman's silence with the warning 'If you complain, it'll only be your word against mine.' Implicit in this statement is the belief that, given her subordinate position, a woman's word has no value. As feminists we must forcefully battle against such sexist assumptions.

With the help of precise questions we ask the woman to use her memory to reconstruct events (deeds, dates, words spoken, atmosphere etc.) and to gather witnesses. As soon as we are convinced that she has a valid case – and this does not mean that she has to have proof – we send a detailed letter to her employer. We do not write to the perpetrator or to management but go right to the top, to the managing director of the company concerned.

These letters are essential in establishing our credibility as well as that of the woman in question. The contents are also important as they may be used as a basis for libel action on the part of the protagonist or can aggravate the woman's position, even leading to her dismissal. We emphasize the employer's duty to look after the welfare of his/her staff and the right of everyone to be treated with respect in the workplace, using arguments from the specific case to show how these principles have been breached. We ask the employer to launch an inquiry and at the same time clarify his/her own position. Employers' refusals to take part in unravelling such a 'complex' train of events are unacceptable; it is their duty to launch an inquiry into both sides of the story (not just listening to those in top positions) and to make a stand without antagonizing either of the case's main protagonists. Needless to say, the employer's responsibility does not exclude the man guilty of harassment from responsibility.

We refuse to adopt any false modesty when it comes to phrasing denunciations, on the grounds that this would be condoning that aspect of women's experience that claims that 'such things', in other

Extract from Sexual harassment at Work: a primer. Pilpina Legal Resources Center, Philippines.

words anything pertaining to violence and sexuality, should be left unsaid. All too often, reluctance to speak of these subjects leads women to use understatements and allusive terms, thus helping to reproduce the mechanisms of oppression that allow men to take for granted women's silence about male violence in the name of feminine modesty or some concept of 'good education'. Our letters deliberately spell out the actual words used and describe the gestures and action of the man accused.

One of our guiding principles, as feminists, is not to substitute our voice for that of the woman concerned. Just as no one should ever be used 'in the name of a cause', we refuse to speak 'in the name of harassed women', or even 'in the name of women who approach the association'. Every derivative of totalitarianism began with a group assuming the right to speak 'in the name of ...' So what rules can be applied to the essential function of politics? Obligations to clarify the grounds for one's legitimacy would be a good start.

Our respect for the woman who comes to us conditions the process by which she regains control of her life. We never take a case any further or less far than she wishes. In order for this to work – acknowledging that we have a certain power over the women who come to see us, often in distress, desperate or furious – certain cases demand flexibility. For instance, if we have built up a very strong case that we have worked on for hours on end and the harassed woman suddenly announces, 'I'm stopping. I can't take it any more. I want to forget the whole thing', we always put forward arguments for what we think is in her best interests – in this case probably to continue. If she stands by her position, however, we have to concede and close the file. This does not mean that we have to stop denouncing her ordeal – we simply cannot expose it in its specific context.

Photocopies of these letters are sent to the Employment Minister, who informs the regional office, which then urges an investigation. At this point it is important that the employer is aware of the Work Inspector's investigation into charges of sexual harassment, even though the procedure is likely to be cloaked in language about general workers' rights (wages, work contracts, overtime etc.) without any attempt to examine the problem in depth.

Sometimes other associations join AVFT as civil parties in the investigation. A lot can be gained from a multiplicity of approaches and perspectives. For example, in a case involving the deputy mayor of a northern French town who, for over ten years, had been touching up women and having sex with them in exchange for giving them jobs, we requested the additional participation of the League for Human Rights, which we hope will start to pay more attention to the defence of women's rights; and the French Family Planning Movement, whose stated goals include combating violence against women. The only problem with using several defences is the cost.

There is much to be gained from collaboration between feminist organizations and trade unions, whose weight we have been able to use in several cases. As far as we are concerned, we benefit from our position as outsiders, being less likely to bow to internal pressures. Besides the threat of losing vital public funds, the biggest risk to the survival of AVFT is probably linked more to internal weakness than to outside pressure. In order to be free to highlight any case, no matter who or what company might be implicated, we are very careful to maintain our independence from all institutions.

Defining the problem

Finally, I would like to focus on three further aspects of the problem: the connection between sexual harassment and violence against women; the question of women's responsibility; the issue of building solidarity. These aspects may help women to respond to remarks such as 'Yes, but men are also harassed ...', 'Yes, but women don't support one another ...', or 'Yes, but women are also responsible' (being too seductive, wearing short skirts, sleeping around to gain promotion etc.)

Sexual harassment is an expression of power relations, most often against women by men, reflecting their relative positions in the hierarchy and reflected by inequalities of opportunity in the job market. Since men occupy most positions of power – and determine, through their virtually exclusive control of key government/state positions, the structural values of our societies – sexual harassment, together with other forms of violence against women, is not only commonplace but goes largely unpunished. That these so-called values are evolving to take into greater account the rights of women in no way invalidates this analysis.

Given that in patriarchal societies gender in itself denotes hierarchy, sexual harassment can also occur when a man occupies a position of equal or even inferior rank to his 'victim'. What is then at stake is to illustrate to the victim and others – not necessarily just colleagues – as well as to the harasser himself, the harasser's felt need to maintain the present power balance of gender relations. For those whose identity rests solely on their gender, this necessity is absolutely fundamental. The murder on 6 December 1990 of 14 women students at the polytechnic in Montreal by a man who 'hated women and feminists' serves as a reminder that the menace of violence and death hovers over all women.

Given that the sexual division of power is the expression of a misogynistic, phallocentric, sexist and anti-feminist culture (separately or in combination),[5] sexual harassment can be said to represent the culture of the workplace, as expressed in sexist pleasantries, the display of pornographic pictures, and the denial of women's skills by reducing them to the status of sex objects. Consequently, any judgement concerning sexual harassment that fails to take into account the relationships of power that make up the structure of gender relations effectively reinforces them. The abstract analogy between a man harassed by a woman and a woman harassed by a man has only limited meaning precisely because it leaves out these relations of power that are the very foundation for sexual harassment. It also denies the existence of patriarchal values which condemn women who transgress the status quo.[6] A woman who 'insists' on sexual relations with a man has about as much chance of being defended in our courts as a prostitute; she can even expect to be accorded more than usually harsh treatment for wanting to enact impulses hitherto symbolic of male power. Nevertheless, as a woman exerting a power of authority, she may partially profit from that role as practised by men. On the other hand, the man 'brave enough' to report such advances is likely to find himself basking in the sympathy and admiration of male colleagues, both for having been the object of a woman's sexual demands and for having dared to unmask them. He who gives in to the pressures risks being sent back into the much-despised camp of 'office pet'.

This is not to underestimate the seriousness of such abuse of power, not to deny the woman's responsibility nor to obscure the damage a man might suffer. As feminists, we should clearly affirm our solidarity of principle for the harassed man. At the same time it must be recognized that the majority of known cases against men turn out to be the doing of one or more male colleagues. Given that the hierarchical structures of state, religion, education, and the professions are all founded on the sexual division of power, the need for a feminist analysis is, to my mind, incontrovertible. Only by linking the complex connections between the abuse of power, violence and sexuality can we speak out and effectively fight against abuse such as sexual harassment.

In search of a feminist approach

Developing a feminist approach does not mean setting women and men against each other or relying on solidarity among women alone. As feminists, would we caution, justify or excuse a case of lesbian harassment? Would we silently accept acts of violence committed by women against their children, even their partners, or justify – in the name of the male constraints put upon them – the absence of support from female witnesses? I believe that such positions and the silence which reinforces them, stemming from the defence of a sex and the political struggle to make relations of strength between the sexes one and the same, are largely erroneous.

Among other things a feminist approach needs to do the following:

1. Incorporate an understanding of why and how patriarchy has succeeded in creating a situation where so many women reproduce a culture that essentially negates them.

2. Not exclude solidarity with male victims of violence even when it is based on women's initiatives. Rather than claiming that the recognition of sexual harassment and violence against men will only negate the sufferings of women (the masculinist approach), we can use it to reaffirm the importance of standing up against all kinds of violence, and the cultures that condone it, as feminists have always done. Sensitizing all those who deny the existence of injustices and make unreasonable demands on every man and woman's right to dignity is probably the one way in which feminism can be recognized as a truly universal cause. We therefore have the right to demand that society recognizes that women, feminists, have been a major collective force for social change originally in the vanguard of movements for human rights.

3. Feminist commitment does not mean the exclusion of men sympathetic to female victims of male violence. The accusation that women are not supportive enough among themselves could thus be more effectively fought. In the name of what right should men be cleared of the moral and political duty to denounce injustice? How can we hope to improve relations between the sexes without engaging the attention and responsibility of men? How can we believe in feminism as a humanist approach if we exclude men from any possibility for change by trapping them in the role of oppressor?

Sexual harassment is not a 'women's problem', that is, an offence or crime in which the victims are the guilty ones for not knowing how to react or for not supporting one another – in short, the victimization of women for life. This approach no doubt allows us to be more exacting on their behalf; I will refuse to believe any claims of equality so long as male violence as an expression of men's rights over women remains unrecognized. In this respect, the number of women running an organization is not a relevant indicator. The problem is to examine the organization's structure, to identify elements of sexual hierarchy, and to examine to what extent it is designed to remedy this inequality.

Men have to understand that: sexuality is not an excuse for violent behaviour; their desires do not constitute rightful demands; their sex does not hold the monopoly on fantasy; their silence on the issue of male violence amounts to tacit acceptance; the sexual act is also a relation of power.

A feminist psychiatrist from Quebec recently wrote:

Passive, women are made inferior; different and they are made
guilty. Female sexuality is denied to the advantage of the masculine sexual tradition ... From this point of view, the sexual act
amounts to one of the most aggressive acts in society. It represents
the millennial symbol of women's appropriation by men.[7]

Patriarchal culture sets so little store on women that the violence they
suffer is barely even taken into account. Cases of violence are made
so banal that no one questions them or else people explain them away
with references to social background, alcohol, folly, mental
confusion, love ... In short, everything is set up to avoid confronting
the fundamental constituents of male power and hate, and the fear of
women that so often lies beneath.

Those who reprimand women for being responsible for what
happens to them through sheer naïvety, or blame it on some planned
seduction should be told that: being less naïve means recognizing that
men are dangerous for women; being less seductive means denying
men the very foundations of their fantasies and power over women.
Meanwhile, tackling the issue of female seduction, one of the rare
powers granted to women, must be approached without guilt.

Although sleeping with the boss 'for promotion' and sexual
harassment stem from the same system of male hierarchical power
and should be analysed together, they do not occupy the same level.
Therefore it is not possible to excuse, challenge or justify harassment
on the grounds that women will sometimes consent to have sex with
their superiors in order to gain promotion.

With the reality of economic, social, cultural and family hardships,
the burden of extortion which rests on women has not been
sufficiently exposed, nor has there been enough rigorous analysis of
masculine behaviour. A number of men participate by proxy in
sexual exploits, either real or invented, through covetous desires or
transference. For many, this form of mythical identification is
necessary to nourish their hopes and help constitute their identity.
How many men boast about imaginary sexual adventures? How often
do men, encouraged by their peers, foster ambiguity about such
exploits in order to preserve the benefit of the doubt? Male seduction
may just be another myth of our culture.

In other respects, how many women have been wrongly accused of
obtaining a job or promotion on the strength of their 'charms' in
order to devalue them professionally? It is worth noting that women
are never considered more equal and liberated than when they are
regarded as guilty. Remaining in a situation due to personal
dependence on a man has been recognized as one of women's only
means of survival for centuries. But, given the feeble measure of
freedom left for women, we should not have to stand surety for the
type of delegated power accepted by those who, through some

private or privileged connection, find themselves offered undue promotion. Is access to power worth having on those terms? Apart from anything, power conceded does not amount to real power – nor is it recognized as such.

We must learn to extricate ourselves from a feminine culture based on the perceived value of dependent vulnerability, on submission to men's desires, on awaiting their approval of what we do, all of which amounts to a powerlessness to resist them. We must redefine for ourselves those aspects of culture seldom taught to us: the relations of power between women and men. This means deconstructing myths about what is masculine and feminine in order better to assimilate our own identity.

Sexual harassment, perhaps because it immediately places a woman in an exclusively sexual role, and plays with the ambiguity of sexual, professional, even maternal roles, can only reopen wounds arising from the difficulties that women have in constructing their own individual identities, in taking on the different, often contradictory, roles allotted to them by society.

As well as adding more credibility to ensuing accusations, every complaint lodged by a woman contributes to the shifting of some of the countless denials imposed on them. Each case helps to loosen the foundations of identity constructed and based on violence, authority and lack of respect for the other.

I conclude with the words of Dorval Brunelle who, on being asked what the Montreal massacre revealed about the function of our societies in terms of trying to alter the balance between the sexes, replied thus:

> The motives and reasons that pushed a brain to break down one December afternoon have to be looked at in the wider context of the principles and values which animate society. From this standpoint we men are all guilty, we who tolerate the existence and deepening at the heart of societies of this ambivalence towards women, who are worshipped and adored in terms of images, fantasies and hollow sentiments, while at the same time being beaten, even vilely assassinated in our violent intimacies … To give a name to such horrors, we must start by standing up against every kind of discrimination, from the most intolerable to the most insignificant or petty. In delaying, we have lost the privilege of looking upon women with rectitude.[8]

Notes

1. AVFT, *De l'abus de pouvoir sexuel, le harcèlement sexuel au travail* (Paris, Editions La Découverte/le Boreal, 1992).

2. Sylvie Cromer, *AVFT: le harcèlement sexuel au travail* (forthcoming, 1994).

3. Since entitled *Projets féministes*, the journal is available from AVFT (see page 255).

4. The text of our proposals for penal reform is published in *Cette violence dont nous ne voulons plus*, No. 10, June 1990. Our proposals for workers' rights are reproduced in *Projets féministes*, No. 1, March 1992. AVFT's criticism of the French government's texts appear in *La semaine sociale Lamy*. Copies are available with payment from AVFT (see page 255).

5. My analysis is based on the following definitions by the Canadian feminist Nicole Brossard: 'misogyny signifies hatred or contempt for women ...'; 'Phallocentrism valorises and deifies men on the basis of the phallus as supreme signifier. Myself, ego, phallus, we are Man. Phallocentrism, cultivated over millions of years, allows the justification that God and all His emissaries and representatives are male': 'sexism amounts to a discriminatory attitude and practice against women'; 'anti-feminism is men's political response to women's having a political voice in the public arena'. From *Polytechnique* (Quebec, Editions du Remue-Ménage), 6 December 1990, pp. 95–100.

6. This point is also referred to in Michael Rubinstein's analysis, 'Pour une politique au sein de l'entreprise européenne', in *De l'abus de pouvoir sexuel*, pp. 112-20.

7. Andrée Matteau, in *Polytechnique*, 6 December 1990, p. 104.

8. Dorval Brunelle, in *Polytechnique*, 6 December 1990, p. 150.

Child Sexual Abuse: Why the Silence Must be Broken – Notes from the Pacific Region

Fuelled by the press exploitation of several highly publicized cases, Britain and the USA have seen a rush of public concern about child sexual abuse in recent years. However, as Mary McIntosh points out in her introduction to *Family Secrets: Child Sexual Abuse* (*Feminist Review*, no. 28, p. 14), 'It was the women's movement, starting with small beginnings in consciousness-raising in the 1970s, that enabled the breaking of the silence, the formation of Incest Survivors' groups and the whole opening up of the question of child sexual abuse. Rape crisis centres and other women's organizations have played a vital part in bringing the issue to light and they continue to do work in the front line.' Since those early days in North America, Australia and Europe a broadly similar process has been happening in other countries, among them the islands of the Pacific.

Although the following piece from the Solomon Islands, reprinted from the daily *Solomon Star* newspaper (15 November 1991), only touches on the issue, the fact of its publication indicates an attempt to try to break the taboo of silence that has long surrounded child abuse.

The feature by Nicola Baird was supplied by the Pacific Regional YWCA, based in Fiji's capital, Suva – home of the Fiji Women's Crisis Centre and Women's Rights Movement which together helped to organize a three-week Pacific Regional Workshop on Violence Against Women in August 1992. Outside Australia and New Zealand, the centre – in existence since 1984 – is the only one of its type in the Pacific region. As well as providing a counselling service for women and children, the organization runs a community education programme, distributing leaflets on rape, sexual harassment, child abuse and domestic violence and using other media, in particular radio. An extract from one of the leaflets used, 'Child Sexual Abuse' produced by the Open Training and Education Network (NSW TAFE Commission, Australia, 1992), is also reproduced below.

Why the silence must be broken

'Baby, baby, look at the moon caught up in the mango!' The small boy stops crying and is rewarded with a hug as he turns to see what his aunt means. The mango tree does indeed look as if it has trapped the full moon in its branches tonight. This is one of the many happy family scenes in the Solomon Islands' 5,000 villages. But do not be fooled – the lie is that all Solomon Islanders love children. The same ugly practices that spoil one out of every four children's childhood in developed countries are happening here too. The difference is that child sexual abuse is such a taboo topic that it is hardly ever reported.

The United Nations made a promise to children when they put together The Rights of the Child (1990). Article 19 asks that countries take 'All appropriate legislative, administrative, social and education measures to protect the child from all forms of physical and mental violence ... maltreatment or exploitation, including sexual abuse.'

In the Solomon Islands most people know child sex abuse happens. They hear it, they see it, but they do not report it. 'In custom days,' says Jimmy, a 24-year-old Malaitan with an enviable knowledge of traditional ways, 'a man who played around with a child would be beaten up. Then his tribe would put him into exile. Now, because of Christianity that kind of thinking has changed.'

His colleague, Peter, who comes from Guadalcanal province follows a less aggressive traditional approach. 'We'd put the two parties together, the man's tribe and the child's tribe. Everyone would sit down and eat together. Later we would exchange custom money and shake hands. That solves the problem and it gives us peace,' he explains.

Recently Peter stopped a woman from reporting her husband to the police for sexually abusing a six-year-old girl relative who was living with them. 'If you take a man to the police,' explains Peter, 'and report what he's done, it shows you are not forgiving him. It's true that the law guides us and helps give us peace, but if you go to the police, the problem is still not solved. There is the court case and the man goes to prison and is going to stay cross with you.' Peter believes the exchange of custom money and food, and his church's approach of prayer and forgiveness, are the answer.

Katherine works in Honiara. She has a low-paid job and lives with relatives in an overcrowded government house. It's the closest to a slum that Honiara has. She is a committed Christian. She is also quick to agree that the Solomons coconut wireless suggests child sex abuse is widespread. 'If I saw a man abuse a child I'd go and report it to the police straight away,' she says. But what if Katherine only heard about it?

Recently she was shocked to hear a small girl (let's call her Eva) tell Katherine what Eva's guardian had done to her during a drinking binge. It turned out that Eva was given $4.50 to keep quiet. She spent it on ice blocks. 'I knew it was true but because I'd only heard about it, not seen it,' explained Katherine, 'I wasn't prepared to go to the police or go to the court and make public statements. I was frightened to report it.'

In fact the police would have probably suggested Katherine went home and thought again. 'Child sex abuse is brought to our attention,' says a leading figure in the police force, 'but our initial advice on a family problem like that is to send them home to reconsider making the report. Usually they open the case and then the next day they change their minds. This happens especially with assaults and child abuse. I think it is fair advice,' he continues, 'because experience shows that cases like this usually close before they get to court. A lot of time is wasted as a result.' Police usually advise families to sort out this type of problem with custom chiefs, claims the spokesman.

Elizabeth, married with a son, knew she would not report her boss when she by chance caught him playing with a small boy's penis. 'The boy pulled up his pants quickly and jumped off the man's knee,' she said. 'But I didn't want to report something that only I had seen. I needed someone else to be there. Then I could have accused the big man with confidence.'

Cases like this do end up in the magistrates' court, but Elizabeth's boss might easily have been acquitted, says a top legal man. 'There is an old system of law in the Solomons. For indecent assault you need to corroborate your story to link the accused to the offence. This is virtually impossible to do with child abuse.'

Elizabeth judged it was better to stay quiet than find people believing the big man's story and not what she'd seen. 'They might have started saying I made it up,' she says with horror, 'because people always believe the big man.' According to a UNICEF consultant, she was probably right, 'Quite often if people go to the police it ends up as a public humiliation for them. Keeping quiet looks like a good survival method after all.'

Jimmy's respect of the big man nearly ended up with him losing his job when he heard the man was abusing a young girl. 'It's not good spoiling a man's life by reporting him, but I'm not going to keep working with him,' says Jimmy. 'If he'd stayed on at work it would have been me who resigned.'

Many women find it similarly difficult to tell on their husband or relative. 'Usually child sex abuse is reported through a mum or aunties,' says the legal spokesman, 'but it's a very unusual mother who can take her husband to court.' Often women are threatened on the way. Beata Jio at the Social Development office tells how she heard that one man, abusing his small niece, told his wife to pack her things and go if she talked about what he was doing or planned to report him. A few days later Beata was told the story was not true. 'I think the woman was frightened and that made her change her mind,' she explains.

Why Me? a book designed to help adults come to terms with being victims of child sexual abuse, written by Lynn Daugherty, suggests there are two types of child abuse. One is the fixated child molester, a person who has not mentally matured, and the other is a regressed child molester. The latter usually has a family but stress triggers him into a pattern of sexual abuse. 'Most sexual abusers were themselves the victims of sexual abuse at one time,' reports Daugherty. What's more, nearly every child victim (about 80 per cent) is abused by someone they know, often a family member.

The Bible offers clear rules about this in Leviticus 18. 'Do not have sexual intercourse with any of your relatives (6) ... whoever does any of these disgusting things will no longer be considered one of God's people (29).'

Child sex abuse may not mean vaginal penetration or rape. Daugherty says it most often involves unwanted touching of the victim and takes place any time a person is tricked, trapped, forced or bribed into a sexual act. It is wrong because it hurts the child – sometimes physically, but more often it causes them fear, confusion, anger, shame, depression and feelings of uselessness.

Research shows that children of about nine years old are prime targets. Some children are much younger. Katherine told me about a five-year-old girl who had been bribed with money to rub her uncle's penis. When a 12-year-old friend saw what the man was doing she told her parents. The result was all the household's children and the man were quizzed at the police station. 'He didn't go to prison even though it was discovered he had been doing the same thing to another girl,' says Katherine.

There is a strong link between drunkenness and child sexual abuse. Daugherty stresses: 'Alcohol is not the cause of abuse. It "allows" the abuser to do things he might otherwise not do.' Sometimes poor thinking can be blamed too. There is a story in Honiara about a man who was asked by his friends why he made his teenage daughter pregnant. His answer: 'If a man plants something he must always be the first to harvest it.' This attitude may explain why only two cases of incest have made it to the High Court over the last four years.

'I've never heard of a place where child abuse did not happen,' says the UNICEF consultant, 'but it is a very taboo subject and it is difficult to talk about. Often people who have been abused become self-destructive and angry, they find it difficult in relationships, even choosing partners who abuse them. What seems to be effective is talking about it in self-help groups for adults.

'It's very difficult to tell someone what to do,' she continues, 'because there is so much shame attached to sex abuse.'

The story is the same again and again in the Solomon Islands. People who know a man (though it can also be a woman) is abusing a child do not report it. The reasons range from Christian forgiveness, fear of the legal system, lack of self-confidence or too much respect for the big man. The loser is always the child victim who may not even be believed when he or she does tell someone.

At Save the Children Fund, project manager Maggie Kenyon worries about the effects of sex abuse on child victims. 'Kids often do not realize it is something bad. But they've been told to keep it a secret so they start to see the abuse as a special thing between them and their uncle, or aunt, or whoever abuses them.' This means children get very confusing messages when they find out what they are doing is taboo. If they tell, the friend they shared secrets with will end up in prison, and may never talk to them again.

This is one point Daugherty's book takes a strong line on. The abuse is not the victim's fault. The bottom line, points out Kenyon, is that 'a child has rights and is an innocent victim'.

Until child sex abuse becomes a less taboo subject in the Solomons there will never be an easy way to deal with it. People who can offer help include church leaders, chiefs, the women's development division and the Social Development office at the Ministry of Health.

'We'll try and find out why this happened and help anyone put an end to such actions against young children,' says Beata Jio. However, to take up her offer you must visit or telephone her as her department cannot tour.

In the Ysabel villages a Buala-based health worker says child sexual abuse is very common. She claims a police officer brought five girls back for medical checks on a recent tour. The youngest was 11

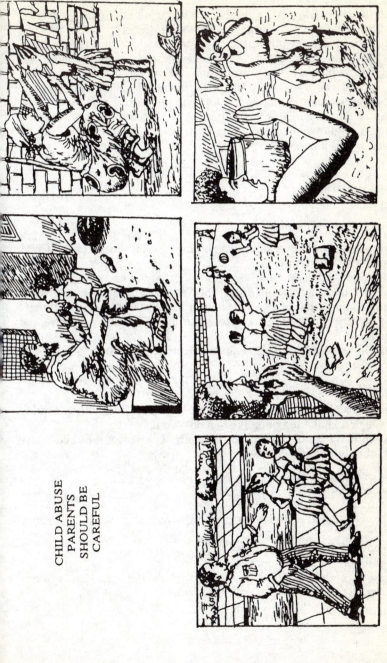

CHILD ABUSE
PARENTS
SHOULD BE
CAREFUL

Special Issue–Sauti ya Sitl, Tamwa, Tanzania.

years old. All were apparently forced to have sex with adults. 'Child sex abuse is a big problem,' she says, 'but the chiefs are not happy when cases are reported. It seems they think it should be settled amongst themselves. I think they want to keep their village's reputation.' This health worker has a message: To stop this problem it's got to be talked about. If someone abuses a child they should go to court or prison. They must learn a lesson. 'But if you keep quiet, or settle in a custom court it will just keep on happening,' she says.

Sooner or later the moon has to come up from behind the shadow of the mango tree. Now is the time for the taboo of silence, which is causing so many little children so much misery, to be broken. Talking about sexual abuse is a start.

Child sexual abuse

What is child sexual abuse?

Child sexual abuse is doing something sexual with a child. **Child sexual abuse is a crime**.

It occurs when an adult uses his or her power or authority over a child, or takes advantage of the child's trust and respect, to involve the child in sexual activity. The abuser may use tricks, bribes, threats and sometimes physical force to make the child take part in sexual activity.

Child sexual abuse is also known as child sexual assault.

When is a child sexually abused?

Child sexual abuse does not just mean having sex with a child – although sexual intercourse is often involved.

A child is sexually abused when the abuser involves the child in any one of these sexual activities:

- touching genitals
- masturbation
- oral sex
- penetrating the vagina or anus with finger, penis or any other object
- showing the adult's genitals
- making sexual comments.

In all cases, the offender has more power than the child – and misuses that power to take advantage of the child.

Who are the victims?

The victims of child sexual abuse are mostly girls (over 90 per cent). And most offenders are men (over 90 per cent). However, it can, and does, happen that victims can be boys and abusers can be women.

How big is the problem?

Child sexual abuse is a big problem all over the world. Research in America (San Francisco) has found that 38 per cent of all women are sexually abused by an adult male before they are 18 years old. Statistics from a study in Britain state that one child in 10 is sexually assaulted by someone they know and trust. Whatever statistics we look at, we know the incidence is high. It is a problem in Fiji too.

However, very few victims of child sexual abuse ever report the abuse. This makes it very hard for us to tell exactly how big the problem is, but there have been so many informal reports that we know that it is widespread. The Women's Crisis Centre has dealt with a number of victims, and doctors, nurses, workers from Social Welfare and other helping agencies report many cases they know of.

Many victims never speak out when the abuse is happening. They only speak out when they become adults themselves and learn that they are not the only one this has happened to. Some victims and their families now report to helping agencies, but few report to the police.

Who are the offenders?

Strangers are not the main offenders. In about 85 per cent of child sexual abuse cases, the offender is a member of the child's immediate family or someone the child knows and trusts.

In studies conducted in Australia, it turns out that in about 50 per cent of cases the offender is the child's father. The next most likely offender is an uncle, then brother, then stepfather and grandfather. Other offenders can be male relatives and acquaintances including friends of the family and neighbours.

In Fiji, 20 cases were seen by the Women's Crisis Centre between 1984 and 1991. Out of these 20, the identities of 12 of the offenders were recorded. In five cases, the offender was the child's father; in three, it was a stranger; and in the remaining four, it was a teacher, an uncle, a family friend and a neighbour.

Offenders are not mentally ill and do not appear to the world as insane child molesters. You cannot pick them out in a crowd. Mostly, offenders appear to be normal, and often people think that they are 'especially fond of children'.

For some people, the idea that someone very close to the child could do such a thing is so shocking that they can't believe it. It's time we started believing it happens. It's time we started speaking out.

Child sexual abuse happens in all cultures and in all kinds of families – rich or poor, large or small, well-educated or not.

The excuses offenders make

Offenders make all kinds of excuses for their behaviour. Some of these are listed below:

- I was giving her (or him) some sex education.
- All fathers do this.
- My wife is frigid (or ill or pregnant).
- I was just showing affection.
- It's our special game.
- I didn't do any harm.
- The child's mother is to blame, she should have known about it (or stopped it).
- It was the child's fault. She (or he) led me on.

There is no excuse for child sexual abuse. Never! These excuses are *wrong*. When offenders make excuses, they are just trying to blame the child or someone else – when they are the only ones to blame.

Many offenders use the excuse that 'the child wanted it'. Children may comply with others' demands but it is out of fear and dependence and sometimes a great need for attention of any kind. They trust adults and this behaviour is a betrayal of their trust.

Children sometimes behave in a way that may seem flirtatious, but usually they are only copying adult behaviour, believing they will gain attention and affection. They are not seeking a sexual response and can never be blamed if an adult involves them in sexual activity.

The adult is responsible – not the child.

Why children don't tell

Most children don't tell anyone what is being done to them. They *do* want the abuse to stop, but there are a number of reasons why they don't tell.

Here are some:

- Often the abuser tells them that this behaviour is normal, and that lots of people do it.
- Children can be told by their abusers that if they tell, they will be in big trouble. They are made to fear that he (if it's the father) will

be sent to gaol and there will be no one to look after the family.

- Quite frequently, when a child has threatened to tell his or her mother about what is happening, the abuser tells the child 'your mother knows already and she doesn't care'. Or, 'if you tell your mother she will think that you're bad and will leave you'.
- The child doesn't know who to trust any more, so doesn't know who to tell.
- Sometimes the child loves the abuser and doesn't want him to get into trouble. She or he just wants the sexual abuse to stop.

Do children lie about being sexually abused?

Often when children try to speak out, they are not believed. There is a false idea that children tell lies about being sexually abused. Children *do not* tell lies about being sexually abused.

Small children cannot make up stories about people doing sexual things to them. They simply don't have enough knowledge to be able to make up such stories. They cannot know about men's penises growing bigger, unless they have seen it and they cannot have seen it unless a man has showed it to them. They cannot know anything about penetration of the vagina unless they have experienced it. Yet abused children can describe such things as 'he puts his finger up my mimi'.

They cannot make it up unless it has happened to them, and if it has happened to them, they are not to blame.

What can the law do?

The Department of Social Welfare has the power to remove a child from a family if it believes the child is at risk. The child is made a ward of the state and taken to a foster home or a place such as the Salvation Army Girls' Hostel. An offender can only be prosecuted under the law if either the child or the child's parent lays charges. However, even when charges are laid, gaol sentences are often light or only suspended sentences are handed down.

Why abuse is often not reported

For all the reasons mentioned earlier, children are very unlikely to report being sexually abused. When the abuser is the child's father, the mother is also unlikely to report the abuse as, in most cases, she doesn't even know about it.

In cases where the mother does suspect, it is often very difficult for her to do anything about it. The Women's Crisis Centre knows of cases where the mother has left the marriage and taken the children so the child will be safe. However, she has been criticized by the rest of the family and her community. It has been very hard for her to find a way to support herself and her children. [...]

What can we do about it?

Children who are victims of sexual abuse are unable to help themselves. It is up to us as a community to join together to protect children. We can work together to stop child sexual abuse.

This is what you can do

- Learn more about the problem.
- Find out what help victims can get.
- Don't pretend there's no problem.
- Stop leaving children in situations where they can be abused.
- Encourage victims and others to speak out.
- Help bring about changes which punish the abuser, not the victim.
- Lobby for legal reform.
- Help victims and their families.
- Talk about your pain, if you are a victim.

Find out more about it

Learn more about the problem of child sexual abuse. Find out how abused children can be helped.

The Women's Crisis Centre in Suva runs workshops and seminars. It gives talks about the problem and what you can do to help. Attend a workshop. Encourage other people to attend. Ask a speaker from the Crisis Centre to give a talk to your community group.

Acknowledge that the problem exists

For too long we've allowed children to be abused because we have pretended the problem doesn't exist. It does. It won't go away because we want it to. Help change the community's attitudes.

Protect children

We must stop leaving children in situations where they can be sexually abused. Be careful who you leave your children with and where you leave them. Remember abusers can be strangers, friends or family members.

Be supportive of victims and their families

Reporting child sexual abuse is very difficult and both the child and the child's family will need a lot of support. If you are unsure of what to do (or the person you are helping is unsure), contact the Women's Crisis Centre to talk it over. They will give you free and confidential assistance to help you work out how you want to handle it.

Help bring about the punishment of the abuser – not the abused
We must work towards bringing about social changes that make sure abusers are punished. For example, why should an abused child be removed from his or her family when the abuser is the one who should be removed? To put this another way, why punish the victim – and why let the offender get away with the crime?

People may argue that you can't remove the offender from the family if he is the breadwinner because otherwise the family will suffer. So we leave the offender with his family and allow the children to continue suffering abuse.

It's odd that we should support this argument in relation to child sexual abuse. If a breadwinner commits another crime – like robbing a shop – we don't say he mustn't go to gaol because he's the breadwinner. We put him in gaol anyway and the family must manage as best it can.

We must work towards setting up financial support for the families of victims so that the offender can be removed and punished and the family does not suffer any further. This may be difficult to do and will take a long time, but we must start thinking and talking about it now. *We must stop punishing the victim*. We must work towards a society where children are protected.

Help promote the fostering of abused children
We must educate and sensitize people to be possible foster parents of children removed from their homes. These foster parents need to be particularly sensitive to the children's special needs as sexual abuse victims.

Encourage children to tell
We must educate children about child sexual abuse so they can tell what is good touching and bad touching, and what is right and what is wrong. They can then speak out when someone tries to molest them.

In some countries there are special units within the education departments with specially trained workers who run education programmes for children in school. While Fiji is not in a position to develop such units yet, we should be working towards it and, meanwhile, non-governmental organizations, such as the Women's Crisis Centre, are conducting sessions for school groups who request them.

In other countries, health departments and education departments also have child protection units which train workers such as teachers to identify victims of child sexual abuse and to help them. Child protection units also help in curriculum development so that 'protective behaviours' can be built into the school curriculums.

Lobby for legal reforms
We need to lobby for a legal process that is not as traumatic for the child who reports the crime as the present one is.

In some countries now, children can give their evidence *in camera*. This means they can give evidence in a small and friendly room with the camera recording the proceedings. They don't have to suffer the extreme trauma of standing up in front of everyone in a courtroom. They can give evidence using words they understand themselves. For example, they can use anatomically correct dolls to show and explain what was done to them.

If these changes to the legal system were made, children and their families may be encouraged to report the crime.

Women and Violence in Post-Communist Czechoslovakia

Jiřina Šiklova and Jana Hradilková

Jiřina Šiklova and Jana Hradilková are founder and co-ordinator of the Prague-based Gender Studies Centre, a multi-media resource centre committed to the raising of gender consciousness in society.

Before the 1989 political change in Czechoslovakia, gender studies was virtually unknown as a term, academic discipline or concept. Furthermore, anything to do with the 'woman question' was dealt with according to Communist Party lines by the universally disliked Czech and Slovak Union of Women. There was no independent women's movement and no real debate about the societal and personal construction of gender. It was simply a non-topic. Research and publication in that field were neither encouraged nor supported, and any inflow of information from the West was severely limited. It is, therefore, not surprising that, when the political situation changed, the impetus and initial materials for the Gender Studies Centre came from abroad.

The centre was founded in October 1991, inspired at first by a book collection donated by friends to sociologist Dr Jiřina Šikova, and then by the encouragement of the Network of East–West Women, an international network of scholars and activists, which donated printed materials and financial support. Since its inception, the centre has been supported and advanced by people from all over the world, and its scope has grown far beyond initial expectations. The original goal was to open a resource centre for the establishment of an academic gender studies programme in the Czech Republic and Slovakia. As the centre developed and responded to the local situation, however, it also began to focus on public outreach and information services; as well as being a library the centre has become a meeting place, co-ordination centre and active catalyst for societal re-examination of the roles, stereotypes and realities associated with gender.

The following report, translated by Susanna Trnka, summarizes some of these concerns specifically in relation to the long-neglected issue of violence against women.

People in post-Communist states are currently beginning to learn their rights, as well as to learn how to be citizens – how to take care of their own interests and to make their own decisions. Along with this process there is growing awareness of human rights and of the rights of women. Just recently we have begun to discuss whether force is a part of sex, whether sexual relations are possible without force, when force is 'still normal' and when it is pathological. This study is one such exploration.

Before the revolution, domestic violence was heavily influenced by the fact that people lived in constant fear of threats and repression and that a large part of the population had to, or thought they had to, conform to the regime. Families then became places where people were able to act naturally, without conformity. Often, therefore, the family was where people reacted to stress and feelings of being demeaned that they experienced at work or during political meetings. Men were more often in leadership positions (in the public sphere) and therefore were subject to more pressure which they then often responded to within a family setting. In relation to their wives they acted typically macho.

Today both men and women are used to such more-or-less accepted behaviour, which is furthermore reinforced by the fact that men are more likely to be the founders of new businesses and to have incomes substantially higher than those of women. Increasing violence in the Czech Republic is, furthermore, encouraged by the loosening of the control and repression which, under totalitarianism, were normally applied to anyone who committed criminal offences; by the shift to a new structure of power and decision-making; by contemptuous feelings toward the previous police regime; by the fact that the police force and judicial system were misused under Communism; by the dilution and transformation of the police; and by the opening up of borders and the possibility of international criminal gangs entering the Czech Republic.

Legal codes on sexual violence

Rape, according to the Czech legal code, is defined as the use of violence, the threat of immediate violence, or the misuse of a woman's inability to defend herself, to force her to consent to sexual intercourse. The offender's punishment depends upon the victim's age and on her relationship to the offender. The object of this law is the right of the woman to make independent decisions with respect to her sexuality. The crime of rape can be committed only upon a woman (and not a man), and not on one's wife. The offender can only be a man, but a woman who hurts another woman through violence or the threat of violence in order to assist a man in forcing the victim into intercourse can be considered a co-offender. Included under rape is sexual violence against a woman with whom the offender lives but who refuses to have intercourse with him. Her physical maturity and sexual experience are not taken into consideration. Intercourse is defined as the joining of the male and the female sexual organs. As long as forced copulation occurs, the crime is considered rape, whether or not the offender experienced sexual gratification. Contact of the sexual organs is not, however, considered sufficient.

Coercion into intercourse according to the law means that the offender used violence, by which is meant physical force with the object of overcoming or preventing serious resistance from the woman, and forced her into sexual relations against her will. Coercive intercourse is, however, restricted to situations in which the woman gives up the possibility of resisting only because she sees that her resistance is completely hopeless. She gives in to the attacker because she has no other choice. If the offender considers her resistance as weak, that it is only in pretence and that in reality she does want to have intercourse with him, legally his behaviour would be considered a factual mistake and the offender would not be held responsible for committing an intentional crime. Included in this case would be situations in which the offender did not know that the situation fulfilled the legal definition of rape.

The laws demarcate conditions under which the victim is limited in her freedom of choice and cannot act independently because, to a certain extent, she is subject to the offender's power; the victim

Isis International Women's Health Journal, No. 18, April–May–June, 1990

submits to the crime because she is dependent in a substantial way upon the offender, for example if he is her father. If she was not dependent upon him, she would not choose to take part in this action. Women who in such cases consent to sexual relations are in fact being violated; this even includes cases where the offender is the woman's ex-husband. This is a fact of which most women who are undergoing divorce proceedings are unaware. Due to the lack of available apartments, many women are forced to live with their ex-husbands during or after the divorce. Even when the ex-husband forces the woman to have intercourse and it happens frequently, the woman does not usually think of using this as evidence before the court or of reporting it as rape. This law also applies to situations where a daughter is sexually abused by her father or stepfather (perhaps with the agreement of her mother who by these means thinks she can hold on to her partner) and doesn't have the opportunity to move out, or doesn't have anywhere to go and doesn't have enough money to support herself. So far, legal awareness that the victim of abuse from a father or stepfather has the right to report this to the court has been limited. Protection of victims of sexual abuse has also been ignored; even victims of legally recognized abuse have had to remain living with those who abuse them.

This law and its interpretation have not been sufficiently used in the interests of women. The primary problem for the victim during the judicial proceedings is the interpretation of what constitutes 'serious' resistance on her part. The victim faces questioning intended to verify that her resistance was not just pretence, that the amount of resistance she showed was proportional to her strength, and that her resistance occurred as soon as possible, along with inquiries into her behaviour preceding the rape and into the context in which the rape occurred. During these inquiries a woman who decides to report a rape is virtually blamed for the crime. She is interrogated, and her words and arguments are scrutinized by the attacker's lawyer, who attempts to show that she should have better protected herself against sexual abuse. The attacker's lawyer also attempts to show that the offender was not aware that he was committing the crime of rape. The victim can't very well disprove this, since she was usually alone with her attacker when the rape occurred, without any witnesses. Thus those who accuse the rapist often end up themselves being accused.

Women's attitudes to violence

Women in post-Communist states often accept brutal behaviour, including sexual harassment, as reflections of 'manhood', and so far have not protested against it. Stereotypes of male and female behaviour have hardly changed. Under totalitarianism, questions of men and women's behaviour were not explored in sociological studies or in the popular press. Until very recently, sociology was reduced to mere state ideology, which is why it did not pay any attention to these questions. Therefore, men and women today do not realize some of the unreasonableness of certain reactions and attitudes. Citizens of post-Communist countries have had an even harder time reflecting on their own behaviour. At present most attention is given to economic questions, issues of consumption, the free market, and political transformation, and again questions of gender are not given much attention.

People generally don't know what is classified under the category of 'punishable crimes of rape'. Even among specialists this classification has been defined just within the last few months. Most people do not accept that a woman has the right to refuse intercourse even after giving the offender the idea that she is interested in having sex with him – for example if she willingly went up to his apartment for a glass of wine – and they do not accept that ignoring her refusal constitutes a crime. Not only men refuse to believe this, but also women who do not know their rights.

Sexual harassment, about which so much is written in the West, is seldom discussed; most women do not know what it is. Obscene comments about women, criticism of women based on their looks, 'playful' smacks, and pseudo-flattery are routine in most workplaces, and it sometimes even seems as if women welcome them. For example, kissing a woman's hand is considered a sign of being a modern gentleman and is seen as opposition to the previously required relation of 'comradeship' between men and women. Sexual relations between bosses and their underlings, usually secretaries but nurses too, verbal allusions to sex and sexual jokes at business dinners (previously at team meetings) are routine and no one – to the surprise of Americans! – objects to it. Only very recently have these problems been discussed and written about. But hardly had we encountered the term 'sexual harassment' when some comic twisted this term into 'sexual rattling' (playing with the Czech word *harašeni*, which sounds like 'harassment' but has a different meaning) and the whole issue had its backbone broken.

Reasons why women don't report rape

- Up until now, there has been an overwhelming distrust of the authorities and of the police.
- Harsh investigations of rape cause further psychological and sometimes even social injury to the victim. Court negotiations last a number of months during which the victim's name and all of the

details of her personal life are made public, causing her repeated social damage.

- The satisfaction from seeing the rapist punished is minimal while the moral and psychological pain of the victim is indeterminate, and neither the victim's psychological damage nor her loss of prestige in the workplace can be replaced or compensated.
- Reimbursement of material damage is minimal and problematic, since the court often requires the victim to collect evidence that damage was done to her, to prove that the damage was done by the offender, to discover the offender's address and place of work, and to pay for the legal costs of the trial.
- The offender is not only treated courteously but is given a lawyer, while the victim is left on the sidelines. The court case can even theoretically proceed against the will of the victim, even though she has to pay for all the legal costs. Once proved guilty, the offender is often given, as a means of softening his sentence, psychological therapy, usually psychotherapy and resocialization, while the court ignores the needs of the victim. She is not even offered psychotherapy.
- Even if the victim wins the trial and the offender is sent to jail, she must still fear that after his release he will attempt to revenge himself upon her for having him convicted.

This situation will be even more complicated in the future when legal costs increase and patients have to pay for their own health care.

The recent period has, however, seen a sprouting of spontaneous self-help groups for women, and organizations that want to solve these problems. The White Circle of Safety was begun in the Czech Republic in 1991. This organization, which primarily offers counselling for all victims of crime, is run on an all-volunteer basis and includes psychologists, psychiatrists, criminologists, lawyers, judges and social workers. During 1993 it gave out personal advice to 84 people, wrote to 135 victims of sexual violence, and fielded 200 telephone calls relating to these issues. The White Circle of Safety sponsors seminars and weekend meetings in which participants learn how to recognize danger signs of sexual violence, practise self-defence, and study their legal rights. Along with the Gender Studies Programme, the White Circle of Safety with the private television company Allegro co-ordinated a televised discussion on sexual violence, which was very successful.

The most important use for all of the research and counselling work is to break through the silence about this form of violence against women; to discuss a subject that is publicly taboo; to speak out on international laws protecting women against rape in a time of war; and to call to the attention of the courts and of the police that it is necessary for them to learn about this topic and to educate specialists who will deal with these problems in ways that are more sensitive than those previously used. It is necessary to write about these problems so that victims no longer feel that they are the 'only one', so that the public won't blame the victim but the attacker, and so that women will recognize their rights on these issues, both in the workplace as well as in relation to their husbands.

Part 3
Health and Sexuality

Gender Violence and Women's Health in Central America

Elizabeth Shrader Cox

A specialist in public health, Elizabeth Shrader Cox has worked in numerous health agencies and women's organizations on projects related to maternal and child health, reproductive health, child care and women's employment, and gender violence. In 1991, after several years in Mexico, she moved with her family to Costa Rica where she continues her work in research, writing and activism on violence, health and development issues. The following article is adapted from an earlier paper entitled 'Violence against women in Central America and its impact on reproductive health', presented at the Safe Motherhood Central America Conference in Guatemala, January 1992.

International health and development projects that choose to listen to women for identification of their needs are finding that gender violence is a major factor in women's strategies for survival and improvement of themselves and their families. Poor women throughout the developing world, whether participating in income-generation projects, childcare co-operatives, primary health care activities, youth organizations, mothering skills classes, AIDS focus groups, child-to-child health training, or Al-Anon meetings, eventually bring the discussions around to the two themes common to their lives: child-bearing and gender violence. They recognize that 'safe motherhood initiatives' will never be wholly successful until all women are safe on their streets and in their homes.

Discussions of women and health in Central America principally focus on reproductive health. In Central American health policy

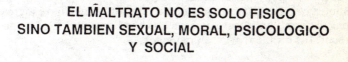

MANY OF US ARE ABUSED WOMEN
–My husband hits me
–Mine throws me out of the house
–Mine insults me all the time
–Mine, too
–Mine, too
From Woman & Violence Training Manual used by the Matagalpa Women's group, Nicaragua

circles, this emphasis on women's reproductive capacity reflects both the relative cultural importance assigned to women's reproductive role and the phase during the life cycle in which Central American women are most vulnerable to disease and death. A reproductive health framework for analysing violence against women is arguably the most appropriate for Central American (and developing country) populations in terms of both defining women's health status and designing interventions.

While recognizing that all forms of gender violence have a profound impact on every aspect of women's lives, this article concentrates on the reproductive health impact of rape, domestic violence and political violence in Central America. I also include an overview of some recent programme initiatives in the region and the critical role health workers can play in ameliorating the detrimental effects of gender violence on women's health status.

The scale of the problem

Epidemiological profiles on women and violence for each Central American country are not available, because reliable, comparable, region-wide data do not exist on rape and domestic violence, a situation that contributes to the statistical invisibility of women's issues.[1]

Some recent figures, however, allow estimates of the prevalence of gender violence in Central America. Approximately one out of every five women can expect to be raped or sexually assaulted during her lifetime.[2] At least one in three women will experience a violent relationship with an intimate partner.[3] Some 15 per cent of Central Americans are considered refugees or displaced persons, a vulnerable population of whom a majority are women.[4] It is not known whether the rates of violence against women have increased in recent years, only that some sectors are beginning to recognize and report the problem in greater numbers.

Sexual violence and reproductive health

In applying a health focus, one needs first to describe the disease, in this instance the 'disease' of rape and sexual assault. The legal and cultural definitions of rape used in Central American countries do not adequately reflect the reality of women's experiences. A necessary first step is to recognize legally, medically, and socially the multiple facets of sexual aggression in order to study it, treat it, and prevent it. The definition of rape employed here is as follows: the unwanted sexual contact of a woman's body perpetrated by one or more

TAMBIEN POR ELLOS RESCATAMOS NUESTRA DIGNIDAD

"Chico Perico
mató a su mujer
la hizo tasajo

y la puso a vender
y no la quisieron
porque era mujer"

CANCION INFANTIL

IT'S ALSO FOR THEM THAT WE RESCUE OUR DIGNITY

Chico perico
killed his wife,
made her into beef jerky,
and put her up for sale
and no one wanted her
because she was female.
            –children's nursery rhyme
*From Woman & Violence Training Manual used by the Matagalpa Women's group,
Nicaragua*

121

persons, whether this contact is with a part of the body or with an instrument. Vaginal, anal, and oral penetration are included in this definition, and ejaculation is not necessarily implied. Rape occurs between strangers, acquaintances, family members and spouses. Furthermore, rape is an act of violence, not an act of sexual expression.

Rape can cause psychological crises that in turn impede a woman's fulfilment of her roles as mother, wife, and wage earner. Studies from various Latin American countries show that more than 60 per cent of rape survivors know their rapist, implying that women are at risk of being raped even by a supposedly trusted person in an apparently safe place.[5] Approximately 40 per cent of reported rapes involve a victim under 16 years of age.[6] The adolescent rape survivor, still in a formative stage of physical and psychosocial development, is especially vulnerable to the negative psychological effects of rape. The situation is further complicated when her family forces her to marry her rapist, a legal and social option that is exercised in many Latin American countries.[7]

In addition to psychological sequelae, rape can cause physical trauma, sexually transmitted infection, including AIDS, and unwanted pregnancy. Data from rape crisis centres indicate that between 15 and 18 per cent of rapes result in pregnancy.[8] Unwanted pregnancy caused by a rape is further complicated by restricted access to induced abortion, a situation common to all Central American countries.

Various forms of rape, specifically incest, acquaintance rape, and sexual coercion, play an unacknowledged role in adolescent pregnancy. In Costa Rica, where approximately 20 per cent of births are to teenage women, government sources estimate that 90 per cent of these pregnancies are the result of a rape.[9] The service statistics from a private Costa Rican organization that works with young mothers further indicate that 95 per cent of pregnant adolescents under age 16 in their service population are incest victims.[10] In a pilot study of Mexican adolescent mothers and nutrition, the researchers had to add three options for rape (that is, rape by a stranger, by a known assailant, or by a family member) to describe adequately the relationship between the adolescent and the father of her newborn.[11] In informal interviews, many adolescent girls refer to emotional blackmail, where their boyfriends threaten to leave them or to go out with someone else if the girls do not have sex with them, as the reason why the girls initiated their sexual activity.

These dysfunctional psychosexual patterns are duplicated in more formalized unions as well. Conjugal rape is frequently the norm for sexual relations between spouses, despite the fact that this form of sexual aggression is not recognized legally in Central America. In studies of battered women, between 30 and 58 per cent say they are raped by their husbands.[12] Furthermore, approximately 12 per cent of non-battered married women report being victims of conjugal rape.[13] Given the shameful nature of the subject, these figures undoubtedly underestimate the actual prevalence of conjugal rape.

Women who do not participate in the decision to engage in sexual relations will have difficulty in following a course of treatment for reproductive tract infections or in using effectively such contraceptive methods as the diaphragm, spermicides, condoms, and natural family planning. AIDS prevention campaigns targeting women for condom use do not take into account that many women play little or no role in contraceptive decision-making.[14] The popular perception in Latin America of the woman who uses a condom is that she is either a prostitute or an unfaithful, promiscuous woman. The mere suggestion of using a condom can provoke a male partner's violent reaction. Psychologically, the woman who does not participate in the decision-making process regarding her sexual activity will likewise be less able to participate in decision-making processes regarding other aspects of her life.

Domestic violence and reproductive health

Conjugal rape constitutes only one aspect of domestic violence. Recent figures from Central America show that woman-battering is as prevalent here as it is elsewhere in the world. A study of 1,000 Guatemalan women concluded that 48 per cent were being beaten by their partner.[15] Another study from Nicaragua of 10,500 women seeking legal assistance revealed that half were doing so because of domestic abuse.[16] In El Salvador, 57 per cent of 200 children surveyed indicated that their mothers were battered women.[17] In Costa Rica, half of women seeking child welfare services acknowledged that they had been physically, emotionally, or sexually abused.[18]

Domestic violence has obvious consequences for reproductive health. For example, battering contributes to maternal mortality through murder and suicide.[19] In Honduras, an average of three women per month are murdered by their partner.[20] Elsewhere in Central America, the impact cannot be easily measured because mortality statistics do not routinely account for gender violence as an underlying cause of death.

Domestic violence also plays a significant role in female morbidity. One in four battered women report being assaulted with a weapon and 40 per cent report being injured seriously enough to require medical attention.[21] Battered women are more likely than non-battered women to use the medical system, visit emergency rooms, take prescription drugs, suffer from alcoholism and drug addiction, attempt suicide, and require psychiatric treatment.[22] Morbidity associated with domestic violence is exacerbated by a lack of health care services, especially in rural areas.

Pregnant women appear to be at an increased risk of being battered. In the dynamics of a violent relationship, any change in family structure or threat to the emotional availability of the woman can cause a violent incident. Many battered women report a change in the pattern of the beatings: the man who previously beat her in the face or back, upon learning that she is pregnant, begins to direct his blows toward her stomach or genitals.

Pregnancy as a catalyst for domestic violence was a phenomenon recognized years ago by women working in battered women's centres. According to different studies from developing countries, between 20 and 65 per cent of battered women report being beaten during at least one pregnancy.[23] Prospective studies in the US report that 8 to 17 per cent of pregnant women are battered during the present pregnancy.[24] Further research confirms that domestic violence has a negative impact on perinatal health as well. Compared to non-battered pregnant women, battered pregnant women are twice as likely to miscarry, and four times as likely to have a low-birth-weight child. Their babies are 40 times more likely to die within the first year of life.[25]

Domestic violence is generational, and if they survive the perinatal period, the children of battered women will confront further obstacles. One-third to one-half of wife-beaters also beat their children,[26] and 28 per cent of battered women report being beaten in front of their children.[27] Children who witness violence, especially boys, are more likely than children from nonviolent homes to grow up to be violent parents and spouses.[28] Moreover, children who witness violence develop the same psychosomatic, cognitive, and affective symptoms as do physically abused children.[29] The psychological trauma associated with domestic violence results in a woman's low self-esteem and devalued self-image, which in turn have negative implications for her capacity to assume her maternal, occupational, and home responsibilities.

Political violence and reproductive health

One cannot write about violence against women in Central America without acknowledging the impact of 15 years of civil conflict. Despite the reduction in political violence throughout the region, its effects are still notable in the existing level of social unrest. Due to many factors, as many as 80,000 women have died in the civil conflict,[30] and perhaps as many as 1 million Central American women are refugees or displaced persons.[31]

Both refugees and displaced persons comprise vulnerable populations at increased risk of malnutrition, physical injury, impaired mental health, sexual assault, and death, conditions further aggravated by the limited access to health care. One element particular to the experience of illegally detained women is sexual degradation and the use of rape as torture.[32] Rape is also a very common experience among female Central American refugees of all ages, and husbands often become abusive when they learn their wife has been sexually assaulted.[33] Refugees and displaced persons live under conditions of extreme poverty and stress, with negative implications for the physical and mental well-being of women and their children.

Health workers' role in eradicating gender violence

These figures indicate that violence against women has a significant impact on reproductive health in terms of maternal morbidity and mortality, unwanted pregnancy, adolescent fertility, the transmission and treatment of sexually transmitted diseases, and decision-making behaviour within couples. Despite the obvious health implications of gender violence, however, the formal health sector rarely plays an active role in efforts to prevent or even treat gender violence and its sequelae.

The minimal level of health sector participation is unfortunate, since health workers are logical advocates and supporters for women who suffer the effects of violence. Women, as mothers, wives, and care-givers to the elderly, are responsible for maintaining health and curing illnesses in the family. In this capacity, a woman is far more likely to use the health care system and come in contact with a health professional than to seek the services of a police officer, lawyer, clergyman, social worker, or psychologist. In particular, midwives, traditional healers, obstetricians, gynaecologists, paediatricians, emergency-room attending physicians, internists, public health nurses and community health promoters should be alerted to the fact that a woman may be battered or raped.

Ideally, these and other health care providers should be trained to identify, assess and refer the physically, emotionally or sexually abused female patient. Where possible, medical examination and testing, psychological counselling, and legal services should be integrated, so that the woman and her support network do not expend precious resources on locating different agencies and service providers. Above all, health services should not revictimize the woman. Stories abound of the rape victim or battered woman who seeks help, only to be treated insensitively or ridiculed by ignorant health care providers.

At this point no Central American country can boast adequately integrated rape crisis and battered women's services. What services do exist are usually legal counselling or public education, and the health sector remains marginal to the process of change. Health professionals often feel at a loss as to what may be done for a battered woman or rape victim who comes to their office or emergency room. The lack of referral options for health service providers leads to frustration and an unwillingness to get involved, when it appears that there is nothing to be done.

Recent initiatives in Central America

Fortunately, several recent developments have shifted the health policy focus to begin to include discussions of gender violence. International donor agencies and multilateral health organizations have raised the issues and encouraged research to define the problem and make policy recommendations. The Pan American Health Organization (PAHO) has targeted gender violence as a health priority and funded research projects on violence against women in each of the Central American countries and Panama. The results are not comparable across countries, since each research team designed its own methodology, and the reports as yet have not been widely disseminated. Still, this effort is significant, since few public sector agencies have addressed this issue.

The public sector has in fact been largely silent, and over the last decade the impetus for programme design and service delivery has come primarily from non-governmental organizations (NGOs). Most NGOs with a gender violence focus are women's organizations offering some combination of medical, psychological and legal services, often including public education, research and advocacy as well. Usually managed on shoestring budgets, these NGOs have made significant gains throughout the region. Many are attempting to make the health sector more responsive to the needs of *mujeres violentadas* by engaging in dialogues with national ministries of health (MOHs), training medical and paramedical personnel, and conducting and disseminating research that focuses on the health impact of rape and battering.

Belize

In Belize, for example, Women Against Violence (WAV) is the country's only organization working directly on gender violence issues. Founded in 1985, WAV has overcome many obstacles to community organizing that exist in Belize and Central America, including geographical inaccessibility, disparate languages and ethnic groups, and extreme poverty. Combining programmes of community education and training, a neighbourhood watch, a telephone hotline, and home visits, WAV has expanded services nationwide. As a result of an agreement forged with the MOH, which has no formal women-and-violence programmes nor specialized medical personnel, rape and battery case referrals are made to WAV service providers. WAV conducts sensitivity training for health personnel and is pressuring the MOH to improve its information and documentation systems, so that raped and battered women will no longer remain statistically invisible.

Guatemala

Like Belize, Guatemala is ethnically diverse and impoverished. Political instability and economic crisis have hindered the MOH's development of community-based health services for much of the country. Responding to the lack of health services, NGOs have sprung up nationwide, often using a community-based health promoter model to provide health education, basic medical services, and follow-up, especially to more geographically and culturally isolated indigenous communities. Organizations such as the Asociación de Desarrollo Todos Juntos (ASECSA) in Totorricapan train health promoters to give community lectures and form women's support groups dealing with family violence, rape and alcohol abuse. Similarly, Al-Anon groups throughout Guatemala are familiar with the link between alcohol and aggression,[34] and assist women in finding solutions to living with men who abuse alcohol and abuse their families.

El Salvador

With the end of the civil war in El Salvador, women's organizations are hopeful that their energies may be more productively channelled toward improving women's lives. Several physicians, frustrated by the lack of services for rape victims, began a rape crisis programme in a hospital emergency room in San Salvador. Collecting information from women on the circumstances of their sexual assault, the physicians then began an education campaign to inform MOH personnel and the public regarding the prevalence of rape. This physicians' group, along with several anti-violence organizations throughout El Salvador, is now spearheading an effort to reform rape legislation.

The Salvadoran experience shows the importance of involving various sectors in eradicating violence. Health services cannot improve until health policies and legislation exist that make women feel safe enough to seek help. Legislation cannot be changed until the public is sufficiently sensitized to and supportive of the issues. Public attitudes cannot change until information is available – information collected, analysed and disseminated in research projects.

Honduras

The Centro de Estudios de la Mujer–Honduras (CEM–H) has focused its efforts on researching the interrelated women, health, and violence issues of rape, battering, AIDS, sexual slavery, and refugee and displaced women. However, few services, in health care or other sectors, exist for abused women in Honduras. The CEM–H is working with other women's groups to change that by lobbying for extensive legislative reform of the penal code, the family code and the labour code, as well as for adoption of a family violence law.

Nicaragua

Once achieved, legal reform must be used in order to make other sectors (health, education, welfare) more responsive to women's needs. In Nicaragua, legal literacy campaigns are combined with health education workshops to inform women of their rights and recourses. The Colectivo de Mujeres de Matagalpa and the Centro de Mujeres de Masaya, with support from the government Secretary of Women, conduct gender violence workshops, first through discussions of the physical, psychological, and social devastation of violence against women, followed by detailed review of the laws that help and hamper women. The Centro de Mujers 'Ixchen' in Managua employs street theatre to encourage men and women to discuss the effects of sexism and patriarchy on their daily lives. The workshops and street theatre build on the experiences of the health brigades and literacy brigades of the 1980s, which helped create a climate receptive to these types of activities regarding gender violence.

Costa Rica

The Costa Rican women-and-violence movement is by far the most sophisticated in the region, incorporating all the elements of other Central American initiatives, with some additions of its own. The Centro Feminista de Información y Acción (CEFEMINA) has assumed a leadership role, sponsoring several national and regional conferences, providing training and services, and conducting research, particularly in the area of legal reform and abused women's support networks.

Costa Rica's Law of Real Social and Economic Equality provides the framework and supportive political climate for the burgeoning public sector and NGO initiatives that combat violence against women.[35] Costa Rican women have a Delegación de la Mujer where they may go to file charges, seek police intervention, and receive referrals for legal services, psychotherapy, couple counselling, women's support groups, and so on. Every woman has access to legal assistance and representation through the Defensoría de la Mujer. CEFEMINA'S Mujer no estás sola women's support network in San José, Alajuela and Cartago sponsors weekly meetings for abused women to confront issues and seek solutions to the problems in their daily lives. The Oscar Arias Foundation for Peace and Human Progress has developed materials for a series of legal literacy workshops nationwide to inform women about their rights, which for battered women include access to restraining orders, availability of the Defensoría and Delegación services, and custody and alimony support laws. There are also several government agencies and NGOs representing children's interests, providing an important referral network for mothers of phsyically and sexually abused children.

Despite Costa Rica's successes, the health sector there remains somewhat marginal to the process. As in other Central American countries, women in rural areas have limited access to services located primarily in urban centres. The legally mandated forensic medical specialist who should provide integrated health services within the Delegación de la Mujer has not been appointed. MOH attempts to deal with the health impact of gender violence have been confined to the valiant efforts of individual women working within the system, particularly in the Departments of Mental Health and Nursing. While some physicians have been working on behalf of abused women for more than 20 years, medical education offers no courses on the diagnosis, prevention, and treatment of health conditions related to gender violence. And while battered women and abused children have been targeted appropriately as beneficiary populations, medical, psychotherapeutic and legal services for adult rape victims remain scarce.

Panama

Several women's organizations in Panama provided education, training and direct services regarding rape and domestic violence similar to the efforts seen elsewhere in the region. The Centro de Estudios y Participación Familiar y Centro de Acción in Panama City has done some interesting work raising sexual harassment in the workplace as an occupational health issue, focusing on the ways in which this insidious violence affects worker morale, absenteeism, stress levels and productivity. Panamanians recently defeated a referendum that included a demilitarization clause. The abolition of the country's armed services would have sent an important message regarding the unacceptability of violence. Moreover, it could have created a situation similar to that of Costa Rica, where the redirection of priorities from military spending to social welfare results in more progressive policies, and programmes that address women's health and gender violence.[36]

Lessons learned

There are dozens, perhaps hundreds of Central American community-based organizations like those mentioned above that address in one way or another issues of violence against women. The most successful of these teach important lessons about strategies to address the health impact of gender violence. First is the importance of considering community needs and listening to women in order to define those needs. Many groups introduce the theme of violence only after gaining the confidence of community women through other health activities, such as family planning or mothering classes.

A second key to success has been the steady building of a community base, where organizations choose their battles regarding violence against women. The imperative to take on all the issues – rape, incest, battering, sexual harassment, sexual slavery and exploitation – ultimately depletes precious economic and human resources without making a dent in any one area of injustice. A single issue, developed over time, has a longer-term effect.

Third, NGOs have exploited openings in MOHs, identifying the one or two health professionals working within the system who are willing to advocate gender violence issues in policy and programme discussions. Subtle internal pressure from MOH personnel, coupled with outside lobbying efforts of activist NGOs, and encouragement from international donors and multilateral health agencies, will eventually compel MOH decision-makers to address the health repercussions of gender violence in their countries.

Taken individually, each Central American country confronts different challenges in designing strategies, reflecting the differences in laws, cultures, health and social indices, and public awareness and acceptance. Collectively, the Central American example illustrates the diversity and dynamism that exists within the larger Latin American violence-against-women movement. The Central American experience highlights the importance of integrating the health sector in the provision of services for abused women and their children. A multi-sectoral approach that involves health care, legislative reform, direct services, public education and debate, sensitivity training for professionals, and research is the key to eradicating gender violence in Central America and worldwide.

Notes

1. Where possible, I have cited existing data within the Central American context, much of which is congruent with findings from other countries. Elsewhere, I refer to statistics from the American continents as well as case studies from Central America.

2. Based on data for US populations and cited by Lori Heise in 'Crimes of gender', *Worldwatch*, Vol. 2, No. 2, March–April 1989. See also 'Violencia contra la mujer: un obstáculo invisible para el desarrollo', *La Tribuna*, No. 40, International Women's Tribune Center, July 1990.

3. Rosario Valdez Santiago and Elizabeth Shrader Cox, 'Violencia doméstica en México', paper presented to the seminar 'Análisis y perspectivas de la lucha contra la violencia de género', Centro de Estudios y Investigación sobre el Maltrato de la Mujer de Ecuador (CIEMME), Quito, Ecuador, 21–25 October 1991. Papers published in the Agencia Latinoamericana de Información (ALAI) Bulletin, *Servicio Especial*, 15 November 1991; Ana Carcedo, 'Algunos datos preliminares sobre la violencia contra la mujer basados en la Encuesta del CID de octubre 1989' (San José, Costa Rica: CEFEMINA, 1991); 'Continua la lucha contra el maltrato', in *Barricada Internacional* (Nicaragua) Year VIII, No. 264, March 1988, cited by *La Tribuna*, No. 40.

4. International Commission for Central American Recovery and Development, *Poverty, Conflict, and Hope: A Turning Point in Central America* (Chapel Hill and San José, Duke University, 1989); Amnesty International, *Women: On the Front Lines*, Madrid, EDAI, March 1991.

5. In a Peruvian study, 60 per cent of rape victims knew their assailant; figure cited by Ana Maria Portugal in 'Crónica de una violación provocada?' *Revista Mujer/Fempress: Contraviolencia* (Chile, FEMPRESS-ILET, 1990). In a study from Panama, 63 per cent of rape survivors knew their assailants; figure cited by Amelia Marquez Perez in 'Aproximación diagnóstica a las violaciones de mujeres en los distritos de Panamá y San Miguelito' (Centro para el Desarrollo de la Mujer, Universidad de Panama, 1990). Figures from Mexico indicate that 67 per cent of women reporting rapes know their assailant; in *Carpeta Básica* (Procurador de Justicia del Distrito Federal de México, 1990).

6. Lori Heise, 'Violence against women: the missing agenda', in Marge Koblinsky, Judith Timyan and Jill Gay (eds.), *Women's Health: A Global Perspective* (Boulder, Colorado, Westview Press, 1993). Data for Panama and Mexico.

7. In El Salvador, for example, a man cannot be prosecuted for rape if he agrees to marry the woman he raped. Many families, in order to avoid public shame and salvage family honour, coerce their young daughters into marrying their rapists. 'Rape and sexual harassment', plenary session of the First Central American and Caribbean Conference on Violence Against Women, San José, Costa Rica, 1–8 December 1991.

Changes effected in Mexican law in 1991 allow for prosecution of a rapist, whether or not he marries the woman he raped. Cultural norms still exist, however, and as in El Salvador families may see marrying the rapist as a way of protecting individual and family honour. For further discussion, see E. Shrader Cox, 'Toward ending violence against women in Mexico', in Margaret Schuler (ed.), *Freedom from Violence: Women's Strategies from Around the World* (Washington, DC, Overseas Education Fund, 1992). For some, there is no fate worse than rape. In an extreme case, a mother in Mexico City severely beat her six-year-old daughter whom she had found being raped on the staircase to their apartment building. When questioned, the mother said that she intended to kill the child, saying that she did not want her daughter to have to live with the shame of everyone knowing that she was no longer a virgin (personal interview with a treating clinical psychologist, Centro de Terapia de Apoyo, Programa de Agencias Especializadas en Delitos Sexuales, Mexico City, July 1990).

8. COVAC, 'Evaluación del proyecto para educación, capacitación, y atención a mujeres y menores de edad en materia de violencia sexual, enero a diciembre 1990' (Mexico City: Asociación Mexicana contra la Violencia a las Mujeres AC–COVAC,

February 1991). Service statistics from the Centro de Apoyo a Mujeres Violadas, AC (CAMVAC), Mexico City, 1987.

9. 'La violencia hacia la mujer costarricense', paper presented to the first Seminario Centroamericano sobre Violencia hacia la Mujer: Un Problema de Salud Pública, PAHO, Managua, Nicaragua, 11–13 March 1992.

10. Tatiana Treguear L. and Carmen Carro B., *Ninas madres: recuento de una experiencia* (San José, Costa Rica: PROCAL, 1991).

11. In the final study of 300 adolescent mothers, 1.7 per cent (N=5) said that the pregnancy was a result of rape. Of all adolescent mothers, 29 per cent were not in a sexual union at the time of the interview; of girls 14 to 15 years of age, 44 per cent were not in a union. These findings are not inconsistent with the possibility that many of their pregnancies were due to forced sexual intercourse or incest. Considering that this was a nutrition study where analysis of rape was not a research objective, these findings merit further investigation. Figures from CORA, 'Estudio sobre la nutrición en adolescentes embarazadas', Mexico City, Centro de Orientación para Adolescentes, 1989.

12. Thirty per cent reported by Elizabeth Shrader Cox and Rosaria Valdez Santiago, *Violence against Mexican Women as a Public Health Problem* (Mexico City, CECOVID, 1992). Studies from Puerto Rico and Bolivia produced the same figure of 58 per cent, cited in 'Campaña sobre la violencia en contra de la mujer', in Bulletin 16–17, Red de Salud de las Mujeres Latinoamericanas y del Caribe, Isis International, Santiago de Chile, April 1988.

13. Fourteen per cent of married women have experienced conjugal rape. Figure cited by Diana E.H. Russell in *Rape in Marriage* (New York, Collier, 1982); 10 per cent of married women reported being raped by their husbands, in D. Finkelhor and K. Yllo, *License to Rape* (New York: The Free Press, 1985).

14. For an examination of the ways in which women's socio-economic context and imbalances of power in their intimate relationships affect high-risk behaviour, see Dooley Worth, 'Sexual decision-making and AIDS: why condom promotion among vulnerable women is likely to fail', *Studies in Family Planning*, Vol. 20 (6), 297–307.

15. Lea Guido, *La Crisis, el ajuste económico y las condiciones de salud de la mujer en Centroamerica*', San José, Costa Rica, PAHO, 1991.

16. Ibid.

17. Ibid.

18. PANI, *Algunas características de la mujer agredida: Propuesta de intervención* (San José, Costa Rica, Patroncito Nacional de la Infancia, September 1990).

19. Lori Heise, 'Beyond reproductive health – nutrition, violence, and mental health', paper presented to the 18th Annual NCIH International Health Conference, Crystal City, Virginia, 23–26 June 1991.

20. 'La violencia hacia la mujer hondureña', paper presented to the first Seminario Centroamericano sobre Violencia hacia la Mujer: Problema de Salud Pública, PAHO, Managua, Nicaragua, 11–13 March 1992.

21. Valdez Santiago and Shrader Cox.

22. Heise (1991). See also Freda L. Paltiel, 'Women and mental health: a post-Nairobi perspective', *World Health Statistics Quarterly*, No. 40 (1987) pp. 233–66.

23. The 20 per cent figure was reported by Valdez Santiago and Shrader Cox. The 65 per cent figure is cited in Heise (1991).

24. The 8 per cent figure is cited by Jacqueline Campbell in 'Correlates of battering during pregnancy', research supported by the US Department of Health and Human services. For reprints contact Dr J. Campbell, Wayne State University College of Nursing. One in six (17 per cent) pregnant women are battered during pregnancy; from Judith McFarlane, 'Battering during pregnancy', paper presented to the 18th Annual NCIH International Health Conference, Crystal City, Virginia, 23–26 June 1991.

25. Heise (1991).

26. In Costa Rica, 35 per cent of battered women report their children were also beaten (PANI). In the US, half of batterers reportedly beat their children; figures cited by Lenore E. Walker in *Terrifying Love: Why Battered Women Kill and How Society Responds* (New York, HarperPerennial, 1990).

27. Shrader Cox and Valdez Santiago.
28. Walker.
29. Heise (1991); Walker.
30. Based on estimates of 160,000 Central Americans of both sexes who have died in the civil conflict, cited in International Commission for Central American Recovery and Deveopment.
31. Based on estimates of 1 to 2 million Central Americans of both sexes who are refugees or displaced persons, cited by Sergio Aguayo, 'Displaced Persons and Central American Recuperation and Development', in William Ascher and Ann Hubbard (eds.), *Central American Recovery and Development: Task Force Report* (Durham and San José, Duke University, 1989).
32. See Amnesty International. Despite the prevalence of rape as a means of political repression, to date only one US political asylum case has been granted, based on the experience and threat of sexual assault by military personnel on a Salvadoran woman.
33. Heise (1993). US health professionals working with Central American populations are particularly concerned with the apparent high rates of sexual assault among Central American refugee women. In interviews with social workers in Harlingen, Texas (near one of the US's largest detention centres for illegal aliens) and with family planning counsellors in Los Angeles, California, many indicated that rape is virtually a universal experience for refugee women over the age of twelve.
34. Alcohol is frequently involved in acute domestic violence situations. Nevertheless, alcoholism is not the primary cause of battering, nor does stopping drinking guarantee stopping the abuse. Therapy groups for batterers often require detoxification and sobriety, but then focus on the root causes of battering, such as gender-based imbalances of power within the family and the community.
35. For a discussion of Costa Rica's Law of Real Social and Economic Equality and its chief proponent and architect, Margarita Penon de Arias, see E. Shrader Cox, 'The Woman Who Would Be President', *Connexions: an International Women's Quarterly*, No. 39, 1992, pp. 14–17.
36. Costa Rica abolished its army in 1948.

'We Have No Rights, Not Even Our Bodies'
Adapted from a Report Compiled for Campaign Free Tibet

Well over 1 million Tibetans have died since the Chinese began their military occupation of Tibet in 1949. Since 1965, when a large part of the country was declared an 'autonomous' region of China, increasing numbers of detailed reports have been leaking out about a consistent programme of forced abortion and sterilization of Tibetan women.

A 1991 survey by the Tibetan Office of Information and International Relations (OIIR) states that 'according to available sources, the practice of forced abortion and sterilization was reported

133

as early as 1955, at that time confined to some parts of the Amdo (Chinghai) region of Tibet'. The ensuing years have seen a systematic spread in the implementation of these measures, as part of what amounts to an overall policy of ethnic cleansing to eliminate the Tibetan people. Refugees also tell of the rape of Tibetan girls by Chinese soldiers, as well as active encouragement for Chinese men to marry Tibetan girls while reverse unions are virtually forbidden by law (OIIR report, 1976).

In terms of analysis and action, only a handful of women's groups worldwide appear to have taken up the cause of Tibetan women. Like government refusals to provide safe birth control or abortion on demand, coercive birth control policies deny the right of women to control their own bodies and, as such, demand recognition, examination and protest as yet another violation of women's fundamental human rights. The reproduction of these testimonies, adapted from a report entitled *Children of Despair: Coercive Birth Control Policies in Chinese Occupied Tibet*, compiled by Martin Moss for the British-based Campaign Free Tibet, is a small attempt to redress the balance.

Pregnancy: a political crime

Dr D.T. worked from 1983 to 1990 in the People's Hospital in Amdo, West of Chapcha. She has since escaped to India.

'The hospital had a Women and Delivery Section, but women didn't come here to deliver children, nor for check-ups. They came only to be operated on. The largest number of "patients" came from faraway nomadic regions, sent under pressure from local birth control offices. It was only when I got married and eventually wanted a second child that I directly experienced what was going on.

'... I was married in 1984, at the age of 22. I soon wanted a child, for which we needed permission from the birth control office, which only allows wives to get pregnant after four years of marriage. In the end we succeeded by bribing officials, and our first child was born in 1986.'

In Amdo couples with more than one child are subjected to so-called financial punishments, including a substantial fine for the second child. Willing to pay the fine, the doctor became pregnant again two years later, but as soon as the news reached her Head of Office a steady onslaught of harassment began.

'Almost every day my boss would appear and try to influence me with birth control policy, trying to brainwash me into having an abortion. He said he wanted to eliminate the child inside me. When I continued to insist that I wanted the child, a Chinese woman doctor named Huang Fen Yin told me to go home and think over the matter carefully, adding that I should have an immediate abortion.

'I decided to delay any decision by asking for maternity leave,

Campaign Free Tibet, London.

again insisting I was still ready to pay any fine. This incensed the doctor, who threatened me by saying "All right. Go ahead and have your child. The financial punishment is nothing compared to the political crime you are committing. From now on, wherever you work, you will only receive 30 per cent of your salary, which will never rise. Your child will not have the right to a ration card, nor be admitted to either nursery or school. You and your husband are fired from your jobs." '

Having initially assumed that such pressures came directly from the Chinese doctors at the hospital, Dr D.T. later discovered that these people were acting in accordance with specific rules and regulations, laid down in secret documents only known to 'certain leaders'. She

135

eventually collapsed under the pressure and, twelve weeks pregnant, agreed to an abortion. Using none of the necessary appliances and no anaesthetic, the termination was carried out on 1 March 1989.

'The complications and pain that I went through during this operation were so terrible that I don't want to tell. Women with much more advanced pregnancies – say seven or eight months – have much greater problems. I have since had irregular periods and constant back pain.'

Many testimonies report health problems attributed to abortion and/or sterilization operations, often carried out under appalling conditions with no regard for the health and welfare of the woman concerned. The symptoms described are remarkably consistent and include, most commonly, erratic menstrual flow, backache, loss of appetite sometimes with attendant gastric problems, weakness and overwhelming fatigue. Some women report fever and headaches. Others even die.

Coercion: the only choice

In addition to severe financial penalties and verbal intimidation, reports of physical force being used to take women to sterilization and abortion centres are also common. A Tibetan man, speaking on 27 April 1991, reported the arrival at his village of a birth control team. The villagers were rounded up into small groups, had their names taken and were told that it was the intention to 'carry out birth control operations on the womenfolk'. He stated that two women who resisted were tied up, 'thoroughly beaten and taken away to be forcibly operated upon'.

In another testimony an English nurse, Valda Harding, describes how she witnessed Tibetan women in Lhasa being captured and taken from their homes:

'Once, in August 1987, I heard a commotion at dusk. Looking out of my window I saw a truck with its back open and three wicker baskets inside. Two contained Tibetan women, caged like animals. The third was empty. A large crowd of protesting Tibetans and a lot of Chinese soldiers were milling around. I imagined the women had committed some crime, but was told they were being taken away for "having too many children". They must have been pregnant for I heard people say that "soon they won't be pregnant any longer". The full significance of what I saw didn't really hit me until later. It sounds strange, but in Tibet you get used to seeing people kicked, beaten and abused.'

Such accounts are widespread and supported by the findings of Indian, American and British doctors, who, on examining Tibetan women in exile, frequently discover scar tissues consistent with some form of sterilization.

The evidence is not easy to obtain, but there seems no doubt from the combination of refugee testimonies, doctors' reports, human rights research and occasional government statistics being gathered by organizations like Campaign Free Tibet, that women are being used (and abused) to facilitate a policy of ethnic genocide that shows no signs of abating, despite heightened international awareness of Chinese human rights violations since Tiananmen Square. In combination with the massive population transfer of Chinese colonists into Tibet, China's coercive birth control programme is seen by Tibetans as being China's 'final solution'.

Female Genital Mutilation
Efua Dorkenoo and Scilla Elworthy

Female genital mutilation is a complex and sensitive issue, involving aspects of sexuality, health, education and basic human rights amid a web of cultural traditions and taboos. Towards the late 1970s, when the practice first began to receive attention in the international press, predominant reactions of shocked indignation in the West (provoked in part by sensationalist and distorted reporting) demonstrated levels of cultural insensitivity and ignorance that upset and enraged many people in Africa. These included feminists such as members of the Association of African Women for Research and Development (AAWORD) who, while firmly condemning the practice of genital mutilation, were moved to put out a key statement on the dangers of Western interference and the need for African women themselves to speak out and lead information and education campaigns in their own countries.[1]

More than ten years later, many dedicated women – from Egypt to Somalia, right through to Western Africa – are doing just that. In the words of Scilla Elworthy, who introduces the report from which the following extracts are taken: 'These courageous women are beginning the sensitive task of helping women to free themselves from customs which have no advantage and many risks for their physical and psychological well-being, without at the same time destroying the supportive and beneficial threads of their cultural fabric.'

The report, published in 1992 by the Minority Rights Group under the title *Female Genital Mutilation: Proposals for Change* (a revised and updated edition of *Female Circumcision, Excision and Infibulation: the Facts and Proposals for Change*, edited by Scilla Elworthy in 1980), presents the facts about genital mutilation, explaining how, where and why it is practised. The authors go on to focus on the views of women campaigners in Africa and what steps African governments, Western states and international agencies can take to end the custom.

A professional health worker, originally from Ghana, Efua Dorkenoo is the director of the London-based Foundation for Women's Health Research and Development (FORWARD), an independent non-government organization promoting the good health of African women and children, with a special emphasis on education against genital mutilation. Scilla Elworthy has worked in health education in southern Africa and as a consultant on women's issues for the Human Rights Division of UNESCO.

The following, slightly edited extracts from the report, reproduced with kind permission from the Minority Rights Group, concentrate on the facts, as well as the issues raised by genital mutilation and the complexities of trying to abolish a custom so rooted in tradition and on such a scale that it has affected an estimated 74 million African women.

The facts

The term female genital mutilation covers four types of operation:

1. *Circumcision*, or cutting of the prepuce or hood of the clitoris, known in Muslim countries as Sunna (tradition). This, the mildest type, affects only a small proportion of the millions of women concerned. It is the only type of mutilation that can correctly be called circumcision, though there has been a tendency to group all kinds of mutilations under the misleading term 'female circumcision'.
2. *Excision*, meaning the cutting of the clitoris and of all or part of the labia minora.
3. *Infibulation*, the cutting of the clitoris, labia minora and at least part of the labia majora. The two sides of the vulva are then pinned together by silk or catgut sutures, or with thorns, thus obliterating the vaginal introitus except for a very small opening, preserved by the insertion of a tiny piece of wood or a reed for the passage of urine or menstrual blood. These operations are done with special knives, with razor blades or pieces of glass. The girl's legs are then bound together from hip to ankle and she is kept immobile for up to 40 days to permit the formation of scar tissue.
4. *Intermediate*, meaning the removal of the clitoris and some parts of the labia minora or the whole of it. Various degrees are done according to the demands of the girl's relatives.

FEMALE GENITAL MUTILATION IN AFRICA

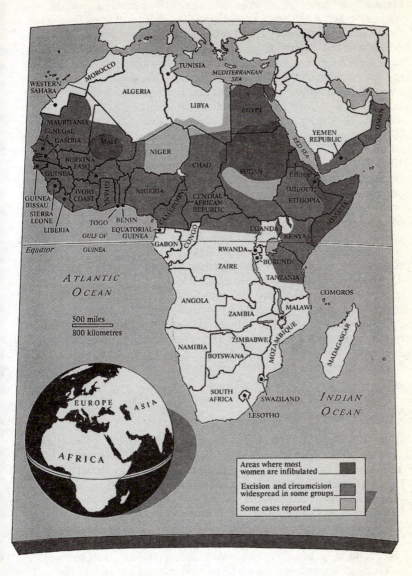

Minority Rights Group, London.

Most frequently these operations are performed by an old woman of the village or by a traditional birth attendant and only rarely by qualified nurses or doctors. The age at which the mutilations are carried out varies from area to area, and according to whether legislation against the practice is foreseen or not. It varies from a few days old (for example, the Jewish Falashas in Ethiopia, and the nomads of the Sudan) to about seven years (as in Egypt and many countries of Central Africa) or – more rarely – adolescence, as among the Ibo of Nigeria. Most experts are agreed that the age of mutilation is becoming younger, and has less and less to do with initiation into adulthood.[2]

Physical consequences

Health risks and complications depend on the gravity of the mutilation, hygienic conditions, the skill and eyesight of the operator, and the struggles of the child. Whether immediate or long term, they are grave.[3] Death from bleeding is not uncommon, while long-term complications include chronic infections of the uterus and vagina, painful menstruation, severe pain during intercourse, sterility and complications during childbirth. Though evidence has yet to be collected, it is also likely that bleeding or open wounds increase the likelihood of HIV transmission and AIDS.

There is great difficulty in obtaining accurate research on the sexual experiences of mutilated women, because the majority are reluctant to speak on the subject and are generally ambivalent on questions of sexual enjoyment.[4] However, in all types of mutilation, even the 'mildest' clitoridectomy, a part of a woman's body containing nerves of vital importance to sexual pleasure is amputated.

Psychological consequences

Even less research has been done to date on the psychological consequences of these traditions. However, many personal accounts and research findings contain repeated references to anxiety prior to the operation, terror at the moment of being seized by an aunt or village matron, unbearable pain, and the subsequent sense of humiliation and of being betrayed by parents, especially the mother. On the other hand, there are references to special clothes and good food associated with the event, to the pride felt in being like everyone else, in being 'made clean', in having suffered without screaming.

To be different clearly produces anxiety and mental conflict. An unexcised, non-infibulated girl is despised and made the target of ridicule, and no one in her community will marry her. Thus what is clearly understood to be her life's work, namely marriage and child-bearing, is denied her. So, in tight-knit village societies where mutilation is the rule, it will be the exceptional girl who will suffer psychologically, unless she has another very strong identity which she has lost.[5]

There is no doubt that genital mutilation would have overwhelming psychological effects on an unmotivated girl, unsupported by her family, village, peers and community. To those from other cultures unfamiliar with the force of this particular community identity, the very concept of amputation of the genitals carries a shock value which does not exist for most women in the areas concerned. For them, not to amputate would be shocking.

These observations concern social-psychological factors rather than the central question, namely, what affects do these traumatic operations have on little girls at the moment of operation and as they grow up? The fact is that we simply don't know. We do not know what it means to a girl or woman when her central organ of sensory pleasure is cut off, when her life-giving canal is stitched up amid blood and fear and secrecy, while she is forcibly held down and told that if she screams she will cause the death of her mother or bring shame on the family.

The practice

The area covered

The countries where one or more forms of female genital mutilation are practised number more than 20 in Africa, from the Atlantic to the Red Sea, the Indian Ocean and the eastern Mediterranean. Outside Africa, excision is also practised in Oman, South Yemen and in the United Arab Emirates (UAE). Circumcision is practised by the Muslim populations of Indonesia and Malaysia and by Bohra Muslims in India, Pakistan and East Africa.[6]

On the map of Africa, an uninterrupted belt is formed across the centre of the continent, which then expands up the length of the Nile. This belt, with the exception of the Egyptian buckle, corresponds strikingly with the pattern of countries that have the highest child mortality rates (more than 30 per cent for children from one to four years of age).[7] These levels reflect deficiencies of medical care, of clean drinking water, of sanitary infrastructure and of adequate nutrition in most of the countries.

The gravity of the mutilations varies from country to country. Infibulation is reported to affect nearly all the female population of Somalia, Djibouti and the Sudan (except the non-Muslim population of southern Sudan), southern Egypt, the Red Sea coast of Ethiopia, northern Kenya, northern Nigeria and some parts of Mali. The most recent estimate of women mutilated is 74 million.[8]

Ethnic groups closely situated geographically are by no means affected in the same way: for example, in Kenya, the Kikuyu practise excision and the Luo do not; in Nigeria, the Yoruba, the Ibo and the Hausa do, but not the Nupes or the Fulanis; in Senegal, the Woloff have no practice of mutilation. There are many other examples.

As the subject of female genital mutilation began to be eligible at least for discussion, reports of genital operations on non-consenting females have appeared from many unexpected parts of the world. During the 1980s, women in Sweden were shocked by accounts of mutilations performed in Swedish hospitals on daughters of immigrants. In France, women from Mali and Senegal have been reported to bring an *exciseuse* to France once a year to operate on their daughters in their apartments.[9] In July 1982 a Malian infant died of an excision performed by a professional circumciser, who then fled to Mali. In the same year, reports appeared in the British press that excision for non-medical reasons had been performed in a London private clinic.

Legislation

In Africa: Formal legislation forbidding genital mutilation, or more precisely infibulation, exists in the Sudan. A law first enacted in 1946 allows for a term of imprisonment up to five years and/or a fine. However, it is not an offence (under Article 284 of the Sudan Penal Code for 1974) 'merely to remove the free and projecting part of the clitoris'.

Many references have been made to legislation in Egypt, but after researching the available materials, all that has been traced is a resolution signed by the Minister of Health in 1959, recommending only partial clitoridectomy for those who want an operation, to be performed only by doctors.[10]

In late 1978, largely due to the efforts of the Somali Women's Democratic Organization (SWDO), Somalia set up a commission to abolish infibulation. In 1988 at a seminar held in Mogadishu, it was recommended that SWDO should propose a bill to the competent authorities to eradicate all forms of female genital mutilation.

In September 1982, President Arap Moi took steps to ban the practices in Kenya, following reports of the deaths of 14 children after excision. A traditional practitioner found to be carrying out this operation can be arrested under the Chiefs Act and brought before the law.

Official declarations against female genital mutilation were made by the late Captain Thomas Sankara and Abdou Diouf, the heads of state in Burkina Faso and Senegal respectively.

In Western countries: A law prohibiting female excision, whether consent has been given or not, came into force in Sweden in July 1982, carrying a two-year sentence. In Norway, in 1985, all hospitals were alerted to the practice. Belgium has incorporated a ban on the practice. Several states in the USA have incorporated female genital mutilation into their criminal code.

In the UK, specific legislation prohibiting female circumcision came into force at the end of 1985. A person found guilty of an offence is liable to up to five years' imprisonment or to a fine. Female genital mutilation has been incorporated into child protection procedures at local authority level. As yet no person has been committed in the English courts for female circumcision but since 1989 there have been at least seven local authority legal interventions which prevented parents from sexually mutilating their daughters or wards.

France does not have specific legislation on female sexual mutilation but under Article 312–3 of the French Penal Code, female genital mutilation can be considered as a criminal offence. Under this code, anybody who exercises violence or seriously assaults a child less than 15 years old can be punished with imprisonment from 10 to 20 years, if the act of violence results in a mutilation, amputation of a limb, the loss of an eye or other parts of the body or has unintentionally caused the death of the child.

In 1989, a mother who had paid a traditional woman exciser to excise her week-old daughter, in 1984, was convicted and given a three-year suspended jail sentence. In 1991 a traditional exciser was jailed for five years in France.

Contemporary practices

Opinions are very divided as to whether the practice is disappearing because of legislation or social and economic changes. Esther Ogunmodede, for instance, believes that in Nigeria, Africa's most populous country, the tradition is disappearing but extremely slowly, with millions of excisions still taking place. She reports that in areas where the operations are done on girls of marriageable age, they are 'running away from home to avoid the razor'. This confirms Fran Hosken's assertion that operations are being done at earlier and earlier ages, in order that the children should be 'too young to resist'. Fran Hosken does not think that the custom is dying out, and she indisputably has the best published range of information concerning all the countries where the practice is known.

An interesting development took place in Ethiopia during the years of civil warfare which only ended in 1991. When the Eritrean People's Liberation Front (EPLF) occupied large areas from January 1977 to December 1978, among many other reforms they categorically and successfully forbade genital mutilation and forced

143

marriage. In fact, the reason given for the large numbers of young women in the EPLF army was that they were running away from home in other parts of Ethiopia to avoid forced marriage and the knife.[11] Although it appears the practice continues in remote areas, because the consciousness of Eritrean women has changed dramatically during the war years, it is easier to persuade men and women to let go of this practice.

Since 1983, the number of educational programmes initiated to raise public awareness of the health risk associated with female genital mutilation at local, national and international level have increased. The media have played a major role in bringing this issue from the domestic to the public domain. As a result of these efforts it can be said that the taboo surrounding even public mention of the practice has at last been broken. There is an increase in public awareness of the harmful effects of female genital mutilation.

It has been noted that female genital mutilation is becoming unpopular amongst the urban elite in some African countries. In Sierra Leone, for example, Koso-Thomas claims that urban men are willing to marry uncircumcised women, in particular when the marriage is not pre-arranged.[12]

In general, among urban educated women, reasons often cited against female genital mutilation include the pointlessness of mutilation, health risks and reduction of sexual sensitivity. The last reason points to a changing attitude towards women's fundamental human rights amongst urban Africans.

In the main, the practice continues to be widespread among large sectors and groups within Africa. Those in favour of the practice are noted in the 1986 UN study to be a passive majority who refer back to traditional society, without necessarily sharing that society's values.[13] In some cases, the practice appears to be spreading to population groups who traditionally never practised female genital mutilation, as observed with city women in Wau, Sudan, who regard it as fashionable, and among converted Muslim women in southern Sudan who marry northern Sudanese men.[14] Furthermore, even in areas where some groups are turning against the practice, the absolute numbers affected may be increasing. Rapid population growth in Africa means greater numbers of female children are born, who in turn are exposed to the risk of mutilation.

The issues

Female genital mutilation is a complex issue, for it involves deep-seated cultural practices which affect millions of people. However, it can be divided into (at least) four distinct issues.

Rights of women

Female genital mutilation is an extreme example of the general subjugation of women, sufficiently extreme and horrifying to make women and men question the basis of what is done to women, what women have accepted and why, in the name of society and tradition.

The burning of Indian widows and the binding of the feet of Chinese girl children are other striking examples, sharp enough and strange enough to throw a spotlight on other less obvious ways in which women the world over submit to oppression. It is important to remember that all these practices are, or were, preserved under centuries of tradition, and that foot-binding was only definitively stopped by a massive social and political revolution (replacing the many traditions which it swept away by offering an entirely new social system, revolutionary in many aspects: land ownership, class system, education, sex equality, etc.) which had been preceded by years of patient work by reformers.

Thus, to be successful, campaigns on female genital mutilation should consider carefully not only eliminating but also replacing the custom. (The example of Eritrea, previously quoted, is illuminating here.) Furthermore, such success may be predicated on long-term changes in attitudes and ideologies by both men and women.

A major international expression of the goal of equal rights for women was taken in December 1979, when the UN General Assembly adopted the Convention on the Elimination of All Forms of Discrimination Against Women. This came into force in September 1981. The comprehensive convention calls for equal rights for women, regardless of their marital status, in all fields: political, economic, social, cultural and civil. Article 5(a) obliges states parties to take:

> All appropriate measures to modify the social and cultural patterns of conduct of men and women, with a view to achieving the elimination of prejudices and customary and all other practices which are based on the idea of the inferiority or superiority of either of the sexes or on stereotyped roles for men and women.

To succeed in abolishing such practices will demand fundamental attitudinal shifts in the way that society perceives the human rights of women. The starting point for change should be educational programmes that assist women to recognize their fundamental human rights. This is where UNESCO, the UN Centre for Human Rights and international agencies could help by supporting awareness-building programmes.

Rights of children

An adult is free to submit her or himself to a ritual or tradition, but a child, having no formed judgement, does not consent but simply undergoes the operation (which in this case is irrevocable) while she is totally vulnerable. The descriptions available of the reactions of children – panic and shock from extreme pain, biting through the tongue, convulsions, necessity for six adults to hold down an eight-year-old, and death – indicate a practice comparable to torture.

Many countries signatory to Article 5 of the Universal Declaration of Human Rights (which provides that no one shall be subjected to torture, or to cruel, inhuman or degrading treatment) violate that clause. Those violations are discussed and sometimes condemned by various UN commissions. Female genital mutilation, however, is a question of torture inflicted not on adults but on girl children, and the reasons given are not concerned with either political conviction or military necessity but are solely in the name of tradition.

The Declaration of the Rights of Children, adopted in 1959 by the General Assembly, asserts that children should have the possibility to develop physically in a healthy and normal way in conditions of liberty and dignity. They should have adequate medical attention, and be protected from all forms of cruelty.

It is the opinion of Renée Bridel, of the Fédération Internationale des Femmes de Carrières Juridiques, that 'One cannot but consider Member States which tolerate these practices as infringing their obligations as assumed under the terms of the Charter [of the UN].'[15]

In September 1990, the United Nations Convention on the Rights of the Child went into force. It became part of international human rights law. Under Article 24(3) it states that: 'States Parties shall take all effective and appropriate measures with a view to abolishing traditional practices prejudicial to the health of children.' This crucial article should not merely remain a paper provision, to be given lip service by those entrusted to implement it. Members of the UN should work at translating its provisions into specific implementation programmes at grassroots level. Much could be learned (by African states in particular) from countries with established child protection systems.

The right to good health

No reputable medical practitioner insists that mutilation is good for the physical or mental health of girls and women, and a growing number offer research indicating its grave permanent damage to health and underlining the risks of death. Medical facts, carefully explained, may be the way to discourage the practice, since these facts are almost always the contrary of what is believed, and can be shown and demonstrated.

Those UN agencies and government departments specifically entrusted with the health needs of women and children must realize that it is their responsibility to support positive and specific preventative programmes against female genital mutilation, for while the practice continues the quality of life and health will inevitably suffer. However, this approach, if presented out of context, ignores the force of societal pressures which drive women to perform these operations, regardless of risk, in order to guarantee marriage for their daughters, and to conform to severe codes of female behaviour laid down by male-dominated societies.

The right to development

The practice of female genital mutilation must be seen in the context of underdevelopment,[16] and the realities of life for the most vulnerable and exploited sectors – women and children. International political and economic forces have frequently prevented development programmes from meeting the basic needs of rural populations. With no access to education or resources, and with no effective power base, the rural and urban poor cling to traditions as a survival mechanism in time of socio-economic change.

In societies where marriage for a woman is her only means of survival, and where some form of excision is a prerequisite for marriage, persuading her to relinquish the practice for herself or for her children is an extraordinarily difficult task. Female (and some male) African analysts of development strategies are today constantly urging that the overall deteriorating conditions in which poor women live be made a major focus for change, for unless development affects their lives for the better, traditional practices are unlikely to change.

Directions for the future

The mutilation of female genitals has been practised in many areas for centuries. The greatest determination, combined with sensitivity and understanding of local conditions, will be needed if it is to be abolished. In every country and region where operations are carried out, the situation is different, as is the political will, whether at local or national levels. In Western countries the way forward is relatively clear. In Africa the problem is more profound and the economic and political conditions vastly more difficult, while international agencies have hardly begun to explore their potential role.

What all three have in common is that, to date, nearly all programmes have been individual or *ad hoc* efforts, with little integration into other structures, with minimal evaluation or monitoring, and lacking in long-term goals and strategies. To achieve real change will require more resources, more detailed planning, and more real, sustained commitment from governments and international organizations.

Notes

1. See Miranda Davies, *Third World–Second Sex* (London, Zed Books, 1983), pp. 217–20.

2. Fran Hosken, *The Hosken Report – Genital and Sexual Mutilation of Females* (third enlarged/revised edition Autumn 1982, published by Women's International Network News, 187 Grant St, Lexington, MA 02173, USA). This is the most detailed and comprehensive collection of information available.

3. The consequences of sexual mutilations on the health of women have been studied by Dr Ahmed Abu-el-Futuh Shandall, Lecturer in the Department of Obstetrics and Gynaecology at the University of Khartoum, in a paper entitled, 'Circumcision and Infibulation of Females' (*Sudanese Medical Journal*, Vol. 5, No. 4, 1967); and by Dr J.A. Verzin, in an article entitled 'The Sequelae of Female Circumcision', (*Tropical Doctor*, October 1975). A bibliography on the subject has been prepared by Dr R. Cook for the World Health Organization.

4. Readers interested to read more about research on the sexual experience of circumcised women may want to read Hanny Lightfoot-Klein, *Prisoners of Ritual: An Odyssey into Female Genital Mutilation in Africa* (New York, The Haworth Press, 1989).

5. These feelings of rejection are clearly articulated by Kenyan girls in 'The Silence over Female Circumcision in Kenya', in *Viva*, August 1978.

6. Q.R. Ghadially, 'Ali for "Izzat": the Practice of Female Circumcision among Bohra Muslims', *Manushi*, No. 66, New Delhi, India, 1991.

7. See map of Childhood Mortality in the World, 1977 (Health Sector Policy Paper, World Bank, Washington, 1980).

8. See Hosken for details and estimates of ethnic groups involved.

9. *F Magazine*, No. 4, March 1979 and No. 31, October 1980.

10. Marie Assaad, *Female Circumcision in Egypt – Current Research and Social Implications* (American University in Cairo, 1979), p. 12.

11. 'Social Transformation of Eritrean Society', paper presented to the People's Tribunal, Milan, 24–26 May 1980, by Mary Dines of Rights and Justice.

12. Koso-Thomas, *The Circumcision of Women: A Strategy for Elimination* (London, Zed Books, 1987).

13. UN Commission on Human Rights, Report of the Working Group on Traditional Practices Affecting Women and Children, 1986.

14. Ellen Ismail et al., *Women of the Sudan* (Bendestorf, Germany, EIS, 1990).

15. *L'Enfant Mutilé* by Renée Bridel, delegate of the FIFCJ to the UN, Geneva, 1978. See also Raqiya Haji Dualeh Abdalla, *Sisters in Affliction* (London, Zed Press, 1982) and Asma El Dareer, *Woman Why Do You Weep?* (London, Zed Press, 1982).

16. Belkis Woldes Giorgis, *Female Circumcision in Africa*, ST/ECA/ATRCW 81/02.

Militarism and the Sex Industry in the Philippines
Sister Mary Soledad Perpinan

Sister Mary Soledad is founder of the Third World Movement Against the Exploitation of Women (TW-MAE-W) which was established in the Philippines on Human Rights Day, 10 December 1980. The organization's aim, to mobilize women in the Philippines and elsewhere towards the liberation of women 'from all kinds of oppression and exploitation based on sex, class or race', has led to numerous campaigns to improve conditions for women workers and, more especially, to expose their abuse as commodities in the international flesh trade. This article and the ensuing anonymous testimony, 'Olongapo: exploited by the army', are reproduced, slightly edited, from *Isis Women's World*, No. 24, Winter 1990–91. The testimony was first published in the American feminist journal *Sojourners*, June 1990.

Whenever I go to Olongapo, my heart goes out not only to my own Filipina sisters but to every fellow I meet, and I think of his mother, sister, girlfriend or wife. Do they know what he undergoes, the state of frenzy he is in after being cooped up in a submarine or ship for weeks on end?

For the good of all we hail the day when troops go home from foreign shores, arms are laid down and uniforms set aside. Will that day ever come, when violence and the war and the abuse of sex are no more?

Sister Mary Soledad Perpinan

It all started in tents that were set up just outside the camps, and which became whorehouses with 15 to 20 beds. Later the *strips* became rows of cardboard shacks. The American needs were catered to with three basic services: laundry, provision of soft drinks and prostitution. Hand in hand with sex strips came drug trafficking, and heroin addiction was a natural consequence. In 1967 there were 400 opium dens; three years later there were 300,000, a 7,500 per cent increase!

149

In Bangkok I reviewed Thailand's own history of sexploitation, which can also be traced to the military. Entertainment centres were established around air bases where 40,000 US servicemen were stationed in the late 1960s. This schooled the Thai women in the art of servicing the foreigner with 'exotic pleasures' to such an extent that Bangkok easily became the sex capital of Asia in the late 1970s.

In the Philippines, Subic Naval Base and Clark Air Base have created and continue to sustain the whoredoms of Olongapo and Angeles where over 25,000 women and girls are given Rest and Recreation jobs to keep American servicemen happy, fit and sane for the military policing of the world.

The girls are recruited from depressed provinces and given false promises of high pay. Often in their teens or early twenties, they find themselves bound to the bar where they work and live with little freedom. They are given a cubicle behind the lounge to serve as their

Tripurari Sharma/Kali for Women

Tripurari Sharma/Kali for Women.

bedroom and workroom. In the course of time some become single mothers. Stories describe how toddlers see what's going on and how babies are placed in a basket under the bed when a customer comes in for sex. At the start of their employment the newcomers are given a bedsheet for which they are charged US$34; board and lodging fees are deducted from whatever earnings they make from drinks and sexual services. The windfall comes when the ships from the Seventh Fleet are on shore. Otherwise these women live during long weeks and sometimes months without a ship, accumulating debts amounting to as much as US$800.

After the change in regimes in the Philippines, *Playboy* published an article, 'Why They Love Us in the Philippines'. It states that 'even as a dictator fell, the more serious business of servicing the US Navy went on as usual'. The author describes only too well Olongapo as this last place 'with beaches and bars and girls and everything cheap,' 'this last frontier where you can have what you want – get a blow job, see a female boxing bout and oil wrestling, and have fun with LBFMs (Little Brown Fucking Machines)'.

Why is it that a military presence has become synonymous with sex and violence? The military system has a way of priming aggression to a high point that unleashes the animal in men. Sexual rampage is the by-product. It happens everywhere.

In South Korea the war games of the Team Spirit exercises usually end up in the raping of village women; even the pregnant ones are not spared. In Olongapo there are many unreported cases of broken bones and brutalized vaginas. In Vietnam the women of My Lai were abused before the massacre. Movies about war are not pure products of the imagination but are based on grim facts.

A number of veterans see the connection of sexism in basic training with the prevailing sexism in military service. Denigration of women leads to the desecration of life: it makes it easier to pull a trigger or push a button to annihilate the living. But when they return to civilian life all this becomes one ugly nightmare that haunts them the rest of their days.

Must Rest and Recreation be at the expense of women? I've asked the question time and again. It seems that it is a must. An American officer in South Korea admitted that they would not know what to do if there was no prostitution. Without an outlet the servicemen would raise hell. There is explicit sanction for sexual exploitation. The men are asked: 'Going out on liberty?' and are offered a box of condoms.

As for AIDS: the very fact that social hygiene clinics are subsidized is an admission that the US government has some responsibility for the spread of sexually transmitted diseases. In 1987 Dr O'Rourke of the US Naval Base in Subic got into a controversy with the Navy when he revealed that Filipino bar girls caught the HIV virus from American servicemen, and suggested that the US Navy should be answerable for this. If STD is addressed, why not AIDS?

His argument was that if the women were given just compensation they might take up an alternative livelihood. However what happened in fact, and is still happening, is that AIDS victims go back to working in bars: in general they remain sexually active and some have even become pregnant. Dr O'Rourke lost his battle to uphold the women's rights: he was fired from the Navy.

With the coming of AIDS to the Philippines, more and more women in the sex strips of the military R and R confess *we are scared of catching AIDS. If only we could get away from here*. In Honduras the AIDS scare has also been triggered off by the US military presence. In 1986, six prostitutes near the base tested positive for AIDS. This brought about street demonstrations and petitions that the Gringos go home.

In Mombasa, Kenya, where there is a liberty port for the Seventh Fleet, AIDS is also a problem. It is debatable who brings AIDS to whom, but the fact remains that when the women recruited from all over Kenya and Tanzania get infected, they take the virus back to their villages and up to the border of Uganda.

The Third World Movement Against the Exploitation of Women (TW-MAE-W) is engaged in the Philippines in direct services for prostitutes. The methodology followed is Paolo Freire's Empowerment Education that would help them become assertive in matters that concern their lives. The prostitutes who come to the 'Belen' drop-in centers share our belief that the most effective intervention in decreasing the potential role of prostitution in HIV transmission is to get out of prostitution and cease being sexually active with many partners.

Knowledge empowers the women, gives them greater self-respect and confidence, makes them less subservient and more an equal to their clients. This transformation has helped a number of them assert their rights, like their refusal to have sex unless the man wears a condom.

With the present curtailment of liberty passes and more rigid curfew hours, places such as Subic and Olongapo have become, relatively speaking, ghost towns. The bar girls are more open to alternatives and thus come to TW-MAE-W's 'Belen sa Subic' and to the Growth Home in Quezon City.

In the meantime the Campaign Against Military Prostitution (CAMP International) continues. To do away with military prostitution is to liberate all parties – the buyer, the seller, the sold. It is dangerous to look at military prostitution as an 'out there' problem of poverty-stricken women from the Third World. The attitude becomes patronizing: *the poor women are in need of money from the GIs who do them the favor of giving them a living*.

CAMP International aims at building genuine solidarity. We tell people in affluent societies to please take care of their men while we attend to our women. We invite real identification with Third World women. What Caucasians do not want to be done to their women should also be condemned when done to the Asian, African and Latin American. There should be a universal sense of womanhood and a universal denunciation of whatever degrades and reduces women to sex objects for sale, and bunnies for play.

Taking class into consideration will throw light on the fact that the marginalized ethnic groups – the colored and the immigrants who get drafted – are as much prey of poverty as their sisters in developing countries.

Olongapo: Exploited by the Army
Anon

I have had many names in my life. I will share all of them with you. Right now it is *AIDS*. I am a carrier, the doctor told me. That settles my future, wouldn't you say?

The first name I remember was *Baby*. That is what my mother and father called me. We were a pioneer farming family. My father was just making a success of our farm when suddenly, without warning, the Philippine National Army came and forced us to leave.

To 'protect' us from the NPA [the insurgent New People's Army] we were made to take everything we could carry and move to a 'strategic village'. There was no village at all, and after building a barracks for the military, we had to start all over again. This event was my first encounter with the military. It changed everything for us overnight. It also changed my name.

I was just 15, and as the eldest I had to do something to help my family. When the captain of our local army squadron introduced a recruiter to my parents, I was ready to go anywhere. He made it sound so nice! I would go to Japan and work in a famous hotel as a professional dancer. It would mean lots of money to send home.

So I became *Mami*! My recruiter wanted me to go to Japan as a prostitute, but I demanded to go as an entertainer. At last, six months later, I left Manila for Japan with six other girls. At the airport a man met us and, after confiscating our passports, obliged us to train as strippers. I was sent first to a bar in Tokyo where I had to work as a stripper. From then on, sometimes I worked in bars and other times in strip halls. I was sent all over Japan, and many times I did not even know where I was. As I went along, I was still paying off my debt so I never received the money I should have. There were several places where I received nothing. My work at this time was just the usual service to customers, with no prostitution. I liked these first few months the best.

Then came the day my name was changed again: *Prostitute*. God forgive me. I was taken to a snack bar where I was told that from now on my work included prostitution; that I had a debt of 600,000 yen to the owner; that I would have to work it all off before receiving a salary; that I could take no tips ... or else! The 'or else' was physical violence and I often had black and blue marks on my body and even on my face.

Long after I calculated my debt was paid off, I was still not free, and still no salary was coming in. I decided to escape. I got away and found good work. But one day, after a month and a half of freedom, the Yazuka (Japanese Mafia) found me and took me back to the bar by force. They beat me up terribly, and from then on I was locked up with one of them 24 hours a day. Through a customer I was able to get a note out and a few days later two men came looking for me by name. I was afraid for my life, but two of us managed somehow to get away. We asked a police officer to bring us to the police station. I still get weak when I think of what might have happened to us. As it was, we were both deported.

By now I thought I had seen it all: Filipino and Japanese recruiters, promoters, agents, managers, traders, club owners, Yakuza, Filipino gangs, prostitution, police, immigration. And of course the customers ...

I thought I had seen everything – until I went to work in Olongapo! As the standards of this business go, I was getting old. I could not last long in Manila, so a barowner friend of mine said he would help me out. He gave me an introduction to one of his cronies, a former US Navy man who ran one of the thousand clubs and bars clustered outside the US Subic Bay naval base. Owners in this town are mostly politicians or ex-servicemen.

After meeting him, my worst experiences in Japan began to look good. If I had not been so desperate for money, I would have gone back to Manila and killed that man who made me think he was my friend. The first thing I was told there was that I would be competing with 16,000 other prostitutes, and if I didn't like what I was ordered to do I could go to the clubs where women do boxing and wrestling to 'entertain' Navy men. So I went to work in the lewd shows that are meant to arouse the customers. It is a fearful thing to see young boys turn into screaming animals and, worse, to have to go off with them after they had 'won' me as a prize. In Olongapo it isn't prostitution we are paid for, it is debauchery!

Whenever I feel sorry for myself, I go out for a walk and take a good look at the street children. There are about 3,000 of them, so they are everywhere. A good many of them are children of US military men. They wander about, some of them on drugs, living off garbage or prostitution. Many are sexually abused by the servicemen, who are often heard bragging about how young 'their kid' was.

These children have lost their identity as Filipinos, and they certainly don't have any future. I make myself think: 'What if my youngest brother had to live like this?' Then I can go back and smile through another day of hell.

The US Navy covers this up of course, and if it doesn't, the owner–politicians do. The other day we were all paid to take part in a demonstration 'demanding' that the government keep the US bases in the Philippines. Well, I for one hate them – I hate the whole place – 'sin city', as it is internationally known. The sailors have their own name for us, 'little brown (sex) machines'. That is one name that infuriates me!

Women are blamed for being prostitutes. All I know is that I had no choice in the matter. For myself and most of the women I know, we live like this because we have to feed and educate our brothers and sisters so they won't have to live like this. Without us, our families would not have survived. The sex industry feeds on our poverty.

I don't know what is going to happen to me now. The doctor put my present name down on my compulsory health report: AIDS carrier. That means I might be fired. If I am, what will happen to my family?

Part 4
Rape and Torture in War

Surviving Beyond Fear: Women and Torture in Latin America
Ximena Bunster-Burotto

Ximena Bunster is a professor of anthropology in the social sciences faculty at the University of Chile, in Santiago. She has written widely on the subject of women and human rights, contributing to a number of anthologies and journals, including a special issue of *Isis Internacional* (No. 15, 1991) in which the following article appeared in Spanish.

Military regimes in Latin America have developed patterns of punishment specifically designed for women who are perceived as actively fighting against or in any way resisting the oppression and exploitation visited upon their peoples by dictatorial governments. The attempts to dominate and coerce women through terrorism and torture have become organized and systematic – administered by the military state. The more generalized and diffused female sexual enslavement through the patriarchal state has been crystallized and physically implemented through the military state as torturer.

Punitive sexual enslavement of female political prisoners is found throughout Latin America. However, the armed, organized terrorizing of women may best be understood in the context of political, economic and social forces present in a given historical– national situation. We, therefore, see a somewhat different profile in the victimization of women taking place in Nicaragua, Salvador, Guatemala, and Honduras than that which has become characteristic of the countries of the Southern Cone: Argentina, Chile, Uruguay, Paraguay, and Bolivia.

In the first cluster of countries – those forming part of Central America – political torture reaches women as daily terror. Women are most often injured or killed in contexts of *generalized* violence: in massacres, attacks on churches during mass, and the burning of villages. This generalized violence affects different segments of the population who happen to be present during the attacks – men, older people, children, and even domestic animals. By contrast, in the countries of the Southern Cone, where a military government or succession of military governments has been entrenched for decades, women are *systematically identified* – with names, addresses, and family composition – as 'enemies' of the government. They are methodically tracked down and incarcerated. There are institutions within the military government dedicated specifically and exclusively to this task.

For the purposes of this article, I have concentrated on an analysis of sexual torture of female political prisoners who are or have been citizens of Argentina, Chile and Uruguay. The Argentinian state has been militarized on and off since 1930 and the Chilean and the Uruguayan states since 1973. I have selected these three countries for the following reasons:
1.   Each at one time was a flourishing democratic government, later aborted by military takeover.
2.   These nations have had years of military dictatorship during which torture as a method of 'security' has become institutionalized. These institutions incorporate scientifically trained torture specialists, physicians, modern hardware, and 'refined' methods in the systematic torturing of political prisoners.
3.   Each of these countries had a highly organized, politically conscious urban proletariat from whose ranks prominent female union and community leaders emerged.

In her work *Female Sexual Slavery*, Kathleen Barry says:

> Female sexual slavery is present in ALL situations where women or girls cannot change the immediate conditions of their existence; where regardless of how they got into those conditions they cannot get out; and where they are subject to sexual violence and exploitation.[1]

My analysis of the nature of the torture endured by Latin American female political prisoners stems from Barry's groundbreaking work. For I believe – and this I have tried to document in the pages that follow – that once one has listened to first-hand and eyewitness accounts and has read and analysed the written testimonies of how pain and suffering are inflicted on women prisoners, a distinctive pattern of torture emerges.

In the state torturers' efforts to force confessions, elicit information, or to punish, a pattern in structure and in content is clearly discernible. These common elements experienced by the female political prisoner in violent sexual attacks upon her body and

CUSTODIAL RAPE

People's Union for Democratic Rights, Delhi, March 1990.

psyche are consciously designed to violate her sense of herself, her female human dignity. The combination of culturally defined moral debasement and physical battering is the demented scenario whereby the prisoner is to undergo a rapid metamorphosis from madonna – 'respectable woman and/or mother' – to whore. To women, through processes of socialization this violent sexual treatment administered by the state becomes most cruelly doubly disorienting; it exacerbates and magnifies the woman's already subservient, prescribed, passive, secondary position in Latin American society and culture.

In order to better understand (while maintaining an awareness of the pitfalls that cultural generalization entails) how societal archetypes and stereotypes are manipulated by the torturers, it is important to look briefly at the delicate balance and complementarity of the male and female roles and the culturally assigned gender differences in Latin American society.

Many authors have discussed the bipolar concept of *machismo/Marianismo* underlying the socialization of men and women in Latin America. *Machismo*, or the cult of virility, has been described as embracing an 'exaggerated aggressiveness and intransigence in male-to-male interpersonal relationships and arrogance and sexual aggression in male-to-female relationships'; *Marianismo*, as 'the cult of feminine spiritual superiority which teaches that women are semi-divine, morally superior to and spiritually stronger than men'.[2] *Machismo* and *Marianismo* are New World variations of Old World themes.

Machismo is obviously a Latin American manifestation of global patriarchy, whereby males enjoy special privileges within the society and within the family and are considered superior to women. *Marianismo*, Mariology, or the cult of the Virgin Mother – she who embodies simultaneously the ideal of nurturance/motherhood and chastity – permeates the world view of Latin America and all aspects of its culture and institutions. Latin American women are supposed to pattern their role as women after this perfect model, inspired through pervasive Catholicism. The patriarchal madonna/whore schema, too, is global.[3] Its particular manifestation in Latin America through the cult of the Virgin shows the extent to which Catholic ideology and the sexual stereotypes it introduced have been assimilated. Latin America has clearly absorbed the Spanish culture introduced by the conquistadores, itself marked by seven centuries of Arab–Muslim domination. The manipulation of these images proved useful to later waves of exploitation through capitalism.

Perhaps one example at this point will serve to bring home the fact of the double brutalization involved in socializing women in particular modes and then using that very socialization as a method of torture. One of the secret detention camps in Argentina, called Olimpo, was opened in the western zone of Buenos Aires in August 1980. Testimony provided by Argentinians who were detained there describes how the torture of detainees involved icons of the Virgin Mary:

> In the very corridor leading to the torture rooms, along which new inmates had passed naked and in which they were beaten when they were first kidnapped, a small chapel was installed. It is a strange kind of Christianity these people have, enjoying punishing and beating until the victim loses consciousness – in front of the image of the Virgin Mary.[4]

Two important characteristics, then, of Latin American culture are crucial to an understanding of the specific nature of female sexual torture in these countries. First, women are basically recognized and valued only as mothers, after the Blessed Virgin Mother. Second, women have adopted and internalized these patterns under the historical weight of Hispanic–Arab and Christian heritage and are now faced and overburdened by contemporary underdevelopment – a situation that must be felt and understood in its dailiness. Latin America has undergone conquest and colonization, and with these has seen Western values imposed over those autochthonic belief systems represented through high Indian civilizations at the time of the conquest. It is in this context that we hear the resonance of the Latin American/Caribbean Women's Collective in exile in Europe today: 'Domination in Latin America has been a prolongation of the history of man's exploitation of man and of men's domination of women.'[5]

In view of this cultural heritage and the ways in which the cultural baggage affects patterned gender differences, it is important to ask whether it matters that the state as torturer is a military state. It seems clear, from the countries examined and the systematic, ordered processes of torture of female political prisoners that are evident, that it does, indeed, matter. The fact that these states where torture has become institutionalized are military states should be kept in mind. It seems that military regimes exhibit the impulse of the state to secure and defend the patriarchal structure and the privileged status of 'masculinity' more blatantly than do other authoritarian states. The military state understands itself to be run for the perpetuation and extension of the values of the military – masculinity, power, and public authority – to a greater extent than do other patriarchal states. It is founded on the assumption that women and notions of the 'feminine' are tools to be used by men; simultaneously, militarism as an ideology purports that women are fearsome threats to public order, to the hierarchy defined and controlled by men. It is important to stress the fact that although other patriarchal states also torture women, militaristic states rely more than civilian states on the use of coercion to strengthen and perpetuate their public authority.[6]

The military elites of Argentina, Chile, and Uruguay have brought internal police forces under their control and have strengthened and further entrenched the institutionalized torture machine through formal co-ordination of internal security bureaucracies and military bureaucracies. Thus, not only have the internal police come within the cloak of the military regimes but the military has also taken an active role in internal security matters. In Argentina, for example, one of the most infamous torture and detention centres is run not by the police, but by the navy. In Chile, separate torture centres are run by the air force, the navy, and the army. In attempts to unify and tighten their bureaucratic torture machines, the military regimes in both Argentina and Chile have brought in the internal intelligence agencies and 'publicly employed' physicians, who supervise torture directly under their control.

The woman who is abducted is made to understand that she is under the control and at the mercy of a military state in every aspect of her life: her socio-economic future, her family life, her sexuality, her internal feelings and sense of herself. Torture is the chosen method to convince her of these 'truths'.

It seems viable to use, as a point of orientation, the definition of torture – the 'standard' definition – as adopted by the Inter-American Commission on Human Rights:

> Torture is understood to be the practice or instigation, by means of which physical or mental pain or suffering is intentionally inflicted upon a person, having taken into consideration the age, sex or condition of the person, for the purpose of intimidation, or in order to obtain a confession or information from the person or in order to punish the person for an act committed or which it is suspected that the person committed.[7]

Although I have used this definition simply for the sake of clarity, and for consistency when using data gathered through various human rights agencies, it is important for us to realize this definition is itself limited and limiting when it comes to an understanding of the special nature of female sexual slavery and torture.

There is a distinctive pattern of torture when female political prisoners are involved. We must recognize and have recognized the fact that when the issue of torture of political prisoners is raised as a human rights issue it never deals with women. We must recognize that the physical and psychic torture of *women as women* – female sexual slavery in patriarchal societies reaching its logical extension and quintessential crystallization in the military state – is made invisible. As the military state so often tortures women as a mode of punishing their 'man', so even to many human rights advocates the 'desecration' of the female is processed as torture of the male.

In order to delineate specific phases and stages of the brutalization and attempted extinction of women as human beings, I have used both composites derived from the large number of recorded violations in Argentina, Chile, and Uruguay, and examples from personal interviews, conversations, and correspondence with women who have witnessed and survived torture.

Due to common elements in their recent histories, a relatively large body of literature exists dealing with human rights violations in Argentina, Chile, and Uruguay. Free public primary, secondary, and university education has provided thousands of women with occupational and professional degrees. From the ranks of the working class and enlarged middle class, female members of the house of representatives (*diputadas*) and senators for the national congress (*senadoras*) emerged. Women committed to change and the abolishment of social injustice have been particularly active in these countries. Human rights organizations such as Amnesty International and the Inter-American Commission have, therefore, been able to amass evidence of the extent of institutionalized torture. These publications document organized phases of terror in the sexual enslavement and torture of female political prisoners.

I must at this point speak to the bravery of those women who have survived what is in fact unspeakable physical and psychological torment and have then come forth to bear witness. We know the psychic pain involved for each of us as we work with these issues; the survivors of these horrors relive their experiences in the telling – their courage and commitment to the rights of human beings must remain for us, here, the inspiration to continue. The bulk of the cases used in this study cover the period 1973–81, when the experiences of these women took place. I have been in touch with women who have survived torture since 1973; the most recent conversations and interviews took place in 1982–83.

It was not deemed necessary to identify the country in each of the cases that follow, as my analysis is directed towards an understanding of the nature of the commonality of pattern of sexual slavery in torture – a pattern that typifies the experiences of all women political prisoners in the Southern Cone of Latin America.

The aim of the first phase in the psychological and physical maltreatment of female political prisoners staged by military, navy, air force or police torturers is to intimidate and create a sense of anxiety in their victims. Two categories of women are targeted for attention.

Captors representing the state as torturer direct their established institutions of violence at the many Latin American women whose political consciousness has spurred them into political activism on behalf of the establishment of a more just social order within their own countries. This has been the case of Chilean women who worked within the Allende government towards the construction of a more egalitarian socio-economic order. This has also been the case of Argentinian, Uruguayan, and – following the coup – Chilean women who became active in the struggle to liberate their countries and peoples from repressive dictatorships and the complicity of those regimes with foreign interests exploiting the human and natural resources of their nations. This group of women, many with public roles – as union leaders, lawyers, doctors, professors – are targeted because of their commitment to a people's struggle.

Institutionalized violence, torture, is also aimed at a second category of women – women who do not have publicly recognized identity of their own but, from the perspective of the state, derive their identity from their relationship to a male. These women are targeted because of the activism of a husband, lover, son, father or brother. The super-macho military system brutalizes these women as an extension of the ego of and as a possession of the male whom they consider the 'enemy' in an 'internal war'. The women undergo imprisonment as hostages in this internal war and are then savagely tortured to get even with their men – the enemies of the military regime in power. The sexual enslavement of women belonging to this category is used to intimidate, emasculate, bring forth confessions from and, in many cases, destroy the men to whom they are legally or emotionally attached.

Intimidation begins with the process of arrest. In the majority of cases, these women have been arrested at home or at their place of work. There are, however, a significant number of seizures in the streets, where women are taken on their way home from a day's work at a factory, office, hospital, school, store – a variety of work sites. A consistent *modus operandi* is used when making an arrest in the street. The woman's way is blocked by three to five men dressed in civilian clothing; only in a very rare instance do these men identify themselves in any way. The woman is grasped violently by the arm by one of the kidnappers while others flank her on each side with their bodies. She is then pushed into a waiting vehicle, handcuffed, and her eyes taped. Sunglasses are usually placed over the scotch or adhesive tape. She sits with eyes lowered and her body tensed with fear. The agents of the government try to use caution lest the fact of their taking a hostage be noted by onlookers. If there are passers-by in a highly congested city area or an oncoming car with passengers, the woman is rapidly thrown to the floor of the vehicle and slapped or beaten with the butt of a revolver.

Probably the most terrorizing arrest is that which takes place when the woman is at home with her family. This violent military operation – envisioned only for the most dangerous criminals in countries with stable democracies – is carried out by an *allanamiento*, a large group of soldiers who come in two or three vehicles and surround the house or building where the apartment of the woman is situated. They carry machine guns and an assortment of other weapons. If any resistance is offered, there is an official housebreaking and search of the home, accompanied by the destruction of furniture, the ripping of mattresses, and the armed intimidation of all the people who are in the house at the moment. This inhumane and cowardly action takes place at night: all reports place such action between midnight and 3 a.m.

Arresting a woman in the home, in front of her children, is doubly painful to the Latin American woman. The family is traditionally run by the mother. The main agent of socialization of children, who has the culturally prescribed role of guardian of the moral values of the society, it is she who must ensure that guidelines for the social and sexually accepted behaviour of family members are adopted and absorbed. She represents the popularly accepted stereotype of the ideal woman exemplified in the Virgin Mother. This cultural pattern permeates all social classes and all adult women, be they mothers or childless. The women are to be morally superior and spiritually stronger than men, sexually pure as opposed to promiscuous, submissive and understanding of the frailties and patriarchal whims of their fathers, husbands and sons, yet strong beneath that submissiveness. The identity of the Latin American woman is derived from her position in the family and especially from her 'sacred' mothering role, where she is overprotective in her nurturing, absolutely devoted to her children, and willing to sacrifice her own desires to please her family – especially the male members. Her love is sacrifice and selflessness personified. It is crucial to understand the extent to which the conceptions are internalized: these attributes provide the foundation on which the edifice of the Latin American woman's self-perception and self-respect is built. These attributes also reflect upon the male members of her family, whose sense of personal honour and dignity is conceived as directly related to and dependent on the sense of moral propriety of the women in their family.

Given all these cultural antecedents, when a woman is imprisoned in her home, the protection and refuge of the home that she represents is shattered, and the control and coherence she maintained in the intimate sphere of the household is destroyed as well.

This assault on a woman's sense of self and the manipulation of her traditional role as wife and mother are used by the torturers to break, punish, and ultimately destroy her. During this violation of her human dignity, torture as intimidation and torture as punishment blend into the same criminal act. This is the stage in an enslaved woman's torment when *family torture* is enacted by her captors. The following case exemplifies this strategy of the state torturers:

> *V.L.*, a young married mother of three children, was assaulted at one o'clock in the morning. Just she and her children were at home when three men in civilian clothing – members of a military torturing squad – broke in. They raped her repeatedly at gunpoint in front of her children, aged five, four, and two, while threatening to shoot her if she cried for help. This heinous act was repeated on six other occasions over a two-month period, creating a constant state of terror for V.L. and her children. Her husband had previously been detained by authorities; she was subjected to this repeated sexual torment in the state's effort to lower her defences and obtain information concerning the husband's political activities.

After the terror of arrest, the hostage woman is forced to face a series of phases of torture through which her state torturers hope to destroy her psychically as well as physically. Again, it is to obtain a confession or information, or as authorized punishment that these 'security' methods are applied.

Both male and female detainees are tortured; some methods are applied equally to both sexes: incommunicado detention, wall-standing, the electric prod, the electric grid, the submarine, the dry submarine, the *pau de arara*, and inventive variations on the theme of beating (see Appendix below).

The overall terrorizing environment of the detention centres should be understood as the backdrop for the torments particularly designed for women. From the institutional perspective, these are orderly affairs. The state's bureaucratic torturing system has incorporated doctors. Physicians are in charge of supervising the physical and psychological torment of prisoners – their scientific knowledge allows them to indicate when a given method of torture should be suspended if the death of the hostage is not desired.

Carefully designed mental torment is applied in counterpoint with the physical torture of detainees in a premeditated effort to increase the total feeling of powerlessness and pain. Simulated executions are staged in the middle of the night; captors threaten that a loved one will 'disappear' or that a spouse, an ageing parent or small child will be tortured if co-operation and information are not forthcoming. Prisoners are forced to witness the torture and death of other detainees or are placed in rooms or cells where they must listen to the moaning of other hostages being beaten with the butts of machine guns, rifles, and revolver. Often, standing naked and blindfolded, survivors report having to listen to the screams and 'almost animal howls of pain' of prisoners being tortured in the same room or an adjacent one. Blindfolds are removed, however, when the detainee is forced through buildings to encounter a flow of fellow prisoners who can hardly walk or talk following torture sessions.

This is a climate, a world, of mounting and disorienting fear. For the prisoner, this is a totally unstructured situation – with 'reality' defined and composed by the torturers. Prisoners have no moment-to-moment, no daily control of their lives; they survive in a dim present with very little hope for the future.

Torture designed for female political prisoners

Female and male prisoners, then, are subjected to many of the same torturing practices, whose aim is to inflict physical pain, mental distress and general suffering. However, the torture of men, while horrible, has as its object something less than the extinction of their sexual, gender identity. The primary form of sexual torture of men is directed toward their sexual confidence; their humanity is debased by placing them in powerless situations, where they cannot defend a female political prisoner – usually a wife, daughter, mother, lover, or friend – from brutal sexual torture performed in their presence.

Women's torment is comparatively much worse than men's

because it is painfully magnified a thousand times by the most inhuman, cruel and degrading methods of torture consciously and systematically directed at her female sexual identity and female anatomy. The processes of imprisonment and torture of women political prisoners is female sexual slavery in its most hideous and blatantly obvious forms. It represents macho patriarchal contempt and misogyny crystallized and implemented through military–police structures of organized violence. These are not simply males 'out of control with permission'; with a demonic irony, the sexual torture of women is named 'control' and is authorized state 'security'. This fact should not surprise us; the military is, by definition, the most sexist and patriarchal institution of the many institutions that reinforce ideological subordination of women in the family and in society at large.

The sexual violence unleashed against women political prisoners is seen as the key in controlling them, through punishment and interrogations. Gang rape, massive rape becomes the standard torture mechanism for the social control of the imprisoned women. Politically committed, active women who have dared to take control of their own lives by struggling against an oppressive regime demand sexual torture – as do the women who have stood by their men in an organized political effort to liberate their country and themselves from a coercive military regime. One of the essential ideas behind the sexual slavery of a woman in torture is to teach her that she must retreat into the home and fulfil the traditional role of wife and mother. It is this role only that provides her with respect in a society where she is ideologically defined as inferior to the men from whom she derives her secondary identity – she is some male's mother, sister, wife, and *compañera*. With a too usual contradiction and reversal, the method of the 'lesson' forcing a return to the *Marianismo* ideal simultaneously violates that possibility. There seems to be not only a willingness to violate cultural notions of what the 'natural' social order is, but in fact to direct torment with excruciating precision just to those areas of societal definition. We can only describe these patterns of state torture, we cannot make them rational.

Behind the sequence of brutal sexual acts committed on a woman's body and mind while she is in captivity lurks the criminal attempt to humiliate, degrade, and morally and physically destroy her through and within the social, cultural, and political environment that is familiar to her. It is, in an important sense, too distancing to speak of culturally accepted and defined gender distinctions. The ideological conceptions, the myths, and the realities of the paradigmatic vision of Woman, are much of the ground from which springs a woman's sense of herself and from which she derives the emotional needs and the gratifications that give meaning to her life: the love and respect of her family and the esteem and caring of her co-workers.

A woman's self-respect, sense of dignity, and physical integrity are shattered when at the hands of her captors she unwillingly becomes the participant-observer of the planned and enforced destruction of her culturally defined womanhood. In every sense of the word, in every level of her being, the torturers' invasion involves radical disorientation.

The sequence of types and examples of torture that follows is from cases of women in Argentina, Chile and Uruguay. There is always a danger, when cases of the torture of people are summarized and then classified. As painful as it is we must not allow ourselves to forget, even for a moment, that we are speaking of pain and torment inflicted upon individuals. Even in the notions of selection of 'evidence' and of a 'viable' methodology, we neutralize the *fact* of the agony for these women, woman by woman.

The woman prisoner is brought blindfolded and hooded to one of the many *casas de tortura* (torture houses) administered by the security forces of these countries. They are most often established in regiments, police quarters, naval and air force bases, and academies, and in houses rented and equipped for purposes of torturing. The woman has already undergone the trauma of arrest and the geographical disorientation of being taken blindfolded to the torture house. She has been cut off from her family; or, if her arrest went unobserved by relatives, neighbours or passers-by, she has 'disappeared' – she knows that no one knows where to look for her. Some victims captured on the streets start shouting their own names aloud so that their family will hear they were dragged away.

While she is presumably at the information desk or in the 'reception room' of the detention centre – 'presumably', because survivors report that it takes a while to look from under the blindfold without being discovered and beaten – her name and address are taken and entered into files with a number. While she is giving the information demanded, her body – especially her breasts, buttocks and entire genital area – is fingered and pawed by countless male hands. Her body is squeezed and explored, producing in her a sense of outrage, sometimes physical pain, shame and despair.

She is then taken to another room, where a group of men undress her, literally tear her clothing and start slapping and beating her up continuously. No sooner has she been able to get on her feet when she is again thrown to the floor or against a wall. Her nose starts bleeding and she aches all over. During the course of this brutal battering, she is given orders to sit down – there is never a chair – so she falls to the floor. She is then given contradictory orders to march in a given direction, obeying, hits herself against a wall, then she is told to kneel and squat because she has to go under a table. In the meantime she is the target of crude verbal abuse and vile ridicule of her naked body. She becomes the pathetic jester who amuses the torturers by her aimless movements directed to make her fall, roll on the floor, crawl on all fours, and jump over obstacles that are nonexistent. Fun is made of the shape of the woman's breasts, her birthmarks, or the scars left on her abdomen after a Caesarean birth. This stage of torture is marked by the captors' sadistic objectification of the women at their mercy.

Questions are interjected during the process of physical and verbal abuse. Depending on her presumed profile, the woman is interrogated concerning the whereabouts of her husband, or a key male political figure who is in hiding, or about whether or not she is active in a specific political party. If the woman political prisoner claims ignorance or refuses to co-operate, the sexual violence of the torture escalates. She is thrown to the floor, splashed with cold water all over her body, and the electric prod is applied to her eyelids, gums, nipples and genital area.

As interrogations continue, sexual torture is increased. Cigarettes are extinguished on the woman's breasts and nipples; her breasts are slashed with sharpened intruments; blades, hot irons and electrical surgical pens are used to brand different parts of her body.

There is a male bonding in the violence of massive criminal rape – performed in succession, by 3 to 27 men in some cases – against women political prisoners. Rape is part of almost every torture sequence endured by women, especially women from 12 to 49 years of age. Power and domination are exerted on the victims of sexual slavery in a torture situation where women cannot leave or fight back. Testimonies of older women political prisoners who have survived correspond in their hair-raising accounts of massive rapes perpetrated on the younger women upon arrival at the 'houses of torture'. Following these vile sessions of rape and other forms of sexual abuse, many women suffered severe haemorrhaging for days with no medical attention.

The use of animals to torture women physically and psychically is yet another phase in this unutterable process. Women's mental stability and physical health have been seriously threatened, sometimes destroyed, by the introduction of mice into their vaginas. Foreign objects, such as sticks and dull instruments, have also been introduced into the vagina and anus; but it is difficult to compare even such abuse with the psychological and physical suffering brought about by a scratching, biting, disoriented mouse forced into a female's genital region. Women, now in exile, who have survived this torture explain that they have not, nor do they believe they ever can, really recover from the trauma. Many of them developed ulcers within their vaginal walls as a result of the rodent's action inside them.

Many female political prisoners in Chile have been raped by trained dogs – usually boxers.[8] This is evidently one of the most brutalizing and traumatic experiences suffered by women in prison. The survivors of this torment find it very difficult to report their exposure to this extreme sexual debasement. With sickening canniness, the torturers traumatize their victims into feeling shame for their own bodies. The women who are able to do so are willing to recall these events in an effort to make known these atrocities although they suffer anew by speaking of them.

The military state – the patriarchal state in distillation – with its dependence on coercion to mould human beings to the ideology that will sustain its authority, uses the paradigm of female sexual enslavement, rape, in as many forms as it can imagine. Patriarchy under stress tends to reveal itself with contradictory zeal. The notion of madonna/whore in the context of male linearity of thinking[9] as it melds with rape systematically applied to exert absolute control is illustrated through the case of A.N.M.R. This courageous young widow, whose husband had been assassinated during a military operation, was seized by the police and mercilessly tortured for long periods. As she refused to talk, she was given electric shocks, sent to her cell for a short while, and then dragged out again by the officer in charge of the supervision of her sexual torture. Officers would shout to groups of soldiers inviting them to rape her with the following order: 'Come and have a good time with this whore, because she needs it.' They did rape her. She sums it up in her own words 'Thus I was debased and raped countless times.' As if continual rape were not enough 'control', her uterus was later ruptured by a high-voltage shock with an electric prod.

Rape is used during sessions of 'family torture', usually to extract information from a non-cooperative male prisoner. It is for this reason, for leverage in interrogations, that women in the family are kidnapped along with the male 'subversive'. Numerous wives and daughters of male prisoners have been sexually debased and massively raped in front of their husbands, lovers or fathers. If a man is wanted and in hiding, his wife and female children are incarcerated in a manipulative attempt to extract information concerning his activities and hiding place. If the wife does not co-operate with her captors, she is raped. If this does not produce the desired information, she is threatened with the rape of her daughters. In addition to the physical suffering, the psychic strain of having to deal with such a clash of loyalties and the consequences of any so-called decision are devastating. Unfortunately, many threats are made good by the torturers, and mothers are forced to witness in shock and powerless pain violent sexual acts committed upon their innocent female youngsters.

An extension of the notion of degradation of a woman in the community of her family is the forced abuse and humiliation of a woman through her peers. As with family torture this method produces pain and humiliation in all those forced to participate in this particular type of sexual torment. A naked woman political prisoner is placed in the middle of a human circle formed by her naked male co-prisoners, many of whom know her. In cases where she is not known personally, she stands as the representative of 'one of their own' ideologically. The men are forced at gunpoint to masturbate while looking at the naked body of the woman and having her as a target when they ejaculate. The woman who finds herself in this type of situation, from which she cannot escape, is degraded in a painfully debasing incident in which male domination not only increases her inferiority as a woman but robs her of her dignity and individuality as a person.

It should be noted that there appears to be a class element and racial component in the most extreme cases of sexual violence. Proletarian women and women with markedly *meztizo* features – the fusion of European and Indian admixtures – have been even more brutalized than their lighter sisters coming from bourgeois families. It is also important, however, to stress the fact that in the highly class-conscious society of Latin America, the sexual torture of female political prisoners has cut across class lines. The common denominator has been the definition as enemy by the fascist military governments, whether the 'security threat' comes directly through the woman's – real or supposed – political activism or through the identity she is seen to derive from a male who is politically active.

Torture of the female psyche

Although, as is quite evident, it is impossible to separate physical abuse from psychological abuse, the state torturers have designed methods specifically aimed at the mental torment of their prisoners – methods that underscore their domination and control. This harrowing of the psyche of women prisoners is used by their tormentors to complement the sexual violence that their bodies are undergoing. Psychological torture leaves scars that are almost impossible to heal. A woman's sympathy and empathy for others is played upon; her deep sense of herself as nurturer is manipulated and torn. The following situations and cases show different aspects of this form of sexual/gender violence.

Many women have reported how painfully humiliating it is to have their physiological processes, basically excretion, controlled and observed by their torturers. They were not allowed to go to the bathroom when they needed to but when their guard felt like taking them. Once in the bathroom, they had to empty their bowels or bladder in front of the torturer, who was aiming at them all the time a shotgun. He would not even turn his head aside.

Many survivors of torture describe the agonizing impact that the sobbing and crying of other women being raped in an adjacent room or a few feet away from them had on the moral integrity that they were trying to preserve in order not to break down. Psychological torture is inflicted with false news of the death of family members and/or by threats that a loved one will disappear. A woman professor of mathematics was thrown against a wall and, holding a revolver against her forehead, her torturer – a marine – shouted, 'Talk, talk, for once and for all, because you are going to be executed and you will never see your small daughter again.'

Psychological suffering is also administered by purposely having female political prisoners become aware of or witness the rape of women in advanced stages of pregnancy – seven to eight and a half months.

The use of children by these state torturers and the manipulation of the woman's caring and nurturing role take many forms. Many women have had to endure having their own children or the children of female friends and political comrades tortured in their presence.

Not only the young offspring of women and men who are sought by a dictatorial regime for their clandestine activities against the government, but also the children of women and men considered a threat to the 'internal security' of the government have been kidnapped by force from their homes. These children are placed in so-called Homes for Children run by the armed forces; they are hostages used to exert pressure on their parents. Most often, a message will reach the mother of the child with an ultimatum – if she does not turn herself in to the security forces, the little girl or boy will remain in captivity and undergo torture or be placed 'under the vigilance of sexual perverts who prefer children'.

Under the threat of having child tortured or 'disappear' altogether, mothers have sometimes confessed the hiding place of their husband or *compañero*. Here again is a most diabolical form of psychological torture: the Latin American mother placed in a situation of conflict between her role as wife/lover and her role as mother will almost always opt for her 'sacred' maternal duty of protecting the vulnerable child. In addition to living with the brutal assault her body has suffered while under interrogation, she must live now, as well, with the 'guilt' of having revealed the whereabouts or activities of her husband. There is shattering moral pain brought about by the disintegration of her family. This is the cruellest attack upon a woman's psyche; it shows us so clearly how the torture of these dictatorial military regimes pierces to the essentials of female sexual slavery. The woman must not only suffer in every part of her being; she must also be faced with a shame that is called a 'choice' and feel herself a 'collaborator' with her torturer, no matter what she does or does not do.

Kathy Barry, in exposing the pervasive patterns and practice of female sexual slavery, begins to weave those threads of connection showing how slavery extends beyond the individual and further enslaves her. We see this with shocking clarity in the selected ways in which the female is tormented as a political prisoner. This cultural sadism not only tries to smash a woman in and through the centre of her being, particularly through her nurturing role, but also zealously spans generations. We do not need to wait 30 years to test a hypothesis of possible damage to the children of V.L., who watched her repeatedly raped, or to the children who underwent the torment of the detention centres. We do not need to wait to ask about the unutterable complexities of damage done to those who both witnessed and served as examples.

The military state sadistically literalizes patterns of female sexual slavery. It is important to speak specifically to the facts of those women taken when pregnant.

When a pregnant political prisoner does not die on the torture table or lose her baby after beatings on the abdomen, being kicked, raped and tortured with electric shock – under the supervision of a doctor – she is returned to her cell, under the same conditions as the rest of the prisoners.

Following her subjection to the pattern of torture described, a young Argentinian woman gave birth to a son. She was tied to a bed by her hands and feet during a five-hour labour, receiving medical attention just as the baby was born; for the duration of their incarceration, the infant was made to sleep on the floor of the cell. Amnesty International doctors examined the woman and the child following their release from prison. Miraculously, the baby appears to show normal mental and physical development. The mother suffers from impaired memory, headaches, inability to concentrate, nervousness, and dizziness.[10]

Amnesty International has documented numerous disappearances of mothers and children, where the child was either born in prison or abducted with the mother.[11] In Argentina, the greatest number of pregnant women and mothers of infants and schoolchildren 'disappeared' between 1976 and 1980. During this period, pregnant women were taken to ESMA – the principal naval training college in Buenos Aires – which was earmarked as the maternity unit for secret detention camps in the capital city district. All pregnant women who survived interrogation were attended at ESMA by a doctor from the naval hospital. After the birth, the mothers were usually 'transferred' and the infants sent to official or clandestine orphanages or adopted by childless couples in the armed forces.

'Transfer', according to surviving witnesses, is the name given to mass-scale assassination in Argentina. Guards tell prisoners at a detention camp that they are to be 'transferred' to another place, to a location where they will not be allowed to take their few possessions or additional clothing as they will be issued uniforms at the next detention centre. In actuality, they are all killed or become *desaparecidos* – missing – the word used to describe thousands of Argentinians who have never been heard from again, and whose bodies have not been returned to their families for burial.

Hundreds of Argentinian women have given birth and been 'transferred'. Their babies have been reported as missing by grandparents and surviving relatives. The toddlers and older children abducted with their mothers have never been seen again. The grandmothers of these missing babies and children, who have also lost their own daughters and sons, have formed an association, The Grandmothers of the Plaza de Mayo – an offshoot of The Mothers of the Plaza de Mayo.[12]

Evidence and documentation concerning the sale of some of these children, both in Latin America and abroad is just surfacing.

Female sexual enslavement is one of the most salient characteristics of the oppressive military dictatorships in many Latin American countries. It is one of the most difficult crimes against women to punish and eradicate because the oppressors, the torturers, the persecutors, and executioners of women are all members of the authoritarian state, the military state, that has done away with all the basic human rights to which individuals are entitled.

The military state depends on the oppression and exploitation of the poverty-stricken masses of Latin Americans; because it is racist, it is against the full participation of ethnic minorities in national affairs. The military state is also the epitome of sexist patriarchal ideology and therefore is against the largest minority, women, who have been made to retreat to their traditional role as reproducers and nurturers of the younger generations.

By protecting the economic interests of the wealthy families belonging to the upper class and by serving as a watchdog for the investment of multinational corporations, the military state endorses the economic exploitation of the bulk of the population and the natural resources of the country it purports to represent. Profits for some are reaped faster when the constitution of a country is ignored; when the congress that is to guarantee the democratic process is closed indefinitely, its politicians banned from participation in government affairs; and when strikes and criticisms of the government are made illegal, a cause for punishment and imprisonment.

If the segment of the population that dares criticize the totalitarian military state is female, the punishment is administered through female sexual slavery in torture. The subservient, dependent, passive and unequal position in society that women experience in a *machista*-patriarchal society is exacerbated in torture. The

173

courageous women who have managed to survive this brutal appropriation, colonization, and objectification of their bodies, as well as the psychological suffering derived from the cruelly premeditated deprivation of their human womanly dignity have set an example of bravery for us all. They have also handed us the banner of struggle by surviving, by not succumbing at the feet of their tormentors, by transcending their sense of shame and humiliation and by offering their personal testimonies to make known the criminal acts of the military state. Their cry is for justice, for the elimination of sexual slavery in torture, for the spread of awareness of its existence and its monstrosity so that it may be stopped, so that it will never happen again.

Appendix

Information gathered through direct communication, reports quoted in the OAS Report on the Situation of Human Rights in Uruguay, and my own analysis of hundreds of recorded cases of human rights violations in Chile, Argentina, and Uruguay, show that female and male detainees have been tortured with all the different methods described below.

Incommunicado detention: This is a type of punishment in which the prisoner is placed in isolation, usually hooded or with the eyes held closed by a blindfold, in a room with no light or ventilation. Women report having been isolated for from ten days up to four months.

Wall-standing: The prisoner is ordered to remain standing in a fixed position, sometimes with arms upraised or holding weighty objects, with legs kept well apart, for hours or days. Sometimes wall-standing takes place nude and in the open air. Many women have been forced to stand, handcuffed and blindfolded, for two to three consecutive days without food and without sleep. Sometimes they have been forbidden to go to the bathroom.

Beatings: Prisoners are beaten in a variety of ways: using karate blows, sticks, iron objects, rubber bludgeons, fists, brass knuckles, kicks, and so forth. Many prisoners have lost teeth and suffered fractured ribs and ruptured eardrums. Women prisoners are usually slapped on the face with open palms and punched in the stomach until they lose their balance and fall; they are kicked until they stand up again. It is common for women prisoners to faint under this agonizing treatment; they are revived by a cold shower followed by electric shocks.

Electric prod: Electric current is applied to the most sensitive part of the prisoners' bodies – gums, lips, eyes, genital organs, breasts. If the torturers are careful and expert, 200 volts exactly are used, as 220 volts are regarded as fatal.

Parrilla electrica (Electric grid): Here the prisoner is tied naked, with arms and legs open, to a metallic bedlike frame. This facilitates the application of electric shocks.

The submarine: The prisoner is repeatedly immersed upside down, in a tank of water – generally mixed with vomit, blood, or urine – until on the verge of asphyxiation. Prisoners often die during this torture.

The dry submarine: This method of torture involves the slow asphyxiation of the prisoner by wrapping his or her head in a plastic bag or sack.

Stocks: The prisoner, generally naked, is tied to four stakes in the ground – always in the open air – so that arms and legs are completely separated.

The horse (this specific type of torture is designed for men): The naked prisoner is made to mount a sawhorse which keeps him from touching the ground. His arms are held open, and the sawhorse is moved backwards and forwards beneath him so that he feels as if he were being sawed in half. This results in serious injury to the genital organs.

Pau de arara: The person being tortured is hung by the knees from a horizontal plank, with hands and ankles tied together. This procedure cuts off the circulation of the blood; the body turns livid and the individual being tortured faints.

Drugs: Pentothal sodium, especially, is administered to produce a relaxed semi-hypnotic state in the prisoner whereby he or she offers little resistance and information is easily obtained.

Violent sexual acts: A variety of methods have been documented. Torturers frequently violate detainees; mutilating devices are often inserted in the vagina or anus. At times male detainees are sexually violated.

Notes

1. Kathleen Barry, *Female Sexual Slavery* (New York, Avon Books, 1979).
2. Evelyn P. Stevens, 'Marianismo: the other face of machismo in Latin America', in Ann Pescatello (ed.), *Female and Male in Latin America* (Pittsburgh, University of Pittsburgh Press, 1973).
3. Mariolatry, 'by any other name', and its attendant conceptions of madonna/whore – Mors per Evam, Vita per Miriam – is indeed *global*, in the socialization of women, in the schematization of women in patriarchy. It is simply more superficially apparent in Latin America, through the entrenched dominance of Catholicism.
4. Amnesty International, *Testimony on Secret Detention Camps in Argentina* (USA, Amnesty International Publications, 1988).
5. Latin American and Caribbean Women's Collective, *Slaves of Slaves: the Challenge of Latin American Women* (London, Zed Press, 1980).
6. Cynthia, Enloe, 'The Military Model', 'Nato: what is it and why should women care?' and 'Nato: the lesson machine', in W. Chapkis (ed.), *Loaded Questions: Women in the Military* (Amsterdam/Washington, DC, Transnational Institute, 1981).

7. *Ten Years of Activities 1971–1981* (Washington, DC, General Secretariat of the Organization of American States, 1982).
8. Comisión Internacional de Investigación de los Crimenes de la Junta Militar en Chile, *Denuncia y Testimonio* (Helsinki, Comisión Internacional de Investigación de los Crimenes de la Junta Militar en Chile, 1975).
9. Barry.
10. Amnesty International, *Children* (London, Amnesty Publications, 1979).
11. Amnesty International Reports 1980 and 1981 (London, Amnesty Publications).
12. The Mothers of the Plaza de Mayo circle in silence for half an hour daily wearing white headscarves and bearing the photos of their 'missing' ones. For Mother's Day of October 1981, over 5,000 women filled the square. The Grandmothers of the Plaza de Mayo share a small office and their placards with the mothers' group but petition on their own for the approximately 800 missing children of missing parents. The grandmothers believe that their grandchildren are in official and clandestine orphanages or that they have been adopted in Argentina and in neighbouring countries. Some of Argentina's 'missing children' have been found in Uruguay, Brazil and Chile. Unfortunately, too few have been found – see *Buenos Aires Herald*, 11 July 1981; *Guardian*, 28 November 1981; *Connexions, An International Women's Quarterly*, Winter 1983, No. 7.

The Rape of Women in Bosnia
Slavenka Drakulić

The widespread media coverage of the rape of Bosnian women by Serbian soldiers, in early 1993, risked presenting it as something exceptional. In fact the use of rape in war is nothing new. As Christine Chinkin, professor of law at Southampton University, pointed out at Amnesty International's second annual conference on women and human rights that same year, the rape and abuse of women in armed conflict has a long history. She went on to cite attacks from Kuwait, Somalia, Peru, Liberia, Burma and Japan before elaborating on the theory that the rape of women during war is a consequence of male power and masculine privilege, both a deliberate instrument of war and a response to it:

> The images and language of conflict are masculinized. There are numerous examples: war makes 'men' out of boys; weapons are judged by their depth of 'penetration'; countries are 'raped'. ...
> An article in the *Sydney Morning Herald* during the Gulf War described the 'rape' of Kuwait. This concentrated upon the pillaging and removal from Kuwait by Iraq of essential

176

transport, industrial machinery, luxury goods and food rather than on the physical rape of Kuwaiti and foreign women. Rape is not merely an image or metaphor of war, but a reality to women as victims of war.[1]

Slavenka Drakulić is a Croatian writer living in Zagreb. Her works include two books of essays, *How we Survived Communism and Even Laughed* and *Balkan Express*, and a novel, *Holograms of Fear*. The following article was first published in *Elle* magazine, April 1993, and is reprinted with kind permission from the author.

The room is tiny, about three metres by four, with one small window barely letting in any light on a gloomy winter morning. Outside, it's bitterly cold. Stiff, frozen pieces of washing are hanging on a clothesline stretched between the barrack huts. This is Resnik, a refugee camp near the city of Zagreb in Croatia, with 9,000 refugees from Bosnia and Herzegovina. Most are Muslims. They have lived here for months now, 10 to 15 in one room. They are not allowed to cook, they have to carry water from outside and the nearest lavatory is along a path 50 metres away.

In the Kahrimanovic family's room are six bunk beds and one stove. All they possess is laid out on the beds: some clothes, toys, cans of food, two or three pots. Yet these people from Kozarac, a village in Bosnia, consider themselves lucky. They have survived.

The crowded room smells of coffee, dampness and unwashed bodies. Eight men, five women and five children are sitting in a circle, eager to talk. I am here to talk about rape, and they know it, but they prefer to talk about war, about how much land they owned, how many cattle, the size of their houses.

Men talk about how they survived Omarska and Trnopolje concentration camps. Time is passing, less and less light comes through the window, but they don't mention the subject. Finally, I have to say it, to ask if they have heard of mass rapes, if they saw any. There is a silence, even among the children, as if that horrible word renders them speechless.

I sense it is the wrong way to ask the question, wrong time, wrong context, but it is too late – I feel doors closing.

Then I get a kind of unison answer: there were no women raped in our village. We were just lucky I guess, says one of the women. But yes, we heard that it happened in other villages, adds Smail cautiously; he is the oldest man in the room. After his words, it is a little easier to breathe, but the conversation suddenly stops. People are getting up and leaving, a sign that I should do the same. As I am walking out, an old woman, Hajra, comes after me: 'Come tomorrow, my child,' she says quietly, 'then we'll tell you what we know. We can't talk about these things in front of men.'

This reaction was not unexpected. Since September 1992, when it became clear that mass rape was happening in Bosnia, women have been exposed to this kind of questioning almost daily. Reporters get off the plane in Zagreb (it's safe, conveniently located, has an airport and shelters a lot of refugees) and walk into one of five or six refugee camps nearby to ask the question a British journalist chose as the title for his 1980s book about life as a foreign correspondent: *Anyone Here Been Raped and Speaks English?*

Most of the time they run into the wall of silence which is driving everyone crazy: reporters, humanitarian and feminist activists, United Nations (UN) representatives, UN High Commission for Refugees specialists, European Community commissions, human rights organizations ... all keep arriving in their masses, passing through tiny, cramped rooms in the hope of getting a closer picture. Most will leave empty-handed, or will go to Tuzla or Zenica in Bosnia, where women and doctors are more open because they are not yet out of the war, not yet in a position to try to forget.

Investigators are disappointed that after all the fuss in the world media, women are more silent than ever. Don't they know it is good for them to talk? Well, the issue is more complicated than that, and the fact that their evidence might identify a war criminal is not their main concern.

Many have lost touch with family members – husbands and sons are still fighting or in concentration camps, or they have disappeared – and they don't know if they are still alive. Talking might jeopardize these lives. But perhaps the most important reason is that they want to hide it. They live in the domain of the unspeakable, suffering the ultimate humiliation. If anyone knows, their lives are ruined. They are ruined anyway; the invisible scar will never heal, but it is better to hide their pain and shame from others, from relatives and neighbours.

What makes us believe that a woman raped in wartime will be any more disposed to speak out than other rape victims? Perhaps we expect her to feel less guilty because she is one of thousands, but it isn't like that. A woman whose family knows she was raped told me none of them ever mentioned it. I asked if women talk among themselves. No, she said, they prefer to go through it alone.

It is extremely difficult to gather reliable information under conditions of war – living and working in cellars with no facilities at all, constant shelling and lack of food. In Bosnia, where a government war crimes commission is compiling evidence, documents are collected at random from the police, the Ministry of the Interior, hospitals or individual doctors. The Bosnians are not using the rapes as a propaganda tool. All they have done is publish estimated numbers and submit a report to the UN, as if they would prefer to hide it. And yet there are enough established facts to

Join **WAR** and fight for Human Dignity.

WAR AGAINST RAPE

conclude that tens of thousands of women is Bosnia and Herzegovina are being raped. The precise numbers may never be known, but numbers are not the issue.

When I returned a second day to Resnik, there were only five women in the room. Then the youngest, 17-year-old Mersiha, who just the day before strongly denied that she'd seen any rapes, changed her story: 'Five of my schoolmates were raped and then killed. They lay in a ditch for days. As I passed I didn't want to look, but I did. Their clothes were torn off and I could see they had been tortured. There were knife wounds on their breasts and stomachs.

'One afternoon, about 50 of us women were walking through the woods back to our village from a concentration camp where my brother was imprisoned when we found armed Chetniks waiting for us. It was impossible to escape. They picked out two. About 10 Chetniks raped them in front of us. We were forced to stand and watch. It was dark when they released us and I still remember how one of them shivered when I took off my jacket and put it on her naked shoulders.'

While she talked, the other women stared at the floor as if they were guilty. I asked Mersiha, but what about you? She looked across at her mother as if asking for permission to say more. 'No, it did not happen to me,' she said, but I was not convinced. Maybe, if I came another day, and yet another, she would tell a different story.

But Mersiha did speak of a cousin's experience. This led me to a refugee camp in Karlovac, to a network of frightened women who know each other's misery, but hide it. The 30-year-old was raped by four Serbian boys barely over 20 – not drunk, not crazy. Boys she knew from a nearby Serbian village.

'After all these months, I still feel branded. I can't get rid of the feeling of being physically dirty and guilty,' she told me. When I asked if she would go back, I received the same reply that I heard from many Muslims, not necessarily raped and not necessarily women: 'Under no condition would I live in the same village as Serbs. I would never let my children go to school with their children. I would not work with them, or even live in the same state.'

These words, more than anything, reveal the nature of the crime and the point where this kind of mass rape gets its proper name: ethnic cleansing.

Women have been raped in every war – as retaliation, as damage to another man's 'property', as a message to the enemy. Rape is an efficient weapon for demoralization and humiliation. In the Second World War, Russian and Jewish women were raped, Soviet soldiers raped German women in their hundreds of thousands. Chinese women were raped by the Japanese, Vietnamese by Americans. There is nothing unprecedented about this case except that there is a visible political aim behind it. It is an organized and systematic attempt to clean (to move, resettle, exile) the Muslim population out of territories Serbs want in order to establish an ethnically 'clean' nation-state of Great Serbia.

Women are impregnated on purpose in great numbers (the estimate of the Bosnian Ministry of Works and Social Affairs is some 35,000) and released only after abortion is impossible, 'to give birth to little Chetniks'.

If Muslim men are killed and exterminated in around 150 concentration camps (some 120,000 have died in Bosnia, and about 60,000 are missing), if women are humiliated, impregnated and expelled from their country, then not only is their traditional cultural and religious integrity destroyed, but the reproductive potential of the entire nation is threatened.

It should not be forgotten that Croats and Muslims raped Serbian women in Bosnia too – but the Serbs are the aggressors and their aim is to take two-thirds of the territory. This does not excuse Croats or Muslims, but they are in a defensive war, and at least do not have organized rape as a political aim.

Bosnian Muslims who have been raped have almost no future. In spite of a *fatwa* issued by religious leaders that men should marry them and raise their children as Muslim, that is not likely to happen. One woman told me she would kill herself, even if her husband would be willing to take her back, rather than endure the shame and humiliation. One of the most frequently used words in connection with rape is death.

Equally disturbing and painful is their attitude towards the babies who will be born from these crimes. Without exception, they said they would kill the child ('I'd strangle it with my own hands,' as Hajra put it), or at best, abandon it. Many are already mothers, and for a woman to have such feelings towards what is, after all, her child too, shows the strength of their emotions.

Note

1. See Christine M. Chinkin, 'Women and peace: militarism and oppression', in K.E. Mahoney and P. Mahoney (eds.), *Human Rights in the Twenty-first Century* (Kluwer, 1993).

Part 5
Government Measures
and the Law

Government Measures to Confront Violence Against Women
Jane Connors

A senior lecturer in law at the University of London's School of Oriental and African Studies, Jane Connors is among an international group of activists, United Nations human rights experts, international law scholars and government officials working towards the elimination of gender-based violence and its recognition as a human rights issue. Among several publications, including the definitive UN study *Violence Against Women in the Family* (1989), she is one of the key contributors to *Strategies for Confronting Domestic Violence: a Resource Manual* (see p. 260). The following is expanded from one of two contributions by Jane Connors published in *Combating Violence Against Women*, a report by the International League for Human Rights (March 1993).

Violence against women, in all its manifestations, has emerged over the last decade as a matter requiring priority attention, with evidence from all over the world revealing that violence in the home, sexual assault and sexual harassment are risks common to all women, irrespective of colour, social class, race, ethnicity, sexual preference, religion and culture.

The following analysis outlines the current strategies employed by governments to confront violence against women. These strategies remain at various levels of sophistication and development from country to country and thus, necessarily, the account is generalized. I

Enough Violence: Raymunda Guillén/Manuela Ramos, Peru.

also examine methods which are now being introduced at intergovernmental level, both internationally and regionally, to reduce and eliminate the problem.

Most governments confronting various forms of violence against women have tended to approach the problem as one requiring legal solutions. Certainly, other initiatives, including shelters and refuges, have also been used, but in general these have emerged as *ad hoc*, grassroots and activist responses rather than the original response of government.

In the context of legal responses to violence against women a number of general issues deserve mention. First, in most countries (except where sexual abuses are concerned) such violence receives no special treatment in the law, meaning that women have to rely on the general law. Second, most legal systems have not displayed a synthetic approach to the problem. In other words, the laws of most legal systems address the various manifestations of violence against women separately, with no suggestion that they may have a uniform or even related structural cause. This has meant that, practically speaking, laws concerning different forms of such violence are located in different legal remedies and texts. From a theoretical viewpoint, this failure to adopt a synthetic legal approach has resulted in a general failure to link the various manifestations of violence against women to subordination of and discrimination against women generally. The failure to adopt a synthetic approach in legal remedy has affected other areas, so that service provision and other strategies employed to address the problem have also developed in a fragmented way.

Through focusing on legal strategies, the following analysis reflects this approach, describing government measures that have been initiated to confront four distinct types of violence against women: domestic violence or violence against women in the household; sexual harassment; sexual assault; and violence related to tradition and culture.

Before these are considered, however, it is important to be aware of three key factors concerning law and law reform. First, despite the important role the latter play in addressing manifestations of violence against women, the law does not constitute a neutral force, but reflects the interests of those who are dominant in any society. Accordingly, no matter how benign legal initiatives in this area may appear to be, they will reflect the interests of that society's power-holders who are, in essence, comprised of the patriarchy. Even where such initiatives and reforms truly reflect the interests of women, they remain part of the wider legal framework and its structures. Therefore, law and law reform regarding violence against women must be constantly challenged so that laws and the legal system do not act, no matter how subtly, to reinforce male control. Second, however important innovative legal measures may be, they of themselves do not provide the solution: they are merely the backdrop to other measures that may be more effective. Finally, as with all strategies to confront violence against women, legal measures must be tailored to the socio-economic and cultural make-up of each community. It is well to be cautious when seeking to transplant any strategy, especially a legal strategy, from one cultural context to another.

Domestic violence

Legal approaches

The central question confronting governments when they address violence against women in the household – whether perpetrated by the woman's partner, parent, child or other relative – is the appropriateness of criminal justice measures as a means of addressing the problem. Two divergent approaches have emerged as dominant responses to this question. One is that the criminal law is totally inappropriate, and that a conciliation/welfare approach stressing mediation and therapy is preferable. The other urges that domestic assault is criminal conduct and should be treated no differently from similar conduct occurring in other contexts, notwithstanding the fact that it takes place in the family and occurs between intimates. While some legal approaches to domestic violence take a purely welfare approach and others advocate criminal sanction in all cases, many others occupy an intermediate place along the spectrum between these two extremes. Western governments have tended to favour a criminal justice approach.

While the relative emphasis on civil and criminal law varies among national legal responses to domestic violence, most countries now have laws that protect women who are the victims of domestic violence. Such laws not only provide individual victims with remedies, should they choose to take advantage of them, but also indicate a national policy commitment to oppose domestic assault. All governments should be encouraged to introduce clear, accessible and well-integrated legal provisions, appropriate to the particular country situation.

General laws applied to domestic violence: Virtually all countries have legal measures, such as criminal tortious sanctions, that are applicable to cases of assault generally and are, therefore, theoretically available in cases of domestic assault. Most countries provide matrimonial relief, such as divorce or judicial separation, for those who are violently abused by their spouses.

But these remedies have proven to be inadequate responses to domestic violence. In most countries, general criminal sanctions are not applied unless the violence suffered is particularly severe. And when these measures are used, the general criminal law is not sufficiently responsive to the particular issues that arise in the case of domestic assault. While matrimonial relief provides a remedy for some women, it is of course available only to those who are married, and even in those cases may not be desired by the victim, who often seeks to end the violence rather than the relationship with her partner.

Special laws adopted to address domestic violence: Some countries have introduced special legal approaches to confront domestic violence. In general, these have developed from two existing legal remedies: the breach of the peace procedure and the injunction.

In many countries there is a procedure for lodging a complaint of threatened or actual violence before a magistrate or justice, who then can request the violent party to enter into an undertaking, with or without a pledge of money, to keep the peace or be of good behaviour. If the undertaking is breached, the offender forfeits a specified sum of money or is imprisoned. The process is criminal, but the standard of proof is lower than that ordinarily applied in criminal proceedings. While this procedure holds forth some potential as a remedy for victims of domestic assault, enforcement of the remedy may be unduly cumbersome, requiring a further court appearance, initiated by the victim or the police.

Some countries have modified and strengthened this procedure to make it more useful in the context of domestic violence, while others have adopted similar remedies, usually known as 'protection orders', that apply specifically to such violence. Generally, the remedy available through this procedure is a court order, obtained on the balance of probabilities, that can protect the victim from further attacks or harassment. Breach of the order is a criminal offence and the police can arrest, without warrant, a person who has contravened a protection order. The offender need not be present in court and the order is granted if it is shown that it is more probable than not that he caused or is about to cause damage. Ancillary orders can be obtained. These may include a direction that the offender is forbidden to approach the woman or her home, which he may have shared with her or, indeed, may legally own.

The role of police: Governments that emphasize the criminal nature of domestic abuse have generally recognized the central role of the police in responding to this form of violence. Recognizing that police traditionally have been reluctant to intervene in such cases, these governments have introduced strategies to encourage such intervention. These strategies have included legal measures, such as clarification of police powers of entry, arrest and bail procedures in cases of domestic violence and enactment of legislation that compels women to give evidence against their abusive spouses; and introduction of police force policies, such as presumptive arrest and charging policies and police training in the dynamics of legal approaches to and support services for domestic assaults.

Civil remedies: A number of governments have emphasized civil remedies, rather than criminal procedures, to protect individuals against domestic assault. These approaches have often built upon existing injunction or interdict proceedings in national law. In countries where these remedies can be obtained, they generally are available only incidentally to a principal cause of action, such as divorce, nullity or judicial separation. In some countries where these remedies have been made available to victims of domestic violence, these restrictions on access none the less persist in national law. In others, however, a victim of domestic violence can apply for injunctive relief independently of any other legal action. Usually, the relief available is of two varieties: an order prohibiting the offender from molesting or harassing the victim, and an order excluding or evicting the offender from a part or all of the matrimonial home or the area in which the home is situated. The orders are usually supported by a provision entitling the police to arrest the offender, without a warrant, if he breaches the order.

Implementation strategies: While appropriate legislation is an important step towards providing protection against domestic violence, law reform alone does not guarantee implementation, and indeed implementation of such laws has been disappointing in most countries. Even in countries where governments have made a high priority of reforming the law relating to domestic assault, implementation has been hampered by the attitudes of police, prosecutors, judges and magistrates and other major actors in the legal system, who have tended to view their role in such cases as one of mediation.

An effective legal response requires that, at all levels of the legal system, principal actors understand the dynamics of domestic violence; there is a consistent response at all levels of the legal system; offenders receive appropriate disposition and treatment at each level; and victims and their families receive appropriate services. Effective legal response and implementation requires, above all, that the government and society recognize that domestic violence is intolerable and that strong sanction is appropriate. This recognition should result in a response integrating legal approaches, service provision and training, and education measures.

Service provision

Although governmental responses to domestic violence have focused upon legal reform, legal remedies are generally the last resort for victims of domestic assault, who typically turn for help first to family and friends, religious leaders, health care professionals and social workers. While some non-governmental sectors have long recognized the problem of domestic violence, most societies have been slow to provide services for victims, offenders and their families.

Overall, the response of the health and welfare sectors to domestic violence has been disappointing. Professionals in these sectors, usually uneducated in the dynamics of domestic assault, have chosen to concentrate on the victim, rather than the offender, as the key to their response. In general, both sectors have looked at such violence as an individual rather than structural problem, and have stressed the importance of the maintenance of the family.

In many countries, services for victims of domestic violence have become available as a result of efforts by individual women or groups of women rather than at the initiative of the government. Often, however, once services have been made available by the efforts of such women, governments have stepped in and either taken over these services or introduced their own services modelled on those introduced by the voluntary sector.

Kenton Penly, 1993.

Shelter provision has proven to be the most important service for victims of domestic violence. Shelters, which were originally conceived as advice centres for women at risk and ultimately developed to provide residential accommodation for them and their children, exist in such varied countries as Trinidad and Tobago, Egypt, Malaysia, Zimbabwe and India. Although many are now government-staffed and funded, most were initiated by volunteer women who themselves had been victims of violence. In many countries where the government has adopted the shelter model, shelters are established for specific groups of women, such as immigrant women, women with disabilities, and aboriginal women. Unfortunately, even countries that have introduced shelters generally do not provide sufficient funding, and shelters are overcrowded and understaffed. Other services that exist for victims of domestic assault include toll-free advice lines, counselling services and advice centres.

Some governments have implemented programmes for offenders. Like shelters for battered women, many of these programmes began as community-based responses to domestic violence and many were linked to shelters. In some cases these programmes are part of diversion schemes or a court sentence. These schemes are new, and should be approached cautiously until their effectiveness can be assessed.

Research, training and education

Government-funded and -sponsored research into various aspects of violence against women in the family is well developed in various countries, some going so far as to have information clearinghouses on the subject. In most, however, research has not progressed beyond the rudimentary. Careful and rigorous research, particularly into strategies to confront domestic assault, should be a high priority.

A number of countries have initiated training programmes for professionals involved in domestic violence. Most of these programmes focus on the police, regarded as the front-line of response. While the programmes vary considerably, few countries offer police comprehensive and in-depth training in the dynamics of domestic violence, available forms of legal recourse, and the services available for the victims of domestic assault. Police in most countries receive no training in this area.

In some countries, law students, lawyers, magistrates and judges are made aware of domestic violence during their training, as are other professional groups, such as nurses, doctors, welfare and social workers. Again, this training is not routine and varies in quality and duration.

Some governments have recognized that domestic violence is the result of social norms and values that provide stereotypical roles for men and women, and have concluded that these views can best be addressed through education, both formal and informal. In some countries, the subjects of family violence and peaceful methods of conflict resolution form part of the primary and secondary curriculum.

Many countries have relied on informal education strategies both to inform women of their legal rights, available options and support systems, and to convey to both women and men that family violence is to be deplored. Such strategies have included poster campaigns, distribution of booklets and videos, television and radio advertising and folk theatre productions. It is perhaps in Australia that the crucial role of education in its widest sense has been most appreciated (see pp. 239–45). The federal government there initiated a National Domestic Violence Education Programme for the period 1987–90, the aims of which were fourfold: to raise awareness of domestic violence as a matter of community concern; to provide accurate information on domestic violence; to encourage widespread community participation in the campaign against domestic violence; and to change attitudes that cause such violence.

In the first year of the programme, a national survey was undertaken to develop information on community attitudes to abuse. This revealed, alarmingly, that one in five of the respondents condoned the use of physical force by a man against his wife in some circumstances, one-third of the respondents regarded domestic violence as a private matter, more than one-quarter would ignore a case of domestic violence in their neighbourhood, and nearly half knew either a victim or perpetrator of domestic violence personally.

In light of this response, revealing that the Australian community viewed domestic violence as a private, non-criminal matter, the government sponsored National Domestic Violence Month. Activities, including local debate, the preparation of information kits, posters and pamphlets, were co-ordinated at the local level. The month was launched by the Prime Minister and particular attention was paid to the development of materials for Aboriginal and Torres Strait islander women, immigrant women, women in isolated and rural communities, and young women. Videos, booklets and radio programmes were developed. The programme ended with a National Forum of Domestic Violence Training attended by over 500 people, which stressed the need for training for those who work with domestic assault.

Although the programme has now concluded, it established a strong momentum which will doubtless affect any further domestic violence strategies. It resulted in increased government funding, and an evaluation of community attitudes after the programme indicates that the Australian community no longer views domestic violence disinterestedly.

Sexual harassment

Legal approaches

Legal approaches to sexual harassment tend to vary with the nature of the offensive conduct and according to the circumstances in which the harassment occurs, with different remedies applying to harassment occurring in the street or in the workplace, respectively.

Most countries fail to provide remedies for harassment falling short of rape, sexual assault, indecent assault or common assault occurring outside the workplace. In exceptional cases, however, specific legislation prohibits sexually offensive behaviour, which is variously described as insulting the modesty of a woman, even as teasing.

A number of governments have recognized the importance of sexual harassment in the workplace and educational institutions, and the impact of such harassment both on the individual woman and on the effectiveness of an organization. These governments have allowed women who have been subject to such treatment to seek remedies under legislation pertaining to employment, such as sex discrimination or equal opportunity statutes, concluding that harassment in the workplace amounts to less favourable treatment on the basis of gender. Still others have enacted legislation specifically prohibiting sexual harassment in the contexts of employment, the provision of goods and services, and educational institutions; and providing remedies where such harassment occurs.

Although these laws are broadly similar in approach, some statutes are more effective than others, having wider definitions of harassment, extending coverage to contract and commission agents, allowing representative actions by unions, and fixing employers with vicarious liability for the harassment of their employees.

Non-legal approaches

In general, government measures to prevent sexual harassment have been confined to the introduction of legislation, leaving campaign and other publicity efforts to the initiative of trade unions, workers' associations and private organizations. A number of governments have, however, produced protocols or guides indicating how sexual harassment can be eliminated in both government and non-governmental institutions. A limited number of governments, such as that of New Zealand, have drafted standard form contracts, used when government contracts are concluded, that contain clauses forbidding harassment.

Some government bodies have promoted greater awareness of sexual harassment, its serious short- and long-term implications, and the educational strategies that can be used to confront the problem. The latter have included the production of pamphlets, protocols and advertisements. In 1990, the Human Rights and Equal Opportunity Commission of Australia conducted a poster, magazine and advertising campaign, which incorporated a toll-free complaint line, aimed at young women in vulnerable occupations. Women responded positively to the campaign, which has had a continuing impact.

Sexual assault

Legal approaches

Virtually all countries criminalize sexual offences against women through such crimes as abduction, defilement, indecent assault, procuration, unlawful detention for immoral purposes, and rape. Over the last decade, most countries have, however, witnessed demands for reform of both the substantive and the procedural law governing such offences.

In general, the areas of debate have been as follows:

• the scope of the offence
• whether sexual assault in marriage is a crime

- the question of the consent of the victim
- the related issue of the accused's perception or the complainant's consent
- evidentiary requirements, including the law of fresh complaint, the introduction of evidence as to the victim's past sexual history, and corroboration
- amelioration of court procedures
- sentencing
- the treatment of sexual assault complainants

Most countries that have reformed their law of rape and sexual assault have widened the definition of assaults regarded as particularly heinous beyond those involving penetration of the vagina and the anus by, for example, penalizing forced oral intercourse and treating this offence equally seriously. Further, a number of countries have made their legislation 'gender neutral', defining the crimes so that women and men can be both victims and offenders. Some have graded sexual assault in terms of seriousness, providing higher penalties where sexual contact is forced by violence or where sexual assault is perpetrated by a group. Some countries have removed the word 'rape' or its translation from the statute books, being of the opinion that use of this word militates against the acquisition of conviction.

A number of countries' laws now provide that unwanted sexual contact within marriage is unlawful, thus removing the rule that a wife, by the act of marriage, consents at all times to sexual contact with her husband. But criminal actions under these laws are rare, and successful prosecutions even more uncommon.

Substantive legislative reform in some countries has sought to change the focus at trials for sexual assault from the complainant to the accused. This effort has addressed the law's treatment of two issues: the question of the complainant's consent and the offender's perception of the complainant's consent.

In most jurisdictions, the prosecution must prove that the complainant did not consent to sexual contact to establish the crime of sexual assault. In the absence of fairly severe injury, this may be difficult, and in most jurisdictions is virtually impossible if the complainant knew, had a past sexual relationship with, or was involved with the offender in some way. Some reforming statutes have sought to shift the focus from the complainant's consent by defining situations in which the complainant's consent will be deemed to be absent. These include, for example, situations in which the complainant or another person is threatened with physical or economic retaliation; situations in which the accused falls into a particular category, such as a hospital worker, employer, prison official or police officer.

Many jurisdictions require an accused to have a particular mental state before he can be regarded as having sexually assaulted the complainant. In general, the prosecution must prove that the accused intended to have sexual intercourse with the complainant against her will or that he was recklessly indifferent to her wishes. In effect, this means that an accused must be acquitted if he is able to show, no matter how unreasonably, that he believed his victim consented to his attentions. Some countries, aware that this allows the accused to allege that the complainant enjoyed sexual contact in demeaning circumstances, have introduced reforms requiring the accused, once the prosecution has proved that the woman did not consent, to show that he believed, on reasonable grounds, that she consented. Such reforms thus preclude allegations by an accused that, although most women would be averse to sexual contact in the circumstances proved, the complainant had unusual sexual habits and desires.

Although there has been significant focus on the reform of the substantive law of sexual assault, evaluations of legislative reforms that have been instituted reveal that most women place more significance on reform of evidentiary and procedural aspects of this area of law. Thus, modifications of the requirements of fresh complaint and corroboration and of rules allowing introduction of evidence of the past sexual history of complainants have been welcomed as significantly ameliorating the complainant's ordeal and limiting the humiliation that she endures both in the courtroom and beforehand. Other measures, which have included provisions assuring complainants' anonymity, court procedures that hide the identity and deny the offender bail, or at least inform the complainant of the offender's whereabouts, have also been enthusiastically received.

Supports and services

Supports and services for victims of sexual assault, as with services for victims of domestic violence, have usually been initiated by individual women and women's groups. As with domestic violence, the models established by these women and groups have often later been adopted by the government.

In many countries, rape crisis services, toll-free advice lines, advice services and accommodations for women who are the victims of sexual assault are available. Some of these services are run by women's groups with no government support; others are operated by the government; and still others are operated by a combination of private and government sectors. Some operate autonomously, while others co-operate with the police; some are integrated formally with the police.

In most countries, police stations have traditionally been the principal sexual assault reception agencies. Overall, little attention has been paid to the singular ordeal that a rape complainant endures, and police stations generally are not equipped to alleviate this. Some, however, have taken account of the particular needs of sexual assault complainants, and offer a multidisciplinary approach to such complaints, often co-operating with hospitals or special clinics. In some countries, police have introduced special examination rooms, away from the station, to minimize the victim's ordeal.

Training and education

Victims of sexual assault are usually ashamed, guilty and afraid of how people will react to them. Many are humiliated, ridiculed, scorned and stigmatized by police and other workers, and treated with hostility and suspicion by their family and friends.

The negative response to the victim of rape stems from attitudes towards women, rape victims and rape that are the product of popular myth and prejudice. Women are believed to provoke sexual assault by the way they dress, where they go, and the way they move and behave. They are considered to be responsible for their own protection and are expected to ensure that they do not arouse male sexuality.

Evidence from many countries suggests that the police are particularly at risk of being misinformed by these stereotypes. They are thus frequently suspicious of complainants, particularly in cases where there is no obvious sign of injury, where the offender is known to the complainant, she delays reporting her assault, or appears calm and unemotional. If the complainant is perceived to be morally dubious, as, for example, when she is sexually experienced, her allegation may be deemed completely not credible.

Police suspicion may manifest itself in various ways: the complainant may be totally disbelieved and discouraged from pursuing her complaint; the investigation may be conducted in such a way as to test her story – insensitive, bullying interrogation may take place, for example, involving a series of officers and a medical examination in unpleasant or threatening circumstances; or the complainant may be kept uninformed of the progress of the investigation. Insensitive police procedures not only add to the ordeal of the complainant, but obstruct acquisition of the best evidence and militate against conviction of offenders.

In most countries, police officers receive basic training in the law and practice relating to sexual assault, but in most countries this training is brief and under-resourced. Some countries have recognized the importance of special police training and education in this area, and have introduced specific training and education at both the initial course level and at refresher and advanced levels. This training has typically emphasized methods of obtaining the best evidence for conviction, and has thus been technical, but some has included attitude training and sensitization. Most of this has taken the form of training courses, but some countries have employed kits and protocols that the investigating officer is directed to use in cases of complaints of sexual assault, which not only ensure that officers are meticulous in their collection of evidence, but also that they direct their inquiries sensitively.

Police officers are not the only group that needs to be educated in the dynamics of sexual assault. Prosecutors, defenders, judges and the general public require such training. Unfortunately, although some countries conduct specialized training in sexual assault for lawyers and judges, this area is not as developed as, for example, training in the area of domestic violence, and requires further attention. Again, although poster and advertising campaigns organized around domestic violence and sexual harassment have been conducted in many countries, sexual assault has not received the publicity it warrants.

Violence related to tradition and custom

In a number of countries, women are subjected to violent or harmful treatment by virtue of practices that are regarded as traditional, customary or prescribed by religion. These include violence related to dowry, widowhood rites, sati and genital mutilation.

There have been efforts to eradicate each of these practices by criminalizing them. However, here more than in other contexts where women are the subject of abuse, the law alone cannot be relied upon to change practices that are rooted deeply in tradition and culture and which, to a certain extent, are defended by both women and men, despite the fact that they have patently harmful consequences.

Harmful traditional and customary practices will be eradicated only when there is fundamental societal change, which will occur only with attitudinal changes at all levels. This sort of change can be achieved only with a combination of short- and long-term measures aimed at the particular practice and at the underlying cause: inequality. Such measures include formal and informal education, effective use of media and a clear commitment from government, which must be prepared not only to condemn such practices legislatively, but also to ensure that such legislation is implemented in good faith.

Legal measures

A succession of statutes in India and Bangladesh have sought to

195

criminalize violence related to dowry. These statutes establish the crime of dowry death, and establish severe penalties for those who demand, give, take or advertise dowry. Some of these laws include provisions that presume that the crime of dowry death has occurred in specified circumstances, and also strengthen police powers to respond to these crimes. India also criminalizes sati and its glorification. Some countries, such as Ghana, have been prepared to criminally sanction those who perpetrate harmful widowhood rites.

In general, criminalization of genital mutilation has occurred in countries, such as France and the United Kingdom, where the practice is confined to immigrant groups. In countries where the practice is customary, governments have more typically relied upon education, information and consciousness-raising campaigns to eradicate the practice.

Education

Legal strategies have not proved to be very effective in the context of traditional and customary practices. Certainly, dowry has not been eradicated in South Asia, and deaths and injuries occurring as a result of the practice continue to rise. Sati, on the other hand, is not a common practice, while widowhood rites appear unaffected by legal reforms. The incidence of female genital mutilation in countries that have criminalized the practice continues to rise.

Some commentators argue that stringent legal measures in the context of traditional practices may be counterproductive, serving to drive the practice underground or, indeed, encouraging it, as such legal measures may be perceived to be an attack on the particular tradition or cultural and societal system, rather than on the harmful practice itself. These commentators accordingly advocate education strategies.

In South Asia, education and information campaigns have been introduced to discourage the practice of dowry and its related harmful effects, and to eradicate sati. The Indian government, for example, has instituted television and cinema advertising campaigns that employ uncompromising commercials to discourage these practices. Further, in India a number of special police dowry units, headed by women officers, have been established; public lawyers have been appointed to assist women in the prosecution of dowry related crimes; and many women's organizations have actively campaigned on the issue.

Activity to eradicate genital mutilation has not been as focused as that to stop dowry-related violence, but in some countries where the practice is customary, poster campaigns and training modules for service providers have been introduced. These have sought to transform the social, religious and cultural bases of the practice.

Further, in a number of these countries, high-level government officials have publicly condemned the practice, drawing attention to the attendant health risks to girls and women (see pages 137–48).

Intergovernmental measures

Violence against women has been one of the concerns of the United Nations Division for the Advancement of Women since the beginning of the early 1980s. Its first Expert Group Meeting on the issue was held in December 1986; it published a research study on violence against women in the home in 1989, and collaborated with the Crime Branch of the United Nations in the production of a manual for criminal justice workers working in the area of domestic violence, which was released in 1993. The United Nations Committee on the Elimination of Discrimination Against Women (CEDAW), the supervisory body established under the International Convention on the Elimination of All Forms of Discrimination against Women, has formulated three recommendations on violence against women.

Recommendation 12, made in 1989, directed states to 'take appropriate steps to protect women from any form of violence within the family, at the workplace, or in any other area of social life' and report on those steps in their country reports required under the convention. In 1990 Recommendation 14 urged the eradication of female genital mutilation and the removal of cultural, economic and other pressures that help to perpetuate it and other harmful traditional practices. Recommendation 19, made in 1992, provides the most detailed guidance for states parties to follow where all forms of violence against women are concerned. Importantly, it links violence against women and gender discrimination, stating, 'Violence against women is both a consequence of systematic discrimination against women in public and private life, and a means by which constraints on women's rights are reinforced. Women are vulnerable because of disabilities imposed on them in economic, social, cultural, civil and political life and violence impairs the extent to which they are able to exercise *de jure* rights.'

The activities of the CEDAW committee in the area of violence against women have been complemented by work to formulate an International Declaration on the Elimination of Violence Against Women, the drafting of which was sponsored by the Commission on the Status of Women. Drafting of the declaration began in November 1991 at an Expert Group Meeting and was finalized at an Intersessional Working Group of the Commission on the Status of Women in September 1992. The draft declaration, which received the approval of the full commission, and the Economic and Social Council and the blessing of the World Conference on Human Rights in June 1993, was recently accepted by the United Nations General Assembly.

The declaration is significant in that it locates violence against women within the rubric of discrimination against women, categorizes it as a violation of human rights, and requires states to condemn violence against women and not to invoke any custom, tradition or religions or other consideration to avoid their obligations with respect to its elimination. It encourages states, without delay, to pursue by all appropriate means a policy of eliminating the problem. To this end, it encourages ratification of CEDAW, urges states to refrain from engaging in violence against women, and advocates that states exercise due diligence to prevent, investigate and punish acts of such violence, whether perpetrated by the state or by private persons. The declaration further includes specific programmatic suggestions aimed at eradicating violence against women.

Both the work of the CEDAW committee and the drafting of the Declaration on the Elimination of Violence Against Women testify to the seriousness with which the United Nations organisation and various of the member states view the differing manifestations of violence against women. The seriousness of the issue was underlined by the violent experiences of women in the former Yugoslavia during 1992 and 1993. Although women throughout history have suffered considerably during international and internal wars, and although women in current conflicts other than those in former Yugoslavia have proved to be similarly vulnerable, the visibility of, in particular, sexual abuses against women in a European conflict shocked the international community (see pages 176–81). Reaction included activities specifically designed to assist the women of former Yugoslavia and, also, greater support for strategies that had been considered in the context of the general problem of violence against women. Thus, the draft declaration attracted greater support, as did the proposal for the establishment of a United Nations special rapporteur with the dedicated brief of investigating violence against women. Indeed, the significance of the problem was acknowledged in the Declaration of the World Conference on Human Rights, held in Vienna in June 1993, while the programme of action agreed by the conference commended both the draft declaration and the proposed special rapporteur.

Intergovernmental activities on the issue have not been confined to the international level. The Council of Europe, following a number of meetings on the question, in 1991 issued a Solemn Declaration on the Elimination of Sexual Violence, while the Organization of American States (OAS) is involved in the preparation of an InterAmerican Convention on the Prevention, Punishment and Eradication of Violence Against Women. The OAS draft convention, like the UN declaration, links the various forms of violence against women to subordination of and discrimination against women generally and then seeks to bind states to various important measures of a legal, service and educational kind, which might lead to the reduction and ultimate elimination of women's victimization.

Conclusion

The diverse measures that have been introduced to confront the various forms of violence against women at country level are still relatively new, whilst, as we have seen, those promoted by intergovernmental bodies are still being developed. To a large extent, those measures that have been introduced have emerged in an *ad hoc* and reactive fashion. Further, many, particularly legal measures, have been put in place without adequate analysis of context. For example, legal approaches of Western states have often been introduced, without modification, in developing countries. Finally, many of the strategies introduced in this area have not been monitored or evaluated appropriately.

The importance of monitoring and evaluating strategies, and the wide dissemination of the results of such assessment, cannot be overrated. Their significance is illustrated by the 'pro-arrest' policies in cases of domestic violence which, as indicated above, have been widely advocated by activists and scholars who stress the criminal nature of violence against women in the home. Recent evaluations of these policies, however, suggest that, where certain groups are concerned, mandatory or presumptive arrest policies are counterproductive and, indeed, highly dangerous.

It is highly likely that the various forms of violence against women are linked and are based on a common cause – the subordination of women. It is likely, therefore, that many of the measures that are now employed to address this violence are merely treating the symptom, rather than the cause of the phenomenon. Work is now required to ensure that all measures interrelate and encompass effective approaches to address the legal, social and economic injustices that women face. One of the keys to the elimination of these injustices and the linked phenomenon of violence against women is global and state condemnation of the conduct, which will encourage a culture of justice for women in private and public life. There are various ways this condemnation can be conveyed – by constitutional provision, as in Brazil, by laws, by media campaigns and by education. It remains the case, however, that until such condemnation occurs, the measures employed to confront this specific form of injustice will continue to obscure the root cause of the phenomenon and perpetuate its existence.

Violence Against Women as Bias-motivated Hate Crime: Defining the Issues in the USA
Leslie Wolfe and Lois Copeland

For more than two decades, activists in the US movement against violence against women have campaigned for such violence to be treated by legal institutions as criminal behaviour. The following extracts, taken from a policy paper of the same name, examine the problem in the context of widely accepted definitions of bias-motivated hate crimes. Published by the Washington-based Center for Women Policy Studies, the paper was written in response to two related yet disparate events: the passage of the Hate Crimes Statistics Act of 1990 without inclusion of crimes based on gender, and the murder in the same year of 14 women engineering students in Montreal by Marc Lepine, who declared his intention to 'kill the feminists', lined up the women against the classroom wall, and opened fire with a .22-calibre automatic rifle. The authors seek to show that acts of violence based on gender – like acts of violence based on race, ethnicity, national origin, religion, and sexual identity – are not random, isolated crimes against persons who happen to be female. Rather, these are crimes against individuals that are meant to terrorize the larger group or class of people – women.

Definitions of hate crime: including crimes against women

While women often are the victims of violence for the same reasons men are (robbery, burglary, larceny, motor vehicle theft), women also are victims of violence simply because they are women. This continuum of hatred of women is expressed in forms ranging from sexist language and harassment to explosions of violence such as rape, assault and battery, and murder. Although such violence is traditionally seen as individual and 'personal', it is much more.

Yet the suggestion that violence against women as women should be defined as bias-motivated hate crime and included in anti-bias crime legislation has met with some resistance. Allies and partners in efforts to ensure equal rights for all have expressed doubts about the efficacy of including gender in hate crimes legislation, about the usefulness of defining rape, battery, and murder of women as bias-motivated hate crimes, and about the legitimacy of fashioning civil rights remedies for such crimes.

Violence against women does indeed meet the requirements of widely accepted definitions of hate crimes, which are acts of terrorism directed not only at the individual victims but at their entire community. It is violence directed toward groups of people who generally are not valued by the majority society, who suffer discrimination in other arenas, and who do not have full access to institutions meant to remedy social, political and economic injustice.

The most comprehensive definition of hate crime, which has been accepted by various anti-bias crime organizations, was originally developed by the California Attorney General's Commission on Racial, Ethnic, Religious, and Minority Violence.

> [a hate crime is] any act of intimidation, harassment, physical force or threat of physical force directed against any person, or family, or their property or advocate, motivated either in whole or in part by hostility to their real or perceived race, ethnic background, national origin, religious belief, sex, age, disability, or sexual orientation, with the intention of causing fear or intimidation, or to deter the free exercise or enjoyment of any rights or privileges secured by the Constitution or the laws of the United States or the State of California whether or not performed under color of law.[1]

It is interesting to note that this definition originally included 'sex' as a protected category; indeed, its history is instructive. While 'sex' was included in the definition itself that was adopted by the state of California, the journal article explicating the definition and the concept of hate crime did not include any discussion of gender-based hate crime.[2] This omission undoubtedly reflects the fact that even when violence against women is understood to be a pervasive form of hate violence, it remains ill-defined and often invisible except in feminist analyses of the kind cited above.

Other organizations have adopted the California definition, but have deleted 'sex' from the list of protected groups.

The Women's Project of Little Rock, which monitors hate crimes in Arkansas, includes violence against women in its definition of hate crime. In fact, the project adopted the definition of the California Task Force and, without realizing that 'sex' had originally been included in that definition, incorporated gender in its definition, believing it was the first group to do so. Indeed, the Women's Project

Women and Violence

RAPE AND THE LAW

The legal definition of rape is as provided by section 149 of the Fiji Penal Code;
Any person who has unlawful carnal knowledge of a woman or girl, without her consent, or with her consent if the consent is obtained by force or by means of threats or intimidation of any kind, or by fear of bodily harm, or by means of false representations as to the nature of the act, or in the case of a married woman by personating her husband, is guilty of the felony termed rape.

Section 150 — Punishment of rape —
States — Any person who attempts to commit rape is guilty of a felony and is liable to imprisonment for seven years, with or without corporal punishment.

Section 151 — Attempted rape —
States — Any person who attempts to commit rape is guilty of a felony and is liable to imprisonment for seven years, with or without corporal punishment.

In Fiji there are no categories of sexual assault — rape is rape provided that the victim did not consent, and penile penetration occurred. The age of the victim is not relevant and the degree of injury suffered only arises when the judge is sentencing the rapist i.e. if the rape is accompanied by other injuries the sentencing will be heavier. All other assaults fall into the category of indecent assault i.e. where penetration did not occur.

Defilement in Fiji is different from rape i.e. a defilement charge is laid where the victim is under the age of 16 and has consented to the sexual assault or is not capable of giving her consent. Frequently sexual abuse of children falls into this category where penetration has occurred.

On the face of it the definition of rape as provided by Section 149 of the Fiji Penal Code appears to be a reasonably wide one. In practice however, it is given the narrow interpretation by the Courts that rape must involve penetration of the vagina by the penis. Any other type of sexual assault is regarded as being indecent assault which carries a much lighter sentence.

Because of this interpretation, the definition of rape needs to be broadened to include instruments other than the penis, and the vagina should not be the only part of the body protected by the law relating to rape.

Rape and the Law, complied by Fiji Women's Rights Movement, 313158.

is one of very few that monitors sexist, racist, anti-Semitic and homophobic hate violence. In support of its inclusion of violence against women as hate crime, the Women's Project states that 'hate violence comes from generalized hatred or prejudice toward a group of people who hold in common a single difference from the defined norm – religion, race, gender, sexual identity – and it evolves out of a societal system of oppression such as anti-Semitism, racism [or] sexism'.[3]

Peter Finn suggests that hate crimes can range from threatening phone calls to murder; they include the full range of words or actions intended to intimidate or injure an individual because of his or her race, religion, national origin, or sexual identity.[4] He also suggests guidelines for identifying whether a crime is bias-related, which have been adopted by the National Institute of Justice:

- common sense (such as burning a cross on a lawn)
- language used by the perpetrator (such as slurs)
- severity of the attack (including mutilation)
- lack of provocation
- previous history of similar incidents in the same area
- absence of any other apparent motive (battery without robbery, for example).[5]

Acts of violence against women – from threatening, obscene telephone calls to street harassment, from battering to rape to serial murders with mutilation – clearly include many of these characteristics.

Hate language

The use of racial, ethnic, and homophobic slurs characterizes either a verbal attack or the defacing of property as a hate crime. Women too are subject to hate language – sexual innuendos, catcalls, threats and other street harassment – that are meant to intimidate, harass, and denigrate each woman and all women. Such hate language often accompanies violent assaults on women, including rape and wife abuse, yet women are the only group in society that is expected to view such harassment as 'flattery'.

The intimidating effect of hate language is being recognized on many campuses, for example. Confronted by an increase in racist, homophobic, and sexist hate language, colleges and universities are adopting restrictions on such verbal violence, acknowledging that racist and sexist speech disrupts students' lives and destroys the learning environment.

Absence of motive

Many experts believe that so-called 'motiveless crimes' – such as battery without robbery, or murder without an apparent motive – are indicative of hate crimes.[6] Both media and police reports officially define virtually all serial murders of women and many individual murders of women by men as 'motiveless crimes'. The 'motive' for rape is increasingly understood to be hatred of all women, rather than sexual desire for a particular woman – thus suggesting hate crime. Further, wife abuse is clearly a 'motiveless' crime of domination and control. In virtually all of these cases, the 'motive' is hatred and anger at women, and a desire to control, acted out on a particular woman.

Federal and state law reform for the 1990s

Despite this and much more evidence, crimes motivated by gender hatred are not included in most anti-bias crime legislation at either the federal or state levels. While the law alone cannot change attitudes, laws do make a statement about a society's values. Laws that punish hate crimes declare that such violence will not be tolerated.

In response to the increase in the number of hate crimes across the country during the 1980s, a number of groups united to push for enactment of laws that would confront bias crime and improve the response of the criminal justice system. At the federal level, a broad coalition representing people of color, gay men and lesbians, religious minorities, and women, have come together to document and combat the pervasiveness of hate crimes. Among them are the private advocacy organizations that have been collecting statistics on hate crimes, such as the Anti-Defamation League of B'nai B'rith, the Center for Democratic Renewal, the Southern Poverty Law Center, and the National Gay and Lesbian Task Force.

The Hate Crime Statistics Act of 1990

Largely in response to the coalition's efforts, the Congress passed the Hate Crime Statistics Act in the spring of 1990, requiring the Department of Justice, for the first time, to collect statistics on hate crimes.

When the bill first was introduced in the 99th Congress, it only required data collection on crimes motivated by racial, ethnic, or religious prejudice. Crimes based on sexual identity were included in the revised legislation, introduced in the 100th Congress. But the bill was amended to change the term 'sexual orientation' to 'homosexuality or heterosexuality', because some Members of Congress felt the definition was too broad.[7] While the bill passed the House of Representatives, it languished in the Senate because conservative Senators, led by Jesse Helms, disapproved of the inclusion of sexual identity.

Strong lobbying efforts by the Coalition on Hate Crimes Prevention helped pass the bill, which was signed into law in April 1990. The Hate Crime Statistics Act of 1990 (Public Law 101-275) mandates the collection and publication of data about crimes that manifest prejudice based on race, religion, homosexuality or heterosexuality, or ethnicity.[8] For the first time, the US Department of Justice is required to include data on the extent and nature of such crimes in its official crime reports. These statistics will help pinpoint the geographical location and extent of hate crimes and will identify both the perpetrators and the victims. Law enforcement agencies and public officials will be able to use the data to focus on problem areas, to promote new programs to improve community relations, and to punish perpetrators. In addition, the process of data collection will assist in evaluating the effectiveness of anti-bias crime legislation.

Crimes motivated by gender hatred are not included in the statute's mandate. Thus, although the Act's enumeration of violent crimes for which data are to be collected includes 'forcible rape', for example, 'gender' is not included as a protected category. An act of sexual violence against a woman can only be categorized as a hate crime, therefore, if she also 'fits' another protected category and can claim that she was raped because of her race, ethnicity, sexual identity, or religion.

Although women's groups that were part of the Coalition on Hate Crimes Prevention introduced the idea of including gender, the coalition decided not to do so, for a variety of reasons. The first was a strategic one: some members of the coalition wanted the bill to pass quickly and believed that including gender would delay passage; they suggested that the coalition could consider including gender bias at a later time.

Some groups also expressed the concern that including gender would open the door to lobbying by other groups for inclusion of violence based on age, disability, position in a labor dispute, party affiliation, or membership in the armed forces. Others believed that including gender would make the Hate Crime Statistics Act too cumbersome and complicated, thus hampering enforcement.

Others who opposed inclusion of crimes against women in the Hate Crime Statistics Act suggested that data collection would be too difficult, because violent crime against women is so pervasive and not all acts of violence against women fit the definition of hate crime, particularly if the violence is committed by an acquaintance. To clarify these arguments, a staff member of the Anti-Defamation League's Civil Rights Division prepared an internal document that presented arguments for and against including gender in hate crimes statutes; one argument against including gender, for example, is that:

Women and Violence

a substantial majority of women victims of violent crimes were previously acquainted with their attackers. While a hate crime against a black sends a message to all blacks, the same logic does not follow in many sexual assaults. Victims are not necessarily 'interchangeable' in the same way; in cases of marital rape or date rape for example, the relationship between individual perpetrator and victim is the salient fact – whether the defendant is a woman-hater in general is irrelevant.[9]

Feminist theorists and advocates for battered women and rape survivors would not agree. As we have shown above, much of the violence against women that is not now defined as bias-motivated hate crime does indeed qualify for inclusion in that category. Rather than eliminate such crimes from consideration, careful analysis of data and crime reports – using guidelines for defining characteristics of hate crimes – could be mandated. As with crimes motivated by other forms of prejudice, a determination could be made whether a particular crime against a particular woman meets the criteria of a bias-motivated hate crime.

Further, the suggestion that 'the relationship' or acquaintanceship between victim and perpetrator is 'the salient fact' and that 'whether the defendant is a woman-hater in general is irrelevant' assumes the legitimacy of male ownership and domination of women. The notion that violence committed by an acquaintance or partner cannot, by definition, be motivated in major part by woman-hating in general ignores the reality of these crimes against women. Victims are indeed 'interchangeable' when a batterer abuses a second wife or a college student commits multiple date rapes, for example. We must identify the crime itself and its motivation rather than perpetuate old patriarchal notions. And we must also remember that crimes based on race, religion, ethnicity and sexual identity all have their own particular qualities as well; they are not necessarily identical but – as bias-motivated hate crimes – they share certain essential characteristics in common.

The Violence Against Women Act

The issue has been raised in Congress[10] by Senator Joseph Biden (D-DE), whose Violence Against Women Act, introduced in 1990 and again in 1991,[11] for the first time labels crimes of violence based on gender as bias or hate crimes that deprive women of civil rights. In his statement to a hearing of the Senate Judiciary Committee on the Violence Against Women Act, Senator Biden said:

This bill is to declare that sex crimes violate a woman's federally protected civil rights ... for too long, we have ignored the rights of women to be free from the fear of attacks based on

206

their gender. We as a nation – as a whole nation – will not tolerate these crimes perpetrated against women simply because they are women.[12]

Title III, 'Civil Rights', of the Violence Against Women Act provides civil rights remedies for survivors of gender-motivated crimes, defined as 'including rape, sexual assault, and sexual abuse, or any other crime of violence committed because of gender or on the basis of gender'.[13]

State anti-hate crime laws

In addition to the federal response, the increase in the incidence and severity of hate violence against people of color, gay men and lesbians, and Jews also has pressured virtually all of the states to enact some form of anti-hate crime legislation in recent years. According to Michael Lieberman of the Anti-Defamation League, 'the rationale for hate crime statutes is that this kind of crime has a greater impact ... than your average day-to-day crime'. It is a 'crime against society as well as the individual – and should be treated more harshly'.[14] Leaders in many communities that have enacted such legislation say that these laws have been effective in deterring crime and in sending a message to the community that prejudice and the violence it brings will not be tolerated.

All state hate crime laws cover acts of religious vandalism, most include ethnic and racial crimes, and a few include crimes based on sexual identity. In addition, some states have included age, disability, political affiliation, or membership in the armed forces as protected classes. However, while many states have taken the lead in combatting crimes based on prejudice and bigotry, only a few have included gender bias crimes. Minnesota, for example, is the only one to include sex – along with race, color, religion, sexual orientation, disability, and national origin – in its intimidation/harassment statute, its data collection requirements, and its training requirements for criminal justice personnel.[15]

All of the states (including the District of Columbia), with the single exception of Utah, have passed some form of hate crime statute. These state laws fall into five major categories:

- laws against institutional vandalism
- laws against intimidation
- civil action laws
- parental liability laws
- hate crimes statistics laws.

Statutes that punish the offender are an important part of a long-range effort to confront hate-motivated crimes. Under the criminal codes in most states, these acts already are prosecuted as assault and battery and murder, for example. Hate crimes statutes add specific prohibitions and punishments for these crimes when they are motivated by hatred of a protected group.

Some states have gone further by enacting statutes that enhance criminal penalties for hate-motivated crimes; these laws include protection from assault, harassment, intimidation, or destruction or defacement of property. Some include harsher penalties in cases of institutional vandalism, while others treat harassment – such as cross burnings and interference with religious worship – more harshly. Some state laws, such as Vermont's, increase penalties for any crime motivated by hatred for one of the groups named in the legislation.

A bill introduced in the New York Assembly would create new criminal offenses for hate crimes. An assailant motivated by racial, ethnic, religious, or sexual bigotry could be charged with additional felony counts and suffer harsher penalties; the proposal also would create a new crime of bias-related violence or intimidation in the first and second degree and would include 'sex, disability, age and sexual orientation' among the covered categories.

In addition, some states have added civil remedies, which allow victims to sue those who committed bias crimes against them for actual damages, unlimited punitive damages, and attorney's fees and costs.

Some states have enacted hate crimes legislation in response to brutal attacks on citizens. For example, a Vermont man was beaten outside a gay bar by an attacker who admitted he was attacking him because he was a 'fag'.[16] The statute that was subsequently passed by the Vermont legislature has been described as one of the toughest in the nation; it is one of the few state laws that includes age, gender, and sexual identity among its protected categories.

Robert Appel, Assistant Attorney General for Civil Rights of Vermont, described the importance of comprehensive hate crimes legislation:

> [T]his legislation was specifically designed to appropriately and proportionately punish crimes against minority persons based on an irrational hatred of said person because these crimes impact all members of the minority involved and not just the actual victim. These hate motivated crimes were intended to, and had the effect of, sending a message to all that they were not wanted in the community.[17]

But far-reaching as Vermont's legislation is, it does not require collection of data on hate crimes, thus limiting the community's knowledge of the nature and extent of hate violence.

Most law enforcement agencies do not keep separate records of bias crimes; thus, for example, they report anti-Jewish graffiti on a synagogue as vandalism, beating of a lesbian as assault and battery, and burning of a cross on an African American family's lawn as arson. Only states that have passed data collection statutes similar to the federal Hate Crime Statistics Act mandate the separate reporting of these acts as hate crimes.

To confront hate violence, states should enact comprehensive legislation that provides both criminal and civil remedies, mandates data collection, and provides for education of criminal justice and social service personnel about hate violence. State hate crimes statutes should include crimes against women among the covered categories, despite the specious reasoning that the huge number of crimes against women as women 'would overwhelm the system'.[18] This in itself suggests the urgency of confronting hate violence against women.

Monitoring hate crimes

Prior to enactment of either federal or state anti-bias crime statutes, private organizations responded to hate violence by monitoring hate crimes and tracking the activities of hate groups, drafting model legislation, and implementing anti-violence educational programs. Without the commitment of these organizations, no data would be available on these crimes. Their work remains essential, despite enactment of some data collection laws, because most states have not yet provided sufficient funding for data collection, there are inconsistencies in state and federal requirements, and many states have not yet begun to implement their recently passed laws. Further, these organizations play a crucial role in monitoring enforcement of hate crimes statutes at both the federal and state levels; and they bring public attention to the continuing existence of hate violence.[19]

At least four women's organizations monitor hate crimes; their work provides models for other local and state women's groups to replicate. More important, their work demonstrates to the larger anti-hate violence monitoring organizations that crimes against women can be included in their own research and monitoring programs.

The Texas Council on Family Violence was founded in 1978 to advance the battered women's shelter movement in Texas. The council also tracks and monitors violence against women, particularly domestic violence, in Texas, and publishes the 'Grim Tally' every month in its newsletter, *The River*. The 'Grim Tally' includes statistics on the number of women murdered and seriously assaulted by their male partners; it also reports the number of men killed by their female partners. The council's statistics come from its coalition of women's groups in the state, who clip news stories from local papers.

The council is a proactive organization that believes that women, not just wives, are the targets of violence because of their sex. In addition, the council states that this violence is not random and that it is inflicted on women without 'social remorse or protest'.[20] Advocacy and the empowerment of women through a strong grassroots movement are key ingredients of the council's mission, and it confronts difficult issues – such as AIDS in the shelter, understanding cultural differences among battered women, and violence against women as gender-bias hate crime. The council also conducts workshops on the needs of older battered women, of African American women experiencing violence, and of battered women in Hispanic communities, for example.

The Women's Project of Little Rock, Arkansas was founded in 1981 to eliminate sexism and racism; to achieve this ultimate goal, the Women's Project believes that classism, ageism, anti-Semitism, heterosexism, and gay- and lesbian-hating also must be eliminated. While the project is concerned for all women, its work focuses especially on those women who are traditionally underrepresented: – poor women, aged women, women of color, teenage mothers, lesbians, and women in prisons.[21]

The Women's Project has been monitoring hate violence in Arkansas since 1989,[22] and has created a monitoring model that can be replicated by women's groups in other states. Unlike other groups, the Women's Project monitors sexist violence along with racist, anti-Semitic and anti-gay and lesbian violence. In addition to monitoring hate violence and the activities of hate groups in Arkansas, the Women's Project holds workshops on understanding racism, gay- and lesbian-hating, and sexism and on developing methods to eliminate them and to educate the public and the criminal justice system. The Women's Project systematically collects data on *all* forms of violence against women.

The Women's Project uses a community organizing approach rather than a staff-centered approach to collect and document hate violence. More than 200 volunteers around the state track hate violence and their evidence is augmented by newspaper reports. The Women's Project's local volunteers help organize community responses to hate crimes, including protests, letters to the editor, victim support and advocacy. For example, the Women's Project organized the community to respond to gender violence by holding a funeral service for the 26 women killed in Arkansas during the first five months of 1990. On each tombstone was the name of the woman killed and news articles reporting how she was killed.[23]

The Women's Project believes that the local approach works best in organizing because it empowers the community of women to confront violence rather than to feel helpless. The project also is committed to working at the local level as the most effective way to bring about justice and social change. When the community works together, its members can develop an understanding of the groups that are victimized by hate violence, whether they are women, people of color, Jews, or gay men and lesbians.

Finally, two organizations have developed clearinghouses of information on crimes of violence against women. The National Clearinghouse on Marital and Date Rape was founded in 1980 to research, compile, and educate the public regarding the myths about rape that deny the fact that most rapes occur in the home and that many are committed by women's dates, partners, or husbands. The Clearinghouse follows current cases nationally and compiles files of legal briefs, legislative and litigative testimony, bills, statutes, law review articles, newspaper clippings, magazine and journal articles, statistics, anecdotal data on marital and date rape incidents, published and unpublished studies, and letters. The Clearinghouse provides testimony and assistance in preparing legislation to criminal justice personnel and policy-makers. In addition, the Clearinghouse staff makes presentations on marital and date rape on college campuses, to professional associations, and to the media.

The Clearinghouse on Femicide was founded in 1989 to confront the problem of murders of women. Its goal is to make femicide, defined as the murder of women and girls because they are female, an international crime under the United Nations mandate. The Clearinghouse does both activist and educational work; it maintains a database on victims of femicide, provides research for scholarly work in this area, and also works against misogyny and woman-killing through non-violent means. One of the Clearinghouse's first projects is to have 6 December declared an International Day of Remembrance.

Until women can live and work without fear of victimization and annihilation, we will not achieve our goal of a free and equal society. During the 1990s, hate violence against women must be confronted through the diverse strategies described in this report. Passage of federal and state laws such as those described above will send a message of support and encouragement to women struggling every day against abuse that ending hate violence and protecting women's equal rights remains a national priority.

In addition, local women's groups – including rape crisis centers, battered women's shelters, campus and community-based advocacy and service organizations – will continue to be the cornerstone of all efforts to define, monitor, and confront hate violence against women.

Notes

1. California Department of Justice, Attorney General's Commission on Racial, Ethnic, Religious, and Minority Violence, *Commission on Racial, Ethnic, Religious, and Minority Violence Final Report* (Sacramento, CA, Office of Attorney General, 1986).

2. Office of Criminal Justice Planning, California Department of Justice, 'Emerging criminal justice issue: When hate comes to town – preventing and intervening in community hate crimes', *Research Update, I,* (4), 1, 1989.

3. S. Pharr, 'Report from the women's watchcare network', *Transformation*, 3, Summer 1989.

4. P. Finn, 'Bias crime: a special target for prosecutors', *Prosecutor*, 14, Spring 1988.

5. Ibid.

6. Ibid.

7. US House of Representatives, *Hate Crimes Statistics Act Report 100-575* (100th Congress, 2nd session, 20 April 1988).

8. US Congress, *Hate Crime Statistics Act of 1990*. Public Law 101-275, 23 April 1990.

9. S.M. Freeman, *Policy Background Report – Hate Crimes Statutes: Including Women as Victims* (New York, ADL, 1990).

10. Other federal programs are designed to provide services to women who are victims of violence. The Family Violence Prevention and Services Act, administered by the Department of Health and Human Services, provides grants to states to establish, maintain, and expand shelters, and to provide counseling and related services to domestic violence victims and their dependents. The Victims of Crime Act (VOCA), administered by the Office of Justice Programs, Department of Justice, provides grants to states for programs serving victims of crime, primarily victims of domestic violence, sexual assault, and child abuse; funds are available for rape crisis programs and battered women's shelters, and for victims' compensation. The Office for Victims of Crime (OVC), administered by the Office of Justice Programs, established in 1983, administers sexual assault and abuse prevention programs.

During 1990, several bills were introduced in Congress on violence against women, and hearings have been held on rape, domestic violence, and abuse of women worldwide. Representative Constance Morella (R-MD) introduced a Sense of Congress Resolution on Domestic Violence that calls on judges to consider evidence of spousal abuse in child custody cases; Representative Morella also introduced Domestic Violence/Judicial Training Grants, a bill that would authorize the State Justice Institute to award grants to carry out research and develop judicial training relating to child custody litigation involving domestic violence and to develop training curricula for state judges. Both bills were reintroduced in the 102nd Congress (1991). Immigration Reform for Battered Spouses, introduced by Representative Louise Slaughter (D-NY), was passed as a provision of the omnibus bill restructuring the US immigration system; it allows immigrant abused spouses to file for permanent residency without having to remain in abusive marriages in order to qualify for permanent resident status.

11. Representative Barbara Boxer (D-CA) introduced the Violence Against Women Act in the House of Representatives in July, 1990 and introduced a somewhat modified version, H.R. 1502, 20 March 1991.

12. J. Biden. Opening statement, *Hearing on Violence Against Women Act* (Washington, DC, Committee on the Judiciary, US Senate, 20 June 1990).

13. Committee on the Judiciary, US Senate, *Violence Against Women Act of 1990*, Report 101-545 (Washington, DC, Committee on the Judiciary, 2 October 1990).

14. R. Sherman, 'Hate crimes statutes abound', *National Law Journal*, 12, (37), 3, May 1990.

15. Anti-Defamation League of B'nai B'rith, *Hate crimes statutes: A response to anti-Semitism, vandalism and violent bigotry, 1990 Supplement* (New York, ADL, 1990).

16. R. Sherman.

17. R. Appel, unpublished correspondence. Montpelier, VT, 2 May 1990.

18. Heinzerling, cited in Sherman.

19. Editor's note: the organizations referred to are the Anti-Defamation League (ADL) of B'nai B'rith, the National Institute Against Prejudice and Violence, the Southern Poverty Law Center, the Center for Democratic Renewal, and the National Gay and Lesbian Task Force (NGLTF). Details of their work are included in the full policy paper.

212

20. L. Heise, 'Crimes of gender: an issue of human rights', *The River*, VIII, (11-12), 9, 1989 (excerpted from *World/Watch*, March/April 1989).

21. S. Pharr, *Homophobia: a Weapon of Sexism* (Inverness, CA, Chardon Press, 1988).

22. S. Pharr, 'Hate violence against women', *Transformation*, 5, (1), 1, January 1990.

23. S. Pharr, Press statement, Little Rock, AR: the Women's Project, 30 May 1990.

The Experience in Pakistan
Farida Shaheed

Farida Shaheed is a founder member of the activist women's collective Shirkat-Gah, and of the Women's Action Forum, a consortium of women's groups that monitors developments concerning women in Pakistan. She is also one of three co-ordinators of Women Living Under Muslim Laws, an international network of groups and individuals concerned with the status of women living under Islamic law in over twenty countries.

The overview below is largely drawn from *Combating Violence Against Women*, a report by the International League for Human Rights (see page 259). It is followed by a short article by Beena Sarwar, reprinted from the *Frontier Post*, Lahore, 25 November 1991. Beena Sarwar is a journalist and active member of Shirkat-Gah.

The year 1991 was a particularly bad one in Pakistan, both in terms of violence against women and in terms of the erosion of human rights through a series of legislative acts. The year began and ended with campaigns protesting violence against women and calling for justice, particularly in the growing number of cases of torture and rape by members of the state's law enforcement agencies.

Hand in hand with this mounting violence has come the passage of a series of laws that have seriously eroded human rights and the independence of the judiciary. These laws include the Shariat Act, the Twelfth Amendment to the Constitution, the Terrorist Affected Areas Ordinance, and the Special Courts for Speedy Trials Ordinance. The effect of these laws is to undermine the work of grassroots organizations fighting violence against women and other human rights abuses.

The forms of violence against women and their causes

The forms of violence against women have remained constant. A much earlier survey by the Women's Action Forum indicated that there are three primary categories of gender-specific violence:

Acts perpetrated against women as individuals for a wide range of specific, individual acts

Thus, women have been killed, mutilated and abducted for:
- rejecting marriage proposals
- refusing to return to abusive husbands
- inability to fulfil the financial or material demands of their in-laws (dowry deaths)
- even something as trivial as not having dinner ready.

Violence in which women's bodies become the ravaged battleground for disputes between men

These cases include violence against women as a tool of political repression, and violence against women as a form of retaliation in disputes between men over property or insults to honour. In the latter cases, the worst punishment a man can inflict on another man is to insult, injure, torture or rape the latter's female relatives.

In 1984, for example, a group of well-to-do landlords in Nawabpur, a city in southern Punjab, murdered a peasant, who was suspected of having an amorous relationship with a landlord's wife, by beating him to death. The landlords then stripped the women in his house who had witnessed the murder, dragged them out of their home, molested them and forced them to walk naked through the village. The women thus became the targets of retaliation in a vendetta perpetrated by the landlord whose 'honour' had been violated by a man from a lower class.

Acts of violence against women as a class

Women, as the least powerful and least organized section of society, are systematically victimized as a class. The less powerful a woman is, the more likely she is to become a victim. The victimization of women occurs when a man, any man, asserts his power in society over any woman.

Much of the violence against women in Pakistan stems from an attitude that is also found in many other societies to greater or lesser degrees, that human beings are defined as men. Women are defined as 'non-men' and therefore less than, or something other than, 'human beings'.

Isis International, *Women in Action*, 2/88.

The role of the state

While violence against women is not new in Pakistan, a particularly disturbing development is the increasing involvement of the state. The state not only condones the abuse by turning a blind eye to specific acts of violence, but has itself become a leading perpetrator of violence against women. The state's failure to adopt adequate punitive measures has the effect of sanctioning violent abuses. Domestic violence and marital rape are not cognizable as crimes – much less punishable as such. Under the Hudood Ordinances of 1979, women have effectively been deprived of the protection of the law in all cases of rape.

The Offence of *Zina* (Enforcement of Hudood) Ordinance converts extra-marital intercourse (*zina*) into a crime against the state. Previously, extra-marital intercourse that was not acknowledged by the husband did not constitute a criminal offence. If the

215

Isis International, *Women in Action*, 2/88.

husband did acknowledge the adultery, only the other man stood accused. With the conversion of *zina* into a crime against the state under the Hudood Ordinance, any third person can file charges against another person without any proof. The ordinance has been abused by persons who file charges as a means of harassing their rivals or enemies.

The ordinance blurs the distinction between rape and extra-marital intercourse. It requires an extremely high level of proof to support imposition of the maximum penalty in cases of both rape and *zina*; the maximum penalties for rape and *zina* are stoning to death for married persons and 100 lashes for unmarried persons. The death penalty can be imposed only on the basis of the testimony of four adult male Muslims of good repute who witnessed the act of penetration, or on the basis of a voluntary confession before a competent court. The burden of proof falls on the complainant. Requiring the same level of proof for imposition of the death penalty in cases of rape as in cases of *zina* ensures that no rapists will ever receive the maximum punishment.

For example, in a widely publicized case, a 16-year-old near-blind girl named Safia Bibi filed a rape charge against her employer, who was acquitted due to lack of evidence. However, the judge convicted her of *zina* because she admitted to having borne a child out of wedlock. Following her conviction, the Women's Action Forum launched a massive protest at the national and international levels which resulted in the Federal Shariat Court taking *suo motu* notice of the case and overturning the judgment. The court held that pregnancy alone could not support a conviction for *zina*.

Simultaneously, the Law of Qisas and Diyat appears in some respects to have converted murder into a crime against the individual rather than the state. The law gives the family of a murder victim the right to ask either for punishment (*qisas*) or blood-money (*diyat*). On the face of it, it appears to have very damaging repercussions in cases where a person is murdered by another family member. The language of the law suggests that in cases of intra-family murders dependants cannot ask for *qisas*. The concept of *diyat* loses its meaning within the family. Although it is still unclear how the law will be applied in practice, it may be a means by which the state abdicates its responsibility to control violence in the most common type of intra-family murder – the killing of a female member by the male head of the family.

Rape, as the least reported crime, probably has the lowest rate of conviction. It is difficult to determine the reporting and conviction rates because no distinction is made between rape (*zina-bil-jabr*) and extra-marital intercourse (*zina*) when registering a First Information Report. The police have the discretion to register the First Information Report under the category they think appropriate. In 1981, for example, Fehmida Bux eloped with Allah Bux, married him, and went to live with him and his first wife. Their marriage was not registered until after she became pregnant. After Fehmida's parents failed to persuade her to return home and tried unsuccessfully to bribe Allah Bux to divorce her, they reported a case of abduction to the police. The police registered the case as one of adultery rather than abduction. Fehmida and Allah were convicted of *zina* and each was sentenced to 100 lashes. The sentence was overturned on appeal and the case was dismissed on remand.

The state law enforcement agencies are increasingly directly involved in perpetrating violence against women. It is estimated that of the hundreds of women taken into police custody every day, 80 per cent are raped in the police lock-ups. When the Women's Action Forum asked lower-class women to join a protest against the rape of women by police officers, they responded, 'If we are picked up by the police, we will be raped. What will you have to offer us then?' Unfortunately, I don't yet have an answer to that question.

The state has used rape to intimidate and punish activists and members of the political opposition. For example, in Karachi on 13 November 1991 Khurhseed Begum, the wife of a political prisoner,

এখন সময় উন্মোচনের

Isis International, *Women in Action*, 2/88.

was raped by men wearing police uniforms. On 27 November 1991 Veena Hayat, an activist in the Pakistan People's Party and a personal friend of Benazir Bhutto, was gang-raped by five masked men in her house in Karachi. Veena Hayat's case received considerable international attention and the government appointed a tribunal to investigate the case.

Women's organizational response

Women's organizations in Pakistan have demanded that the government take steps to end violence against women. Public outrage and pressure from women's groups following the events in Nawabpur led to the swift passage – within two weeks – of the Martial Law Ordinance, Section 354-A of the Pakistan Penal Code, which states that: 'Whoever assaults or uses criminal force to any woman and strips her of her clothes, and in that condition exposes her to the public view, shall be punished with death or imprisonment for life, and shall also be liable to fine.'

This law was promulgated in response to the specific incident in

Nawabpur, and was intended to pacify women's organizations and other groups that had embarrassed the government through their protests. It was not adopted pursuant to a broader concern with violence against women, but as a political manoeuvre of extremely limited practical significance. The law, which applies only in cases that exactly replicate the Nawabpur incident, fails to address the basic problem of violence against women. Additionally, it fails to satisfy the demands of women's organizations. The Women's Action Forum is opposed to capital punishment and considers the law to be severely flawed. It does not appear to have ever been invoked; we feel that it is a clear-cut example of the government passing a law not meant to be implemented.

In 1989, as a result of pressure by women's organizations, the Inspector General of Police for Punjab appointed a Special Liaison Officer to work with women's organizations and agreed to establish a women's police station. Unfortunately, this did not function well in practice; the female police officer appointed was fairly junior in rank and the police substation for women had no telephone.

In response to the abuse of women in police custody, the Lahore High Court passed a ruling that requires the police to ensure that a male relative accompanies any woman held in lock-up overnight. Women activists also tried to involve local women councillors in this process, but without significant results.

At the end of 1991, women's organizations stepped up their campaign on violence against women, especially in instances where members of the law enforcement agencies were implicated. After several confrontations with the present Inspector General of Police for Punjab, it was agreed that the police would recognize and co-operate with a Monitoring Cell composed of women's and human rights organizations. The purpose of this cell would be to act as a watchdog and to receive complaints directly, which would then be referred to the police for investigation. The women's police substation was promoted to a full station and a telephone was installed. It remains to be seen whether any of these initiatives will actually bear fruit.

' ... On Suspicion of Illicit Relations'
Beena Sarwar

'You see that young man who greeted me just now?' asked Azhar, pointing to a tall fellow disappearing into a *galli* (street) at the corner. 'It was just about this time last year that he killed his sister-in-law.'

We were in a small village in Haripur, near the Tarbela Dam. Azhar (not his real name) is a lawyer who practises there, dealing mostly with cases related to land disputes.

Why did the young man kill his sister-in-law, I wanted to know.

'Well, he suspected her of having illicit relations with someone.'

'You think that such suspicions justify murder?'

'No, of course not. But he wasn't just suspicious, he was sure.'

'And that makes it alright?'

Azhar smiled, suddenly not so sure of himself. 'Well ... ' he said, and told me the story as we walked between rows of flowering cornfields in the October sun, lagging behind the rest of our party. With us was Tahir, also from the village and 'Maulvi Sahib' [Muslim priest], who belongs to a politically active group in the Hazara area. Azhar said that the young girl (let's call her Mehreen) was Riaz's wife's sister. She was sixteen, and studying for her matriculation. Besides this relationship, she was also Riaz's second cousin. Apparently Riaz didn't like her going out of the house, and had repeatedly rebuked her for this.

That particular day, he accosted her as she returned home in the afternoon, and asked her where she'd been. She replied that she had gone to give some *kheer* [a sweet dish] to a relative living nearby. He didn't believe her and accused her of going to visit her lover. Mehreen retorted that it was none of his business. Riaz was hiding a loaded pistol behind his back. At her reply, he whipped it out and fired several shots at the girl, at point-blank range, killing her instantly.

Because Mehreen's family and Riaz's family were basically the same, nobody made a noise. The girl's mother was silenced by the heavy weight of family honour, and in order to keep this honour intact, Mehreen was buried quietly and the incident was hushed up. Later, someone leaked their secret to the police and a case was instituted. Mehreen's body was dug up and sent for post-mortem. Riaz was arrested for murder. As his lawyer, Azhar had been able to get him off on justifiable homicide, and at this particular moment he was out on bail.

'Do you think that it's right for someone to kill another human being, whether it's on suspicion or whether the "guilt" has been proved?' I asked.

'Well, perhaps not,' answered Azhar. 'But here you see, it's very different. We are still very backward, compared to other parts of the country.'

'How could you defend someone who had killed a young girl, on whatever grounds?'

'It's my job. And even if I hadn't got him released on bail, most people thought that he did right.'

'He's probably thought of as something of a hero, isn't he?'

Azhar agreed that this was so.

It was at this point that Maulvi Sahib unexpectedly put in a word taking my side of the argument. 'It's wrong,' he proclaimed. 'Very wrong. The right to take a life rests with Allah alone. Nowhere in our religion is it said that a man may kill another for such reasons.'

Finally Azhar grudgingly admitted that perhaps we were right, 'but what can I do? This is how people here think.'

'You are a prominent figure in this area,' I argued, 'It's up to you to take a stand, to discuss such issues with people and try and bring about some kind of change in their minds. How can a society progress if its men are allowed to kill women on such pretexts?' It was becoming quite a heated debate. I was trying to control my temper, while Azhar was torn between fulfilling his duties as urbane host and projecting himself as a progressive-minded individual, and the deep-rooted thinking which had developed over centuries.

We went to a wedding that night, and watched traditional dances performed by relatives and friends of the bride and groom. The only women present in that large, open courtyard were 'visitors' – myself included. Although we were practically blinded by the glare of a huge spotlight and the dust raised by the men's stamping boots, it was great fun. Then our hosts insisted that the guests should join in, and almost dragged poor Tito into the arena. It was only his vehemence and promises to join in 'later' which saved him.

'What do the women do while the men celebrate out here?' we asked.

'Oh, they also celebrate. But inside. We don't allow our women to mix with other men.'

It was later that an economic researcher from the area pointed out, 'They wouldn't have minded if you [women] had joined in. Purdah is only necessary for their own women. Someone should ask them about their double standards.'

The next day we met Azhar's wife, an educated and extremely pretty young woman. She said that she had obtained a law degree through a correspondence course. 'So you can practise with your husband now?' we asked.

'I could practise if we were living in Lahore or Islamabad,' she replied, 'But I can't practise here, with my own people.'

Since she can't practise law, she teaches instead, at a local primary girls' school. Azhar and his friends are among those who advocate more schools for girls, and lobby for a secondary school in the area as well.

Awareness about the need for greater female literacy seems to be quite acute in the area. A young man from a nearby village says that his younger sister goes to school, and that the family wants her at least to do her BA. That is, they may not actively encourage her to go to college, but they won't mind if she does.

'A decade ago,' he says, 'it was considered a sin for girls to study. So you see, times are changing.'

Perhaps they are. But while successive governments pay lip service to various human rights issues – after all, that's what you have to do to get aid these days – for the majority of Pakistanis living in rural and tribal areas these changes will never make a difference to the quality of their lives. Girls may go to school, even college. But when it comes to controlling their own lives, they will always have to bow before the wishes of their menfolk: grandfathers, fathers, uncles, brothers, brothers-in-law, cousins, husbands and sons.

Killing a woman 'on suspicion of illicit relations' is considered justifiable by the majority of people in our society. The insecurity of Pakistani men can perhaps be judged by the fact that the various family planning services run by government and non-government agencies pussyfoot around the issue of birth control, while a woman can't even undergo an operation without her husband's written permission.

Part 6
Education for Change

Talking Feminist Popular Education
Popular Education Research Group

Feminist popular education and international solidarity have been central themes for Toronto's Popular Education Research Group (PERG) since its formation as a non-profit organization in 1981. In September 1992, as part of its occasional publication series *Talking Feminist Popular Education*, the group produced a compilation of articles focusing on 'Educating to End Violence Against Women'. An extract from the introduction to this valuable compilation appears below, followed by contributions by Honor Ford-Smith from Sistren, Jamaica, and Lucrecia Oller, co-ordinator of the Violence Prevention Programme of Lugar de Mujer (A Woman's Place), Argentina. Many thanks to Lynda Yanz of PERG for permission to reprint this material.

Introduction

When women explore their social roles, if the issue of violence does not arise, the workshop methodology is not addressing the issue of gender.

Correspondencia, Mexico, August 1992

When we speak of male violence against women, a myriad of images come to mind; a battered wife, a rape victim, pornography, or the fear on a woman's face as she walks down a dark street at night. Our images of violence against women are shaped by the context in which we live, by our social class, personal experience, education, culture, and – of course – the media. These images are different in different societies and cultures.

Yet despite the differences, male violence against women is a daily reality for women everywhere. As women, we all live our lives circumscribed by the threat, if not the reality, of violence. And a disturbing trend seems to be increasing violence in all our countries.

Women's groups worldwide have organized to resist violence. They have been successful in bringing violence against women into public consciousness, in organizing and empowering women who are and/or have been victims of violence, and in educating and mobilizing (within communities, across countries, and internationally) to demand an end to male violence against women. They are challenging patriarchal claims and images that suggest male violence against women is a 'natural' state of affairs. They are exposing its roots in male power and control. Violence against women is a manifestation of deeply unequal gender relations in our societies, relations that cut across class and race divisions.

The work of women educators, organizers, and grassroot leaders – including the courageous efforts of women who themselves have begun to resist and take control over their lives – has in many respects been groundbreaking. This organizing has implications beyond the issue of violence. It presents a challenge to more traditional notions of political organizing, popular education and feminist pedagogy.

Popular education is a type of education which:
- *takes place within a democratic framework;*
- *is based on what learners are concerned about;*
- *poses questions and problems;*
- *examines unequal power relations in society;*
- *encourages everyone to learn and everyone to teach;*
- *involves high levels of participation;*
- *includes people's emotions, actions, intellects and creativity;*
- *uses varied activities.*

Popular education also follows a cycle of stages. It:
- *begins with people's own experiences;*
- *moves from experience to analysis;*
- *moves from analysis to encouraging collective action to change oppressive systems;*
- *reflects and evaluates its own process.*

From *On Our Feet, Taking Steps to Challenge Women's Oppression*, a handbook on gender and popular education workshops by Liz Mackenzie. Available from the Centre for Adult and Continuing Education (CACE), University of the Western Cape, Private Bag X17, Belleville 7535 South Africa or PERG. Cost $20.00, includes postage.

Women Educating to End Violence Against Women is an attempt to share examples of the work being done in this area. It focuses on the educational methods and strategies that women in different countries, working in radically different contexts, have developed to empower women, challenge unequal gender relations and stop violence.

No! to Sexual Violence in Jamaica
Honor Ford-Smith

Honor Ford-Smith was founding artistic director and drama tutor with Sistren, a working-class women's popular theatre collective in Jamaica. In an interview with Heather Chetwynd of the Popular Education Research Group (see above) she described Sistren's early efforts against violence against women.

Sistren began in 1977, with a core group of 13 black working-class women. It developed different areas of work: theatre, popular education workshops, a screen-printing operation, and a research and documentation department which produces the *Sistren* magazine.

Sistren was one of several different initiatives for organizing women, but it was the only group concentrating on how women make meaning out of their experiences. This was key to Sistren in those years. It represented in theatre how women see themselves and make meaning of their lives, in relation to sexual violence, work, and relationships with men and with other women.

As a cultural force, Sistren was important precisely because it looked at these issues at a time when women's sexuality was being portrayed very negatively through the media. Sistren gave women the chance to talk back to those images.

Originally, all this work was carried out by the central group. But later, Sistren began to organize other small groups of women in different areas of the country. These were called Friends of Sistren.

No! to sexual violence

One of the groups in Kingston decided to work on the issue of sexual violence. In 1984, it produced the pamphlet *No! to Sexual Violence*, and the Sistren theatre group produced a play to accompany it.

The aim was to stir up concern and awareness around the rising sexual violence against women, and to look at the causes for this kind of violence. The pamphlet was distributed to schools, community organizations, interested groups and political parties.

Its format made it quite popular. In the late 1980s, a revised edition was produced, taking into consideration criticisms which had been made. The original cover graphic was changed and statistics were updated.

Using theatre

The publication of *No! to Sexual Violence* served as a discussion starter, and produced various spin-offs. For example, the theatre and the popular education groups at Sistren began to do short workshops looking at different aspects of sexuality. These combined theatre and discussion, and were done all over the country, in schools, in community centres, in the street, and at Sistren headquarters.

REAL MEN
DON'T ABUSE
WOMEN

© Wave Belize and Sistren Jamaica.

We discussed issues like birth control, female and male sexuality, and domestic violence. We attempted to get the audience to define what they felt were expressions of violence against women as opposed to affectionate sexual experiences. We did this by presenting scenes which showed acts of violence between men and women and children, and then stopped and asked people what the problem was and how it could be solved. This allowed women to give their own interpretation of positive solutions. We then continued the play, incorporating their suggestions.

The idea was to create a critical attitude towards domestic and sexual violence, so that it wouldn't be seen as a natural outgrowth of the hierarchy in the home and society. We wanted women to see that men don't have the 'right' to beat and force women, and that women are not naturally required to submit to this. We also looked at the link between domestic violence and issues of class.

The Sistren theatre group produced pieces which highlighted the fact that women were being raped or battered in a way that was particularly violent. We produced theatre which didn't romanticize sexual violence or make it look like women's fault. We presented violence in a way that made the audience uncomfortable and helped them to understand it as a social issue, as something that needs to be changed.

Often the portrayal of rape on stage makes people laugh. We had to find ways of representing sexual violence that distanced it in such a way that the audience felt uncomfortable. In 1978, we presented an incident of rape where we used stocking-faced characters. We elevated the woman who was being raped, and had the rapist use his fists to pummel the woman's vagina. The audience was absolutely hushed.

That way of representing rape, in a metaphorical or symbolic manner, can be more frightening and bring home the violence of it. A naturalistic representation tends to blur or make people forget they are witnessing an incidence of violence. You have to shake up people's ways of seeing in order to help them see that sexual violence is freakish. Violence against women must be portrayed so that it can in no way be confused with a sexual act that is an expression of affection. This is not done on television, where even if the woman is screaming while the man attacks her, people often still go away with their stereotypical views that women bring it upon themselves, that we ask for it.

Looking at the media

Sistren also questioned the media's relationship to sexual violence against women in society. Reggae music, for example, which was in all the dance halls, has a whole genre called 'slack' songs, which often support sexual violence. And the tourist industry was putting out a series of posters which focused on women's bottoms as part of Jamaica's sexual imagery. Around 1987, *Sistren* magazine began to wage a campaign against those images, and particularly against the popular portrayal which invites men to view black women as animals or as having a bestial sexuality.

At the same time, Sistren research carried out a participatory research project which looked at women and culture. We wanted to identify the most strategic issue for mobilizing women. It wasn't so much a question of what women felt most needed changing. Most women felt that unemployment was the most critical issue. But we felt it important to identify the issue women felt they could do the most about, and could gain most from mobilizing around. Sexual violence came out on top.

Out of this initial work, a group called Women's Media Watch emerged. They write to the newspapers, the television, popular artists, all kinds of people who they feel are producing work which is really anti-women. They maintain a constant critical eye on the media. The idea is that there is a link between the violence shown on television and violence shown towards women in society, that the images portrayed by the media have a direct effect on the way men feel and act towards women.

Women's Media Watch also stress that young men and boys can be raped. This has been to get the alliance of men around the issue. Rape is seen as a social issue which affects both sexes, an issue of violence rather than an issue of sexuality. This in no way denies the fact that more women are raped than men – and we certainly stress this – but it allows men to see that sexual violence is a direct concern for them.

Working with young people

In the late 1980s, there was a dreadful incident in a low-income housing complex in Kingston called Sea View Gardens. A young woman in her early teens was sent to the shop to buy something for her mother, and on the way she was raped, murdered and hung by a group of boys. The community mourned and demonstrated against the incident; they were absolutely horrified by the brutality of it.

Just after that, a member of Sistren who lived in the community helped to form a group of young teenagers, now called Teens in Action. This group began by doing drama and critical reflection within the community around the issue of sexual violence. They continue to focus on sexuality, on how men and women deal with each other, through ongoing workshops and forums. They also participate in different types of community service work.

Much of Sistren's theatre work has been with young people. Some of these experiences were quite incredible: taking place out in the middle of the road in hillside villages, for example, with young men and women who were obviously just discovering their sexuality and wanting a chance to discuss it. These 'workshops' provided an opportunity for young people to discuss sex, in a humorous way, and to clarify the boundary between aggression and affection.

Women's Media Watch also works with teens. They do theatre in the schools – showing a scene of sexual violence for example, and then taking it apart with the kids, discussing it, having character interviews, etc. – so that young people can really grapple with sexuality and sexual violence. They look at the way sexual abuse perpetuates itself over generations, how the sexually abused are likely to become abusers themselves, and they look at the link between the media and sexual violence.

Teens in Action and Women's Media Watch are groups that grew out of work initially begun by Sistren. Although they continue to be supported by Sistren, they are autonomous.

Since 1977, there has been enormous increase in the level of women's activity that is autonomous. It has an identity as women-based rather than as an adjunct to a mixed political party, or subordinate to a mixed male and female organization. There is now considerable diversification of work around women, particularly in the area of violence against women. More attention is being paid to it. Much of this work grew out of Sistren's activities. They opened a space for women's issues to come to the forefront.

Domestic Violence: Breaking the Cycle in Argentina
Lucrecia Oller

Lugar de Mujer (A Woman's Place) in Buenos Aires has been working on the issue of violence since 1984. 'As the demand grew, we began running workshops in the community, through unions, women's groups, political parties, mothers' associations, schools, churches, etc. We also produced popular education materials about what we were doing, all aimed at sensitizing the public and promoting reflection' (taken from a letter by Lucrecia Oller, 1990).

Lugar de Mujer's Violence Prevention Programme made a political decision not to open a shelter, but to focus instead on legal assistance and self-help support groups. They strongly believe that communities themselves must take responsibility for ending violence.

Working on domestic violence requires a deep understanding of what the abused woman faces and how she feels.

The battered woman finds herself submerged in a situation of fear, self-deprecation, lack of self-confidence, and sometimes panic. She no longer believes herself capable of getting out on her own strength. Guilt and embarrassment push her further and further into isolation, and her extreme lack of self-esteem makes her think that no one will listen to her, believe or respect her.

The abused woman tries, over and over again, to make her relationship revert to its original state. She ignores her own desires and needs in an attempt to please the abuser, often carrying submission to extremes. This leads to the distortion of her relationships with other people. She often attempts to cover up insecurity by acting defensively and rejecting others.

One of the questions asked repeatedly, often with irritation and impatience, is why women continue to stay with an abuser. This question assumes that women themselves are responsible for the situation in which they are immersed.

The search for alternatives

Our experience has forced us to adopt a perspective which takes into account both the subjectivity of the battered woman and the social dimension of the problem. It is based on the recognition of conditioning factors which affect men and women – factors which are manifested in the way both sexes feel and live.

Within this framework, self-help groups for battered women have proven to be a suitable and efficient instrument for developing solidarity among women, and for strengthening women's individual sense of self-worth.

Women who have suffered domestic violence and who have been able to escape it recognize that during long periods – in some cases for many years – they felt paralysed. They were able to find refuge only in isolation, while hoping that something magical would get them out of their distressing situation.

No in-depth studies have analysed the internal processes which lead women to ask for help. In some cases it may be the shock of ever-increasing violence that forces a woman to act. Although, tragically, there are many unfortunate cases indicating that proximity to death is not sufficient in itself.

Undoubtedly, women feel greater support as domestic violence becomes more visible in the public sphere – as it is identified as a social problem shared by many women. In this way domestic violence begins to transcend the personal and private space.

Perhaps the search for outside help is linked to the battered woman's particular life stage. Our experience is that many of the women who are willing to take steps to resolve their situation, even breaking off their relationship with the abuser, have already finished raising children. Perhaps once children are no longer the central focus of women's lives, women are able to take a fresh look at themselves.

Self-help groups: working towards an end to domestic violence

In her search for a way out, the battered woman may have spoken to a friend or neighbour – perhaps she saw a flyer which invited battered women to participate in a self-help group. One day, prompted by fear or an overwhelming desire to change her oppressive situation, she decides to make one more try.

Afraid and full of doubts, she finds herself sitting in a circle with other women who are speaking about themselves, about how they were able to break free from the same violence that she is now suffering.

As she hears their stories, she can see that no one is pushing for details of the violence, but rather that each woman expresses what upsets her. The women support one another and search together for ways to overcome their problems and decide what to do.

Building self-esteem

Identifying with others, accepting them with all their defects, virtues, fears and lack of definition, helps each woman to accept her own values and the different facets of her own personality. This is a critical point in the process: she is beginning to develop self-esteem.

The group becomes a space where the abused woman can begin to visualize her recuperation. She has ongoing communication with women who have been working at this for a long time, and who share what they've gone through with her. Under these circumstances, the first tangible tool she receives from the group is hope; she sees that others have been able to free themselves, and begins to think that perhaps she can too.

On her first visit, she is asked if she suffers from domestic violence. She gives her first name only. She learns that only she defines the length of her stay in the group, and that the only cost is giving back to other women what she herself receives.

When it is her turn to speak, the other participants listen attentively, respecting what she wishes to say. From the start she finds that the other women are understanding, that all have gone through very similar situations, that each word represents a shared meaning, and that each silence is a moment of reflection. All participants are united in solidarity. Pain is shared and begins to fade. Loneliness and isolation disappear for the moment. To feel heard and understood is to begin to feel human. This way she starts to see the need and possibility of changing her relationships with other people. More important, that she is capable of changing her life and the chain of submission and violence.

She discovers that women as a group suffer discrimination. She learns that cultural traditions place men in a position of superiority over women, and that this must change, not only for her own good but also for the good of all women and the society as a whole.

Work methodology

The methodology used in the self-help groups is inextricably linked to the objectives and results desired. The group's structure and actions must reinforce the self-trust, credibility and self-esteem of the abused woman.

With this in mind, the principal characteristics are the following:

- All co-ordinators have suffered from domestic violence and are strongly committed to the issue. Each one is trained in group dynamics, attends bi-weekly meetings with other co-ordinators and an institutional psychologist.
- Co-ordination should be rotated, facilitating the training of new co-ordinators.
- Women are at different stages. Even some recently arrived may have already broken free from violent situations. This offers a strong counter-example for women who still find themselves immersed in desperation and see no way out.
- Each woman defines the length of her participation in the group according to her needs.
- The group does not recognize any rules other than those which the group itself imposes on its members. This favours an attitude which is autonomous, responsible and committed.
- There is an open and trusting atmosphere which helps the battered woman to recuperate her self-esteem and develop a sense of security.
- The group defines weekly tasks for each participant, with the aim of gradually modifying their personal or family situations. Each week the gains made and difficulties encountered are evaluated. This helps to develop self-confidence and the capacity to take initiative.

ardo began to be more withdrawn and to
rn to the house late. Each week he gave
ia less money. He was becoming more
ent, shouting, breaking glasses and
ing the furniture.

One night she tried to talk to him but he said
he did not have to explain anything. He got
very angry and struck her hard.

solated herself more and more, trying to
the neighbours and not discussing her
ems with anyone. She felt alone and
ysed by panic.

But the violence kept growing. Once after he
hit me for burning the dinner, I saw the
expression of desperation on the children's
faces and felt like killing him. I realized I
needed to find help.

One day, when I was getting off the bus, I
saw an announcement by the church about a
talk on domestic violence. I didn't feel too
hopeful but since I was there, I decided to go
in.

233

Storyboards from the violence prevention programme

The cardboard illustrated stories, some of which are reproduced on the sidebars, show domestic violence developing out of different situation. Lugar de Mujer uses these tools to promote reflection on the causes of violence in the home and the possibilities for overcoming it.

In the self-help groups someone either reads the story or a story is made up as the group views the pictures. There is a question guide to encourage reflection on themes such as:

- Domestic violence – social problem or family concern?
- The role of education and culture in creating differences between the sexes.
- How can battered women change their situations?
- Self-help groups for abused women – are they helpful?

The Circle of Healing: Aboriginal Women Organizing in Canada
MATCH International Centre

Canada's Aboriginal peoples, or members of the First Nation, offer unique strategies for change which have arisen both out of their own distinct reality of oppression in Canada and out of the strength of community and culture which they have maintained through the centuries. The following extracts, exploring some of these strategies, are reprinted from *Linking Women's Struggles to End Violence*, a resource kit published by MATCH International Centre, Ontario.

Woman is the centre of the wheel of life. She is the heartbeat of the community. She is not just in the home, but she is in the community; she is the Nation.

An Aboriginal grandmother

The woman is the foundation in which Nations are built. She is the heart of the Nation. If that heart is weak the people are weak. If her heart is strong and her mind is clear then the Nation is strong and knows its purpose. The woman is the centre of everything.

'The Woman's Part', Art Solomon, Ojibwa elder

That violence against Aboriginal women in Canada is particularly extreme is undeniable. Eight in ten Aboriginal women have experienced family violence, or can expect to experience such violence in their lifetime. For Canadian women in general, the (conservative) figure is one in ten.

There are few services available to Aboriginal women and their children who have to flee their homes because of abuse. Often, if they do have to leave the reserve (a piece of land set aside for Aboriginal peoples), they are perceived as abandoning their families and are treated as outcasts when they return. Among others, the Ontario Native Women's Association (whose 1989 study, *Breaking Free: a Proposal for Change to Aboriginal Family Violence*, provided much of the background for this article) has pointed out the need for houses not for the battered but for the abusers, to enable the abused spouse/partner and children to remain in their home.

This strategy fits in well with the Aboriginal notion of crime and punishment. Traditionally, offenders were not imprisoned, and only in the most extreme cases was a member of the tribe banished from the community, and even then only for a limited time. In *Breaking Free*, researchers wrote that, 'The involvement of Elders and spiritual leaders in the treatment of abusers is critical, because only Elders and leaders who are respected in the community, and respected by Aboriginal men, will be able to get through to men to help begin their process of healing.'

Aboriginal people believe that violence is a learned behaviour and that it must be unlearned. So, in dealing with violence against women, they emphasize the need to heal the whole community and to develop holistic, culturally appropriate, community-based solutions based on the traditional 'four directions': honesty, kindness, sharing, and strength.

What follows, then, is first a brief exploration of the Circle of Healing – a traditional model of healing which Aboriginal groups have recovered and revitalized in their struggles against violence. We then take a look at three groups in Canada whose organizing strategies encompass such culturally based models.

The Circle of Healing

The things wrong in Fort McPherson, Northwest Territories

(northern Canada) are that people aren't dealing with their problems. There is a bar called R.J.'s bar. It's where most people think they're fixing their problems but they're not.

Children in Fort McPherson, from a MATCH workshop, 1989

In the province of Manitoba, Aboriginal people are using a Circle of Healing to address the problem of violence in their communities. It was started by five or six women of the Hollow Water Reserve who began meeting secretly to share their problems. About five years ago, they opened their discussions to the community and a new group evolved to tackle wider social issues – violence in particular. The group connected the psychological, emotional and physical violence they were subjected to with the economic, social and political underdevelopment of their community. They realized that unless that violence was dealt with, their community could not move forward.

In 1987, the group decided to tackle sexual abuse head on when two rapists returned to the reserve, after spending three years in jail, and raped again. The people of the reserve turned to the Circle of Healing, a method as old as native society itself and an essential tool used in native medicinal philosophy.

In an article about the circle in the *Winnipeg Free Press*, 8 April 1990, journalist Catherine Mitchell writes, 'The calling together of the people to solve a problem is the root of communal Indian life.' The Circle of Healing involves treating the entire community to exorcise the pervasive illness of violence. There are two programmes within the Circle of Healing. One is a five-day intensive therapy; the other is a thirteen-step process which takes two to five years. The circle insists on an admission of responsibility on the part of the offender before getting involved. And the circle's principle is simple: until the victimizer is healed, there will be more victims.

Key to the circle's power of healing is a special gathering where members of the community, the victim, the abuser, and family members come together to face the crime. The abuser has to acknowledge the crime publicly. At the heart of the meeting is the speaking out of members of the community, who tell the abuser how they feel about what has happened and offer their support for healing. They also speak to the victim and the family or families involved.

The abuser is given a 'healing contract' setting out punishment – usually community work – and arrangements are made to protect the victim. When the contract expires, a cleansing ceremony takes place to symbolize the return of balance to the abuser, the family, and the community. At this point healing is complete and the crime is to be forgotten. Healing can take years.

The Circle of Healing is now used in the South-East Tribal Council region which includes nine reserves.

Ma Mawi Wi Chi Itata Centre

One of the traditional Aboriginal rituals used by the Circle of Healing is the sweetgrass ceremony. The MATCH workshop on global violence facilitators experienced this healing ceremony at the Ma Mawi Wi Chi Itata Centre in Winnipeg, Manitoba. It is a centre for Aboriginal people and one of its programmes addresses family violence. Afterwards the facilitators wrote in their diary:

> The workshop was opened by someone who burnt sweetgrass to strengthen the circle and its work. The grass is not eaten by animals and the Aboriginal people believe that it is put there by the Spirit to take messages into the sky. When sweetgrass is burnt, people are taking part in a cleansing process. However, when there are men in the room, women who are 'on their time' are asked to leave the room. This is because it is believed that a woman who is 'on her time' is at her most creative and powerful. She is asked to leave so that she will not overpower the men. Besides she is already undergoing a spiritual and physical cleansing process so does not really need the sweetgrass ceremony. If there are only women in the room, they can stay because the women are seen as powerful anyway.
>
> It was one of the most rewarding and revitalizing workshops that we did. I personally shall remember the experience with a deep longing and feeling that things can be different – but how hard we'll have to work for it.

Golden Lake Reserve support group

The Golden Lake Reserve is an isolated, rural community in eastern Ontario with a population of approximately 250.

Although the nearest shelter is only 20 minutes away, for the Aboriginal women of Golden Lake, it is in another world – a white world. To leave, then, is perhaps as traumatic as staying in an abusive relationship.

So the women of Golden Lake have decided they need to find solutions to violence that are based in their community. The first step was to establish the support group. Two years ago, under the initiative of Shirley Coocl, the women of Golden Lake Reserve started a support group with women aged 17 to 70. One of the main problems they deal with is that of family violence.

In the fall of 1989, the group invited the MATCH-sponsored workshop on global violence to the reserve. The participants talked about community responses to violence, and the support group used this as a catalyst to further their own efforts to develop community-based actions against violence on the reserve. Now they are turning to their own Aboriginal tradition in their search for solutions.

Sheshatshit Women's Group[1]

In Labrador (northern Canada) Innu women are fighting for their lives, their land and their families. They are fighting against the military's low-level flights over Innu land. The flights, up to 26 per day, are destroying the Innu way of life. The planes fly so low (100 feet) that their exhaust burns the branches off trees and they have permanently altered the traditional migration patterns of caribou, the animal at the centre of Innu survival. The noise pollution, too, has led to medical problems, the extent of which have yet to be recognized.

While Innu women are fighting for the survival of their way of life, they have also to struggle with an increase in violence against them. At the forefront of the Innu women's attempts to overcome the violence is Rose Gregoire. She says, 'They [the young women] have gone to the military bases and become prostitutes and alcoholics. They become pregnant and then are deserted. The military are raping Mother Earth and they are raping our daughters.'

Rose is a member of the Sheshatshit (an Innu community in the heart of the Labrador) Women's Group, formed four years ago in response to the increased military presence. Frustrated with the extent of social chaos in their community, and with the inability of the community Band Council (all male) to react to it, a handful of Innu women decided to take the matter in their own hands. 'They [the men] used to go to meetings and just have a kind of talk. But they would take no action. Besides, organizations like the Band Councils (made up of male councillors and a male Chief) were imposed upon us. They are not Innu and they do not work in Innu society. In Innu society all people, men and women, make decisions,' Rose says.

So the Innu women started to strategize. Based on their belief in non-violence, they have peacefully occupied air strips and test bombing zones around the Canadian Forces Base. In the process, however, many Innu women have had to suffer further through the indignity of imprisonment.

Yet the Innu remain faithful to their heritage and will continue to preserve their way of life. Says Rose: 'If the environment and the land are destroyed, the animals will not be fit to eat and the people will be frightened to go "in country" [to hunt]. They will not teach their children the old ways. The people will be stuck here in the community and they'll drink themselves to death. And that will be the end. Well we're going to fight that!'

Note

1. Much of this information comes from an article by Joanna Manning, called 'Innu women speak their piece', in the *New Catholic Times*.

Helping Women to Help Themselves: Counselling Against Domestic Violence in Australia
Kathy Silard

Kathy Silard is a counsellor and adult educator with Spark Resource Centre, the only organization for single parents in Australia. Since its establishment in 1979, Spark has seen a growing need to focus its counselling, information and referral services, and lobbying skills on the problem of violence in the home.

Kathy Silard is the author of *Peace or Pieces?*, a nonviolent parenting manual.

Yes, there is domestic violence in Australia! It permeates all levels of Australian society and yet only recently has it received recognition as a serious societal problem. Domestic violence (physical, sexual, financial and emotional abuse of a woman by her partner) is experienced by all racial and religious groups in Australia and is accepted by most Australians as the norm.

How much domestic violence is there in Australia? I can only give the results of recent surveys and police statistics. These definitely do not give a true picture, but are horrific in their own right. In 1988 the Office of the Status of Women conducted a survey to find out the Australian community's attitude to domestic violence. It discovered that one-third of people questioned thought that domestic violence should be kept private, over one-fifth thought that domestic violence was not a crime, and one in five also thought that, at times, domestic violence can be justified.

In 1990 the Australian Bureau of Statistics conducted a survey in New South Wales (NSW). It surveyed random residential areas for victims of crime. It found that 36 per cent of the female participants had been assaulted at least once in their own homes and that 44 per cent of these participants had been assaulted two or more times in the previous 12-month period. This could mean one woman (over the age of 15 years) out of three is a victim of domestic violence.

Spark Resource Centre, Adelaide.

More recent work using NSW Bureau of Crime Statistics and Research data indicates that there are 'growing proportions of non-aggravated assaults reported to police' which 'involve a suspect who is the spouse or de facto partner of the victim'.[1] The proportion of reported non-aggravated assaults has risen to 21 per cent of all reported assaults. Yet these figures do not give a true picture of domestic violence in Australia as most women do not report this abuse.

Numerous researches and my own experience with thousands of abused women indicate that the violence starts early in the relationship. One of the main reasons for not reporting is fear of consquences. There has been an increase in homicides which involve spouses and *de facto* partners: 43 per cent of all homicide victims in Australia were killed by family members and 54 per cent of these family killings (that is 23 per cent of all homicides) involved spouses and *de facto* partners. The fear of worse violence and even death is a real issue for abused women who want to leave. One consequence of leaving may be more violent behaviour by the perpetrator; and the

Spark Resource Centre, Adelaide.

social consequences of leaving (sense of failure, ostracism, rejection, stigma, family rejection) also constitute serious reasons for women staying in abusive relationships.

Since the late 1980s, there has been an Australia-wide campaign to change social attitudes and awareness around the reality of domestic violence. It is too early to ascertain this campaign's effectiveness.

In South Australia (SA), my own state, domestic violence cases make up 40 per cent of the SA Crisis Care Unit's workload. 'The SA Legal Services Commission claims that 50 per cent of all family law clients are victims of domestic violence.'[2] This means that in relationships that break down, domestic violence is an issue for half of the participants. However, high as this statistic is, of the clients I see at my own workplace as many as 79 per cent of the women have been physically or sexually abused. All have been emotionally abused.

The legal system is indifferent and casual in its treatment of domestic violence. The family is seen to be a shrine to be protected – violence is called 'a domestic' which totally trivializes the real pain, fear and horror that occurs and also hides the fact that it is women and children who are the victims of this prolific violence.

Unfortunately, the legal system seems to reflect the attitudes of Australian society, and although moves have been made to address these issues, so far they have not been very effective.

'He saved my life …'

I asked her, 'How did you get those scars?' She told me, 'He saved my life, I was in flames and he threw me in the pool and he saved my life …' She smiled at me. I persisted. 'How did you catch alight?' Her smile faded. She looked at her nails thoughtfully and said faintly, so I could barely hear her, 'Oh, he set me alight. With his lighter. But he saved my life …'

I am a counsellor. At last count I realized I have counselled over 5,000 people. Eighty per cent of my clients have been physically, sexually or emotionally abused by the men who 'love' them (I am only writing about heterosexual relationships in this article). They are often totally unaware that they are living in a state of domestic violence, or that abuse is not a necessary part of the marriage contract.

I am often the first person who calls their experience 'abusive'; I am often the first person who calls it violence or rape. And their reaction is usually shock, denial, anger (often at me) and then there is rationalization and minimization of the events. Often there are tears. The tears relieve me, for it is a step towards their healing.

I have a variety of approaches when I am confronted with a client who has just left a violent relationship. Usually I ask her to retrace the relationship, I ask her to validate and acknowledge her own experiences. I affirm her bravery.

I often write down affirmations for her, but sometimes I am forced to confront her denial. Her total inability to face the awful truth: 'The person I love, who said they loved me, has violated me … hurt me …'

Sometimes I ask for details of the abuse and if my client persists in saying 'but I love him', I actually write down the details of the abuse, plus the words 'but I love him'. For example, Harold (all names are fictitious) has repeatedly assaulted Donna, deprived her of money, picked on their young son and raped her. I write the following:

Harold has beaten me on many occasions, but I love him.
Harold has strangled me until I was unconscious, but I love him.
Harold has kicked me, but I love him.
Harold has left me with no money, but I love him.
Harold has stripped me naked and shoved me out of the front door, but I love him.
Harold has slapped me across the face publicly, but I love him.
Harold has punched me so hard he punctured my lungs, but I love him.

Harold has raped me, but I love him. Etc.

I then write these words:

I *AM* IMPORTANT
I HAVE RIGHTS
I *AM* TOTALLY LOVEABLE
I CAN TAKE CARE OF MYSELF
I *AM* INVALUABLE
I *AM* GOOD

I then ask the client to read OUT LOUD each line three times and to make a comment if she wishes. She will usually start out being very embarrassed, become upset, sometimes laugh, sometimes cry. I always encourage her to get in touch with her feelings and also encourage her to express them. Often the 'but I love him' phrases bring out thoughtfulness, occasionally anger at me; however the affirmations will bring the heavy discharge of emotion.

It is in this session I explain the basic inequality of the sexes, some basic concepts of sexism and I gently tell clients I lived in an abusive relationship for a full decade. Often this small amount of personal information will cause a shift in the client.

Sometimes the clients are resentful, particularly when they have been sent to me. Often they are scared, terrified of their ex-partners, terrified of the future. I encourage them to explore each fear fully. I also encourage them to analyse their beliefs around love versus dependency. I often place them in my classes, if they are willing to join a class; then there is an excellent chance they will not return to the abusive relationship.

Sometimes the method of confrontation 'but I love him' causes a client to leave me as a counsellor and seek help elsewhere. I don't mind. I used to take an impartial stance (years ago) and realized that many of my clients were exposing themselves and their children to great danger. I felt sunk and powerless.

One day I was at a women's shelter annual general meeting when I bumped into an old client. She greeted me with great warmth. I was surprised because the last time I had seen her she had yelled at me, 'You bloody bitch I don't care what you say, I love him!' In fact she had returned to him, to her life of forced prostitution and beatings. She reported she had heard my voice in her head saying, 'but I love him', plus the affirmations. It was the affirmations as well as the knowledge that one person, Kathy Silard, believed she was good and had rights. 'That gave me strength to pack the kids up and leave … I'm never going back. Thank you and I am sorry I swore at you.'

That happened three years ago … she hasn't come back for counselling either. I then decided to be more clear and partial about my position on domestic violence.

Spark Resource Centre, Adelaide.

I teach a variety of classes: Co-dependency; Peer Counselling; Peaceful Parenting (using my nonviolent parenting manual *Peace or Pieces?*). No matter what the class, I speak about domestic violence. In my Peer Counselling classes I do a whole lesson on domestic violence. The counselling classes are filled with the survivors of domestic violence plus social work students.

I commence the session with a brainstorming task: What does domestic violence look like, sound like? I write everything on the board. I then read it back to the group. The whole class divides into pairs and I ask them to listen to each other silently while they share their own experience or knowledge of domestic violence. Often at this stage the participants are in tears. As this is a painful exercise I follow it up with a historical/social review of domestic violence. I answer questions. Following the break I divide the group into three. I ask one group to present the abusing male viewpoint, the second group presents the abused female viewpoint and the third group presents society. Each group is given 15 minutes to prepare its dramatic role play. I encourage the group members to think broadly and also state that they can present their case as a panel, as an act, as an interview, but ask them to try to capture the flavour of their role. I remind them all that they are acting.

Each 'act' usually takes three to five minutes and this is followed by individual debriefing in the large group. Group discussion is facilitated and normally goes on for about an hour. I conclude with a final round: 'What did you learn about yourself and what have you learnt about domestic violence?' This is followed by a counselling session (on domestic violence). The group members do this session during the week that follows the topic of domestic violence.

I continue to counsel most of the students in the classes and find that each class leads to more insight, growth and personal development.

There are many times when I do not confront directly but pose key questions to my clients about the quality of their life and their children's lives. Often I encourage them to focus on their childhood: to explore the early abuse which led them to believe (on some level) that they are women who deserve to be hurt, to be beaten.

Spark Resource Centre, Adelaide.

Through my counselling I present: confidence that they can and will cope; support; reality (I never trivialize, or minimize their fears); and great affection. I have become very close to some of my clients and I am always honest. I answer all their questions (especially personal ones) to the best of my ability. Even when I confront I do it gently and respectfully. Lastly, I encourage them to stop asking themselves, 'What is it about me that makes him violent?', but rather to ask, 'What is it about him that he thinks violence is OK, and what is it about society that makes it OK to beat women and children?'

Notes

1. *Crime and Justice*, 1991 Bulletin (NSW Bureau of Crime Statistics and Research).
2. Kay Buckley, 'Domestic violence in an ecological context' (unpublished paper, 1993).

Bridging the Gap: Feminist Development Work in Glasgow

Jan Macleod, Patricia Bell and Janette Forman

The following article, parts of which clearly echo the previous contribution from Australia, first appeared in a special issue of *Feminist Review* on the subject of child sexual abuse entitled *Family Secrets* (No. 28, Spring 1988). The authors have all been development workers with the Women's Support Project, an information, training and education centre based in Glasgow, in the west of Scotland.

The project, discussed below, was started in response to a need to bridge the gap between crisis work, such as that performed by feminist activists in Rape Crisis and Women's Aid centres (see pages 27–31) and the professionals responsible for handling cases of child sex abuse and other forms of violence against women and children. The original article has been updated with the kind collaboration of Jan Macleod.

Traditional images of Glasgow include shipbuilding, engineering, heavy drinking, left-wing politics, great good humour and friendliness, and macho men. In the 1950s, large numbers of families were moved from overcrowded inner-city areas to newly built housing schemes on the outskirts of the city – 'deserts with windows', as described by one comedian.

In 1993, the shipbuilding and engineering have all but gone and the city has high unemployment, particularly in the peripheral housing schemes. Glasgow has also gone through a public relations exercise, presenting itself as a centre for cultural activities, and working hard to change the hard, often violent, image associated with the city. Unfortunately, however, the macho attitude remains firmly in place, at all levels of society. Glasgow does not come out well when a close look is taken at women's experiences, for example of domestic violence and rape in marriage.

However, whilst the 'macho man' image is well known, what is less well publicized is the strength of Glasgow women. It has been common for community organizations and activities to be led by women, and for women to lead political actions, one of the best-known examples of which would be the Glasgow rent strikes of 1917.

The political commitment of Glasgow women is also reflected in the existence of a number of voluntary, feminist women's organizations. These both offer services for women who have suffered male violence, and work against the attitudes that condone and encourage such violence. They include Women's Aid, organizations working on issues of child sexual abuse, and the Rape Crisis Centre, from which the Women's Support Project developed.

In 1981 the Rape Crisis Centre was overstretched and under-resourced – not an unusual position for voluntary and feminist organizations. In among the individual counselling, administration, volunteer training, talks and fund-raising, we spent hours agonizing over two main points. First, what did we have to offer the many women who, with great courage, were coming to us to talk of their experiences of sexual abuse as children? What on earth could we do to meet this 'new' demand? Second, why were we so often left to pick up the pieces after abused women had been to the police, courts, GP or social worker? Why did women have to suffer secondary abuse through the unsympathetic attitudes they often had to face? How could we influence the few specialist services provided within statutory organizations, and so try to avoid the further abuse of women by the system? Why, when we had so few resources, were we supporting field workers who were in contact with abused women and children, whilst their own departments had nothing to offer them? The Women's Support Project grew from these concerns.

In the centre, crisis work had always gained priority at the expense of educational and development work. We felt that we had the ideas and the experience to back them up, if only we had the time and resources to implement them. We decided to attempt to bridge the gap between ourselves and similar feminist organizations, and the professionals; we began to plan the Women's Support Project.

The project, which opened in 1983, was funded by Urban Aid for the first seven years. We now receive a grant from Strathclyde Regional Council, which covers wages, and we have to raise money for running costs and development work. The project now employs two development workers and two information workers.

The style and direction of the project had to change considerably over its first two years. A main initial aim was to 'encourage women to make greater use of locally available services'. However, we found that a vicious circle existed: women did not feel comfortable using local services because they did not receive an appropriate response, the usual initial reaction being to try to refer on as soon as violence or sexual abuse is mentioned. At the same time we were often told by workers that 'violence is not a problem here', or 'women never tell us about violence', because women were not using the services.

We had thought that we could offer some individual counselling and advice work, but it became clear that to advertise this service would swamp the project and repeat the situation of the Rape Crisis Centre. Our job became to stimulate the development of services, to produce educational material, and to work at keeping women on the agenda of services which at worst have women-blaming responses and at best are prepared to refer women on. Since we were not offering a counselling service we worked to provide a first-class information service. Our resource library developed from this work, and is now in great demand, not only in Glasgow but throughout Britain. We have over 700 books and videos available for loan, all dealing with different aspects of male violence, and many unavailable elsewhere.

The main thread of our approach has always been a feminist analysis of male violence, maintaining strong links between the causes and effects of rape, domestic violence, incest and child sexual abuse. We have been prepared to use any openings, and to jump on most (but not all) bandwagons in order to 'bridge the gap' and put our views across.

For example, people can easily persuade themselves that domestic violence is a private, family matter and that battered women choose to stay in a violent relationship. We often have to point out that domestic violence abuses children, too, before people will take the issue seriously. We build on discussions of domestic violence before talking about incest and child sexual abuse. This is partly to minimize the mother-blaming which goes on whenever child sexual abuse is raised, but also to give workers a social and political framework within which to make sense of the day-to-day problems women face. In addition, people feel more comfortable discussing domestic violence since it is a more familiar area than child sexual abuse. This enables us to draw crucial links between the two areas, implicitly challenging male power, particularly within the family.

Our experience of training has convinced us that what is needed is not just clearer guidelines or more procedures but changes in attitudes. To put it bluntly, there is no point in giving people procedures if they don't believe male violence happens or think it is not their job to deal with it. Workers find it difficult to admit that, as 'professionals', they feel deskilled and unable to cope. In trying to isolate themselves from the painful issues, they often separate themselves from the clients who have this problem.

Child sexual abuse, domestic violence and rape are not easy areas to

RAPE IN MARRIAGE

-IT'S A CRIME!

In Scotland, a man can be charged with raping his wife — whether he is living with her or not.

For further information women should write to:
Women's Support Project, 871 Springfield Road, Glasgow G31

WOMEN **NEVER** DESERVE TO BE RAPED

Women's Support Project, Glasgow.

work in. The issues involved challenge our personal beliefs and attitudes. Even with the most concerned and sympathetic of adults there is a great pressure to shy away from the possibility of abuse. A great many adults have been sexually abused themselves as children and, whilst personal experience can make you alert to the signs of abuse, carrying painful memories can be an added pressure against raising the issue. Our training aims to break down these professional barriers to enable people to face their feelings.

We often begin by getting workers to do an exercise on 'burnout'. They are asked to look at their own work situations and answer the following questions: what do you feel, what do you say, what do you do, and, finally, why do you stay? This brings out points such as feelings of inadequacy, exhaustion and failure and, at the same time, a sense of commitment to some areas of the job, the need for money and workers' fears of making changes. The last heading is then changed to 'why does she stay?' and the point is made that the feelings identified by the workers themselves are very similar to those expressed by battered women. The exercise is extremely effective in making people realize that it is not easy to leave a situation, even when you know it is not doing you any good, and so makes workers less quick to condemn women for staying in a violent relationship.

We also role-play a disclosure of child sexual abuse to make workers look at the way they are treating people, how they would want to be treated, and how the service they provide could be more appropriate and responsive to the needs of women and children. In the words of the Incest Survivors' Campaign, we are asking people to look at what they offer and ask at every stage, 'Who benefits and who has to pay?' There is no doubt that this approach to training is very effective. People are less likely to blame incest on the mother, alcohol, children, unemployment or overcrowding and more likely to face up to the position of women and children in our society. Once this has happened, workers can then look at alternative responses to the problem, such as supporting mothers, working with the child within the home and removing the abuser.

Violence against women and children, whether in or out of the home, is not a minority problem. The social position of women and children encourages their daily exploitation. Child sexual abuse exists on such a scale that we need a totally new approach to the problem. Voluntary services cannot meet the need and neither can limited specialist projects run by a handful of experts. In order to respond adequately, we need a community-based response which recognizes the relative powerlessness of women and children and does something to address this. This may involve people in reviewing their whole approach to their work, and facing difficult choices. For example, staff in a community-based project backed away from a campaign on domestic violence in case it upset their relationships with local community activists who were overwhelmingly men. What does this say about the value placed on women in the community?

As part of our education work we developed a series of posters. These highlighted the fact that acts of violence against women are crimes. The posters are unusual in that they were not aimed at women who had suffered violence, but at the public in general. They were intended to provide information that would promote discussion about the whole issue of male violence, and most important, to challenge men's perceived right to abuse.

The project has also worked to make our services and materials accessible to as many women as possible. For example we have been involved in the development of women's self-defence work. A main aim of this work for us has been to create opportunities for women to discuss experiences and fears of violence in a safe and supportive environment. Classes are not based on physical strength and fitness, but on a mixture of discussion, mutual support and simple, practical physical techniques, including use of voice. We have worked hard to make these classes open to a wide range of women, and have for example offered courses to girls' groups, black women's groups, survivors' groups, and pensioners' groups.

In order to address the increased vulnerability of women with physical disability, and to increase our skills in working with women with disability, we organized a training course with Lydia Zijdel, a Dutch self-defence instructor very experienced in this area of work.

The project has also looked at services available for profoundly deaf women. This work was initially undertaken in conjunction with workers with deaf people, and then with a group of deaf women. This collaboration has been very effective and has resulted in a series of education meetings, production of a video in British Sign Language, and a series of information leaflets aimed at deaf women.

Although there are now more resources identified for abused women, for example more organizations offering counselling for adults abused as children, these organizations cannot meet the demand. There is unfortunately little evidence that mainstream and statutory organizations have acknowledged or responded to the extent of violence against women. This also still applies to some voluntary organizations; for example, we often find that drug and alcohol counsellors are offered little training or support on violence, although they report that this is a common problem for women using their services. Instead of training on male violence being seen as an essential component, it still tends to be added as an extra, often being dealt with in one session. All too often a first response is still to refer women on to specialist services.

Channelling resources into specialist centres and individual treatment whilst changing nothing else allows everyone to collude with abuse. It avoids challenging the power of men in families, the power of professionals over clients, the power of adults over children. It particularly ignores the fact that many existing services for children condone, ignore or in some cases actively encourage an environment which is in direct contradiction to any claim of prioritizing children's needs or encouraging their development. For example, workers involved with teenagers in care wanted to start self-help groups for girls who had disclosed previous sexual abuse. They encouraged the girls to talk, but had no way of explaining to those same girls why they had to put up with male staff touching them, making sexual comments and remarking on their dress and appearance. Again, teachers involved in the 'preventive' work of encouraging children to be assertive and to stand up to potential abusers decided not to let the children use role-play because it would 'undermine discipline'.

It is clear that child sexual abuse is an area in which theory greatly influences practice and this is why much of our work concentrates on making people look at their attitudes. It is also important to offer practical suggestions for ways in which workers can build up confidence and skills and develop support networks both for themselves as workers and for those who are suffering abuse. It is common for people to feel so overwhelmed by the scale of the problems that they don't know where to start. We have found it important to point out that very small steps can make an impact. For example, having leaflets and posters on display helps women to realize that sexual abuse is a subject that they can discuss. Having relevant books or games available helps workers to raise the general issues with children in a non-threatening way. And, of course, workers feel more confident in approaching women and children if they are aware that back-up support and information are available for themselves, and so are reassured to hear of the work of voluntary organizations such as Women's Aid, Rape Crisis and Action Against Incest.

Towards this we have built up a wide range of books, videos and resource material. We have developed links with local community groups, offering information on violence, health and regular self-defence courses, mainly with social workers, health centres and nursery staff. This often involves producing new material, as there is little available.

We also offer regular training days which are open to workers from statutory and voluntary organizations, as well as interested individuals. Issues covered include: supporting women whose children have been sexually abused; working with incest survivors; introduction to child sexual abuse; and group work with abused women. Feedback from these days is consistently positive; one aspect workers really appreciate is the inter-agency approach, the opportunity to meet with workers from other fields, and to share concerns over working with abuse.

Another way in which we try to break down professional barriers is in encouraging different agencies to communicate and work together more, and in developing inter-agency contacts. No one agency can deal with all aspects of a child abuse case. If each agency has a different theory, approach and level of 'proof', how does this appear to the child? Can you think of any way to justify this situation to a child?

Previously for example, in conjunction with Glasgow Women's Aid we organized 'local information initiatives' on the problem of male violence. These brought together interested workers from a variety of backgrounds and provided a useful forum both for examining local social work practice and for highlighting gaps in information and service provision. Following these events a multidisciplinary working party made up of local field workers met regularly to share and develop ideas and experience. This group brought together nursery nurses, teachers, health visitors, social workers, community workers and workers from voluntary organizations to discuss issues around violence against women and children, and to look at local service provision. This group also produced a brief information pack on dealing with child sexual abuse. Although the group no longer meets, the information pack is still in print and has been greatly appreciated for the simple, practical information contained.

The work we do is often exhausting in every sense, but it can also be very exciting. Individual crisis work is largely invisible, but with development work the results are more tangible and easier to build on. More and more resources are now being released to tackle the problems of child sexual abuse. It is important that feminists have the opportunity to do more development work, using the experience gained through individual counselling work, so that developing services are appropriate and begin to tackle the real needs as identified by the women and children themselves.

The project provides an opportunity for experience gained through involvement in feminist collectives to be used in helping field workers gain confidence in dealing with the problem of male violence. In doing this the project does walk a tightrope and has frequently been in the uncomfortable position of being criticized and condemned by both the establishment and the feminist community simultaneously. Opportunities to discuss this problem and share experiences are limited, as we do not know of many other groups doing similar work. We hope to see more of such projects, and would appreciate hearing from women anywhere who are involved in, or interested in, similar areas of work. We believe that the only effective way to tackle the many manifestations of male violence is to stimulate a community response equal to the scale of the problem.

List of Organizations

Africa

Musasa Project, c/o PO Box A 205, Avondale, Harare, Zimbabwe.
Rape Crisis Centre, PO Box 15496, Vlaeberg 8018, Cape Town, South Africa.
Sister Collective, PO Box 60100, Katutura, 9000 Namibia.
Tanzania Media Women's, Association, PO Box 6143, Dar es Salaam, Tanzania.
Women's Action Group, PO Box 135, Harare, Zimbabwe.

Asia

All Women's Action Society, 37 Jalan 20/2, 46300 Petaling Jaya, Selangor, Malaysia.
Asian Women's Rights Council, PO Box 190, Manila 1099, Philippines.
Association for the Promotion of the Status of Women (APSW), 501/1 Mu 3, Dejatungka Road, Tungsikan, Don Muang, Bangkok 10210, Thailand.
Association of Women for Action and Research, Tanglin, PO Box 244, Singapore 9124.
Bangladesh Centre for Advanced Studies, 626 Road 20 (Old), 10A (New) Dhanmondi, GPO Box 3971, Dhaka-1205, Bangladesh.
Forum Against Oppression of Women, 120 Safalya Building, 1st Floor, Currey Road, N.M. Joshi Marg, Bombay 400 012, India.
Gabriela Commission on Violence Against Women, 20-B Florfina Street, Roxas District, Quezon City, Philippines.
Philipina Legal Resources Centre, 3rd Floor, GIMA Building, Magallanes Street, Davao City 8000, Philippines.
Sabah Women's Action Research Group, PO Box 12010, 88822 Kota Kinabulu, Sabah, Malaysia.
Shirkat-Gah, 18-A Mian Mir Road, Lahore – 54840, Pakistan.
Sisters in Islam, 172 Lorong Maarot, 59000 Bangear Park, Malaysia.
Women's Aid Organization, Pertubuhan Pertolongan Wanita, PO Box 493, Jalan Sultan, 46760 Petaling Jaya, Selangor Darul Ehsan, Malaysia.

Australia and the Pacific

Broadsheet, PO Box 56 147, Auckland, New Zealand.
Fiji Women's Rights Movement, GPO Box 14194, Suva, Fiji Islands.
PNG Law Reform Commission, Box 3439, Boroko, Papua New Guinea.
SPARK Single Parent Resource Centre, 930 Port Road, Woodville West, SO11 Adelaide, Australia.
Women's Crisis Centre, Box 12882, Suva, Fiji Islands.

Europe

Association Européenne Contre les Violences Faites aux Femmes au Travail (AVFT), 71 rue St Jacques, 75005 Paris, France.
CHANGE, PO Box 824, London SE24 9JS, UK.
Commonwealth Secretariat, Women and Development Programme, Marlborough House, Pall Mall, London SW1Y 5HX, UK.

Curriculum Centre and Library for Gender Studies, Box 695, 111 21 Praha 1, Czech Republic.
FORWARD, Africa Centre, 38 King Street, London WC2E 8JT, UK.
Northern Ireland Women's Aid Federation, 129 University Street, Belfast BT7 1HP, UK.
Southall Black Sisters, 52 Norwood Road, Southall, Middlesex, UK.
Women Against Rape, 71 Tonbridge Street, London WC1, UK.
Womankind, 122 Whitechapel High Street, London E1 7PT, UK.
Women Living Under Muslim Laws, Boîte Postale 23, 34790 Grabels, (Montpellier), France.
Women's Global Network for Reproductive Rights, NWZ Voorburgwal 32, 1012 RZ Amsterdam, Netherlands.
Women's Information Service, Rue de la Loi 200, B-1049 Brussels, Belgium.

Latin America and the Caribbean
Belize Women against Violence Movement, PO Box 1190, Belize City, Belize.
Caribbean Association for Feminist Research and Development (CAFRAD), PO Box 442, Tunapuna Post Office, Trinidad and Tobago, West Indies.
CEFEMINA, Apdo. 5355, San José 1000, Costa Rica.
Colectivo de Lucha Contra la Violencia hacia las Mujeres, Santa Ma. la Ribera 107–8, Col. Santa Ma. la Ribera, 06400 Mexico City, Mexico.
Lugar de Mujer, Corrientes 2817, Piso 5B, 1193 Buenos Aires, Argentina.
Rape Crisis Centre of Trinidad and Tobago, 40 Woodford Street, Newtown, Port of Spain, Trinidad.
Sistren Theatre Collective, 20 Kensington Crescent, Kingston 5, Jamaica.
Violence, Health and Development Project, Apartado Postal 471-1011, San José, Costa Rica.

North America
Canadian Panel on Violence Against Women, Heritage Place, 4th Floor, 155 Queen Street, Ottawa K1A 1J2, Ontario, Canada.
Center for Women Policy Studies, 2000P Street NW, Washington, DC 20036, USA.
International League for Human Rights, 432 Park Avenue South 1103, New York NY 10016, USA.
International Women's Tribune Center, 777 United Nations Plaza, New York NY 10017, USA.
MATCH International Centre, 1102-200 Elgin Street, Ottawa, Ontario, Canada K2P 1L5.
Popular Education Research Group, 606 Shaw Street, Toronto, Ontario, Canada M6G 3L6.
UNIFEM, 304 E. 45th Street, 6th Floor, New York NY 10017, USA.
Women's Leadership Institute, Box 270, Douglass College, New Brunswick, New Jersey 08903-0270, USA.
Women's Rights Project, Americas Watch, 152K Street, NW, Suite 910, Washington DC 20005, USA.

Middle East
Feminist Library and Resource Centre, (Dr Nermin Abadan-Unat), Halic 34220, Istanbul, Turkey.

Select Bibliography

Americas Watch, *Criminal Injustice: Violence against Women in Brazil* (Washington DC, Human Rights Watch, 1991).
—— *Untold Terror: Violence against Women in Peru's Armed Conflict* (Washington DC, Human Rights Watch, 1992).
Amnesty International, *Women on the Front Line: Human Rights Violations against Women* (London, Amnesty International Publications, 1991).
Ashworth, Georgina, *Of Violence and Violation: Women and Human Rights* (London, CHANGE Thinkbook, 1986).
Asian Women's Human Rights Council, *Crimes Against Gender: Rape and Pornography* (Quezon City, Philippines, AWHRC, 1990).
—— *Traffic in Women*, Report on Asian Conference on Traffic in Women in Seoul (Quezon City, Philippines, AWHRC, 1991).
—— *War Crimes on Asian Women: Military Slavery by Japan During World War II* (Quezon City, Philippines, AWHRC, 1993).
Brownmiller, Susan, *Against Our Will* (Penguin, 1975).
Bunch, Charlotte and Roxanna Carillo, *Gender Violence: a Development and Human Rights Issue* (Rutgers University, USA, Center for Women's Global Leadership, 1991).
Center for Women's Global Leadership, *Women, Violence and Human Rights* (Rutgers University, USA, Women's Leadership Report, Douglass College, 1991).
Coalition Against Trafficking in Women, *The Penn State Report of an International Meeting of Experts on Sexual Exploitation, Violence and Prostitution* (Penn State University, USA, 1991)
Commonwealth Secretariat, *Guidelines for Police Training on Violence Against Women and Child Sex Abuse* (London, Commonwealth Secretariat, 1988).
Connors, Jane, *Violence against Women in the Family* (Vienna, United Nations, 1989).
Copeland, Lois and Leslie R. Wolfe, *Violence against Women as Bias Motivated Hate Crime: Defining the Issues* (Washington DC, Center for Women Policy Studies, 1991). Also see the center's factsheets 'Violence Against Women' and 'Girls and Violence' (both 1993).

Dobash, R. Emerson and Russell P. Dobash, *Women, Violence and Social Change* (London, Routledge, 1992).

Dorkenoo, Efua and Scilla Elworthy, *Female Genital Mutilation: Proposals for Change* (London, Minority Rights Group, 1992).

Enloe, Cynthia, *Does Khaki Become You? The Militarization of Women's Lives* (Pluto Press, London, 1983).

Faludi, Susan, *Backlash: the Undeclared War against Women* (London, Chatto and Windus, 1992).

Feminist Review, No. 28, *Family Secrets: Child Sexual Abuse* (London, Feminist Review, 1988).

International League for Human Rights, *Combating Violence Against Women* (report of a conference sponsored in collaboration with the International Women's Rights Project, New York, March 1993).

Isis International, *Bibliographic Catalogue on Violence against Women in Latin America and the Caribbean* (Santiago, Chile, 1989).

Isis International, No. 15, *La Mujer Ausente* (Santiago, Chile, Isis International, August 1991).

Isis Women's World, No. 26, *Freeing Ourselves from Violence* (Geneva, Isis, 1992).

Kelkar, Govind, 'Violence against women: an understanding of responsibility for their lives', in M. Davies (ed.), *Third World – Second Sex 2* (London, Zed Books, 1987).

Kelkar, Govind, 'Violence against women in India: perspectives and strategies', Gender Studies Occasional Paper 1 (Bangkok, Asian Institute of Technology, 1992).

Koso-Thomas, Olayinka, *The Circumcision of Women: a Strategy for Eradication* (London, Zed Books, 1987).

Mahoney, K.E. and P. Mahoney (eds.), *Human Rights in the Twenty-first Century* (Amsterdam, Kluwer Academic Publishers, 1993).

MATCH International Centre, *Linking Women's Global Struggles to End Violence* (Canada, MATCH, reprinted 1993).

Middle East Watch Women's Rights Project, Vol. 4, Issue 8, *Punishing the Victim: Rape and Mistreatment of Asian Maids in Kuwait* (Washington DC, August 1992).

Miller, Alice, *For Your Own Good: Hidden Cruelty in Child-rearing and the Roots of Violence* (London, Virago Press, 1987).

Moss, M., *Children of Despair: an Analysis of Coercive Birth Control Policies in Chinese Occupied Tibet*, Eyewitness Report No. 3, (London, Campaign Free Tibet, August 1992).

Narasimhan, Sakuntala, *Sati: a Study of Widow-burning in India* (India, Viking/Penguin, 1990; USA, Doubleday/Anchor, 1992).

Omvedt, Gail, *Violence against Women: New Movements and the New Theories* (New Delhi, Kali for Women, 1990).

Popular Education Research Group, *Women Educating to End Violence against Women* (Toronto, PERG, 1992).

Projets Féministes, No. 1, March 1992, *Quels Droits Pour Les Femmes?* (Paris, AVFT).

Russell, Diana, *The Politics of Rape* (New York, Stein and Day, 1975).

——— *Rape in Marriage* (New York, Collier, 1982).

Saghal, Gita and Nira Yuval-Davis (eds.), *Refusing Holy Orders* (London, Virago, 1992).

Schuler, Margaret (ed.), *Freedom from Violence: Women's Strategies from around the World* (New York, UNIFEM, 1992).

Sleeth, P. and J. Barnsley, *Recollecting Our Lives: Women's Experience of Child Sex Abuse* (Vancouver, Women's Research Centre, 1989).

Southall Black Sisters (eds.), *Against the Grain* (Southall, UK, SBS, 1990).

United Nations, *Strategies for Confronting Domestic Violence: a Resource Manual* (New York, UN, June 1993).

Velasquez, Roxana (ed.), *Women: Watched and Punished* (Peru, CLADEM, June 1993).

Vickers, Jeanne, *Women and War* (London, Zed Books, 1993).

Index

Index